THE SECRET FILE OF THE DUKE OF WINDSOR

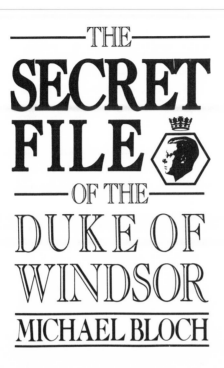

THE
SECRET
FILE
OF THE
DUKE OF
WINDSOR

MICHAEL BLOCH

1817

HARPER & ROW, PUBLISHERS, New York
Cambridge, Philadelphia, San Francisco
London, Mexico City, São Paulo, Singapore, Sydney

This book was originally published in 1988 in Great Britain by Bantam Press, a division of Transworld Publishers Ltd. It is here reprinted by arrangement with Bantam Press, a division of Transworld Publishers Ltd.

FIRST U.S. EDITION

Library of Congress Cataloging-in-Publication Data

Bloch, Michael.
    The secret file of the Duke of Windsor/Michael Bloch.—1st U.S. ed.
        p.   cm.
    Includes index.
    $19.95
    1. Windsor, Edward, Duke of, 1894–1972.   2. Great Britain—Kings and rulers
—Biography.   3. Great Britain—History—Edward VIII, 1936.   I. Title.
    DA580.B538   1988
    941.084′092′4—dc 19
    [B]   88-39284
                                                                                CIP

89 90 91 92 93 RRD 10 9 8 7 6 5 4 3 2 1

To James Lees-Milne – a King's man in 1936

Contents

Contents

Part Three
Postwar Life and Letters

List of Illustrations

List of Illustrations

New York, March 1953: the Duke with his sister Princess Mary, with
    whom he is about to sail to join their ailing mother Queen Mary,
    and the Duchess, who is to stay behind
Crossing the Atlantic in the early 1950s
Sir Walter Monckton (*Popperfoto*)
Sir George Allen (*Illustrated London News Picture Library*)
Sir Alexander Hardinge (*Popperfoto*)
Sir Alan Lascelles (*Keystone Collection*)
Fort Belvedere
La Cröe
The house in the Bois de Boulogne (*Syndication International*)
The Duke's garden at the Mill
Faces of exile

Unless otherwise stated, illustrations are from the collections of the
    late Duchess of Windsor or the author.

Preface

*T*his book tells the story of the Duke of Windsor's exile, the manner in which it was imposed on him, and his attempts to overcome it, from the time of his marriage in June 1937 up to the mid-1950s, when he finally reconciled himself to the fact that he would never be returning to live in his own land. The earlier story of what happened between his abdication in December 1936 and his wedding six months later is a complex one, and I have only attempted to summarize it in the first chapter. It is difficult to unravel all the post-Abdication strands without, first, examining exhaustively the Abdication itself, which is beyond the scope of this book; and, second, having a full view of the other side of the picture, the reactions and machinations of the Government, the Royal Family and the Court, for which it would be necessary to have full access to the relevant governmental and royal archives. Such access has been granted to Philip Ziegler, appointed by the Queen to be the official biographer of King Edward VIII as a British sovereign; and his biography (to which I look forward) will no doubt explain the motives and manoeuvrings of those who were determined that the ex-King should not come home in any guise – a determination regarded at the time with incomprehension by the Duke himself. The present work, largely based on the private correspondence of the Duke and the files of lawyers and advisers who struggled to represent his interests, begins by setting the scene at the moment he began married life abroad, goes on to examine in detail the three most striking measures that were used to keep him out of England – financial pressure, the refusal to accord royal rank to his wife, and the effective confiscation of his old home at Fort Belvedere – and finally charts the chronological progress of the Duke and Duchess of Windsor in exile during eighteen years of marriage.

The immediate history of this project goes back to March 1975, two and a half years after the Duke's death, when the Duchess of Windsor, then in the last year of her active widowhood which came to an end with crippling illness the following November, confided many documents into the care of her French lawyer and confidante, Maître Suzanne Blum, along with written instructions that they were to form the basis of a book relating the unknown story of the ducal exile. In taking this step, however, the Duchess was doing no more than fulfilling a very old intention of her late husband. Ever since his marriage, he had meant one day to explain to the world all that had happened to him after the Abdication; and when, in 1951, his memoirs were published of his years as Prince of Wales and King, he had it in mind to write a sequel in this sense. This was a literary task which he never accomplished, for a variety of reasons; but the Duchess's memoirs published five years later, though very discreet, tell some of the story; and in December 1966, at the time of the thirtieth anniversary of the Abdication, the Duke realized his ambition on a small scale when he wrote a series of newspaper articles – published in America in the *New York Daily News*, and in England (in a slightly subdued form) in the *Sunday Express* – in which he spoke briefly but frankly of his bitter relationship with his family and the many disappointments he had endured.

I have touched on these subjects in three previous publications – *The Duke of Windsor's War* (1982), *Operation Willi* (1984) and *Wallis & Edward* (1986). The first two of these works cover the period of the Second World War and, since I can hardly leave this out here, I have had to go over some old ground in Chapters 6 to 8. But at the same time I have been able to incorporate interesting new material, and to concentrate on the Duke's wartime progress in the light of the exile theme. *Wallis & Edward* is an edition of the intimate letters of the Duke and Duchess of Windsor up to their marriage, also containing the Duchess's journal of their relationship in the form of her letters to her aunt in Washington, Mrs D. Buchanan Merryman ('Aunt Bessie'), to whom she was close. In the present work, I have made full use of the continuing chronicle of the letters to the aunt following the marriage, and I have also been able to publish some fascinating correspondence exchanged by the Duke and Duchess at important moments of separation after the war, correspondence which reveals both the fullness of their love for one another after many years of marriage, and their mingled feelings of resentment and resignation at the way they had been treated by the British royal establishment.

I owe an unrepayable debt to Maître Blum, with whom it is my privilege to have been working since 1979, for all the trust and friendship she has given me over the years. And I am scarcely less indebted to the Duke of Windsor's former secretary Miss Anne Seagrim, for all her interest and advice; to Andrew Best, for his constant support both as literary agent and friend; and to Trevor Langford. Other invaluable helpers include Mark Barty-King, Caroline Belgrave, Peter Bloxham, Vincent Brome, Michael Crowder, Jean-Pierre Dagorne, Dudley Danby, Michael Day, Neil Dawson, Lord Devlin, Bill Elvin, Sir Dudley Forwood, Charles Gornley, Tom Greaves, Hugo Haig-Thomas, Betty Hanley, Richard Hough, Tom Ingram, Alison Joynson, James Lees-Milne, Jean Lisbonne, Frances MacCurtain, Gordon McKenzie, Ursula Mackenzie, Eian MacMeeking, K. C. Malaker, Hans Marcus, Suzy Menkes, Thomas Moraitis, Lady Mosley, Steve Nelson, Raymond de Nicolay, Charles Orwin, Stuart Preston, Annette Remond, Michael Rubinstein, Georges Sanègre, Dr Jean Thin, and my parents. I am grateful to them all – and to the many others I fear I may have left out. Philip Ziegler has always shown me the greatest courtesy and consideration, and I hope that all I have written about the Duke and Duchess will prove a help to him in his great task.

One-third of the royalties of this work are to go to the Pasteur Institute in Paris, the Duchess of Windsor's universal heir, to be used in the fight against cancer and AIDS.

The story told herein is inevitably seen from the Duke of Windsor's own point of view: we see the treatment he received, his struggle against it, his bitter reactions, his disillusionment. Reading it, one must not entirely lose sight of the other side. One must remember the dismay that had been generated by his giving up the throne, and the genuine feeling (albeit a distinctly minority feeling) which continued to exist against him in some quarters. One must bear in mind the personality of George VI, the shy, quiet Englishman who had never sought the throne, and the fear in the minds of himself and those around him that he would be unable to operate as King in the shadow of his more glamorous predecessor. One must also acknowledge the Duke's naïvety in failing to realize how difficult life was bound to be for him as an ex-sovereign, and that he did not make things easier for himself by nursing a permanent sense of grievance and committing several unfortunate errors of judgement. Even so, I venture to suggest that many will be unable to read what follows without a sense of shock and shame.

MICHAEL BLOCH
May 1988

Part One

Causes of Contention

Chapter One

From Abdication to Marriage
1936–37

On Thursday, 10 December 1936, Edward the Eighth, King of Great Britain and Ireland, Defender of the Faith, Emperor of India, accepted the constitutional advice of his Ministers that he could not marry Mrs Simpson, the woman he loved, and remain on the throne. In the most dramatic romantic gesture of modern times, he abdicated in favour of his younger brother and left the country, to be known henceforth as the Duke of Windsor.

The news came to the overwhelming majority of his subjects as a terrible shock. Apart from those in high official circles, or with access to the gossip of London Society or the American press, none of them had ever heard of Mrs Simpson until exactly one week earlier. Even among those who knew of her existence, only a tiny few had possessed any inkling that a constitutional crisis was imminent as a result of the King's desire to marry her. To the millions who, opening their morning newspapers on 3 December, suddenly learned that the sovereign might have to give up his throne for personal reasons, the whole thing seemed incredible. With his good looks and good sentiments, his modernism and flair, his courageous reputation and his sympathy with the common man, he had for a quarter of a century as Prince of Wales been the idol of all classes, built up by the press and official propaganda into an almost godlike figure. His arrival on the throne less than a year before had been greeted with tremendous enthusiasm: his popularity as King amounted to adulation. It was difficult to take in the fact that this great and good personage was in fact a lonely and fallible man, unable to carry on 'without the help and support' of an unknown American woman of forty who had divorced one husband and was in the process of divorcing another.

The Abdication aroused passionately strong feelings among the ex-King's subjects. It is not unfair to say that nothing in the last hundred or more years has caused so much controversy among British people – and the controversy rages to this day. At the time, reactions differed sharply. On the whole, the working classes and thinking people of liberal views sympathized with the former sovereign and found it tragic that he should have had to leave under such circumstances, while the conservative middle classes tended to regard his decision as a dereliction of duty. There was a widespread sense of dismay that so apparently gifted a ruler, trained so well and so long for his task, should be handing over his crown to an untrained, reluctant and embarrassed successor of far less obvious gifts. On the other hand, among what would today be called the Establishment – the powerful circles of government and civil service, church and army, industry and the professions – there was a certain sense of relief at his going: for all his virtues, it was felt that he would have been an inconvenient ruler who would have interfered with the old settled ways, while the new King being unimaginative would present far fewer risks. In any event, the official world, like the aristocracy and the Court that was drawn from it, owed their allegiance not to an individual but to the Crown itself; like the Vicar of Bray, they smoothly transferred their entire loyalty and interest from Edward VIII to George VI.

Against Mrs Simpson there was a general feeling of resentment. In fact very few people knew anything about her, except that she was American (at a time when Americans in England were still regarded with reserve) and had been mixed up in divorce (at a time when this was still considered shocking). It was easy to see her as a scheming woman who had deflected the King from the path of duty, as the person principally responsible for the Abdication. This was not the truth. Her intimate correspondence with the King, published after her death, shows that she tried to disentangle herself from him and so keep him on his throne, that it was his own stubbornness which forced the issue. Those who knew her did not have the impression she was a *femme fatale*: perceptive diarists of London's social world – Marie Belloc-Lowndes, Robert Bruce-Lockhart, Victor Cazalet, 'Chips' Channon, Harold Nicolson – writing of her in the three years preceding the Abdication during which she was the centre of his interest, portray her as a simple and well-intentioned woman, some-what odd in her role but not without dignity, who seemed on the whole to be a good influence on the sovereign. Afterwards, most people preferred to believe that she had 'pinched the King'.

But the considerable majority, whatever their view of the Duke and the future Duchess of Windsor, believed one thing – that it was only natural that the couple after their marriage should eventually return to live in England and play some part in the British royal scene. Doubtless it was right that the Duke should stay away for a period of years to enable his successor to settle in. Doubtless his return might raise some problems concerning family and official relationships, the role he was to play as an ex-sovereign, and whether his wife should be treated as royalty. Doubtless some of the passions engendered by the Abdication would linger. Nevertheless, almost everybody would have agreed with Neville Chamberlain, who as Prime Minister in 1938 expressed the view that 'the right course was for the Duke of Windsor to be treated as soon as possible as a younger brother of the King who could take some of the royal functions off his brother's hands'. Indeed, in January 1939 – only two years after the Abdication – a Gallup Poll taken throughout the United Kingdom found that 61 per cent of the British people wanted the Windsors to return to England and only 16 per cent were against this, while 23 per cent had no particular views one way or the other.

The Duke of Windsor, who achieved his ambition of marriage in June 1937, less than six months after giving up the throne, him-self hoped and intended to return to England with his wife after an interval, and if possible play some subordinate rôle. He took few of his possessions with him when he left his country; and for many years he and the Duchess of Windsor lived in temporary rented accommodation, having no desire to take up permanent residence abroad. At the time of the Abdication, there seemed to be a tacit understanding that they should remain out of the country for no more than about two or three years. But what can only be described as a feud developed between the Duke on the one hand, and on the other the Royal Family, the Court, and conservative officialdom, who seemed determined at his exclusion. At the end of 1938, he was informed by King and Government that his return would not be welcome. In September 1939, when he came back to England to offer his wartime services, he was cold-shouldered and speedily posted back to France. After the defeat of France in the summer of 1940, he was dispatched for the duration to govern the Bahamas – a post conceived 'to keep him at all costs out of England'.

Three issues in particular may be said to illustrate the attitude of what one must call the Windsors' opponents, and the difficulties placed in the way of return. First, there was an attempt to make the pension promised to the Duke at the time of the Abdication conditional on his giving an undertaking never to come back to England except by the consent of the King under the advice of his Ministers. Second, there was an unprecedented decree purporting to deny his royal status to his wife, which amounted to an official censure of his marriage and which he regarded as a humiliating insult. Third, there was a ban on his taking up residence again at Fort Belvedere, the country house he had created near Windsor and come to love 'more than any material thing', in spite of an unwritten promise given by the King in December 1936 that he might one day do so.

By the end of the Second World War the Duke had become demoralized by what he regarded as a campaign against him of banishment and persecution, yet a homesick optimism still caused him for some years to cling to a desperate belief that circumstances would change, permitting his psychological and physical repatriation. In 1945 he hoped to be able to continue to serve his country usefully in the sphere of Anglo-American relations. In 1947 he hoped that he might acquire the use, for some months of the year, of his beloved Fort. In 1949 he hoped that the anguished question of his wife's status would at last be resolved, allowing family reconciliation. In 1951 he hoped that Churchill's arrival as peacetime premier would lead to a settlement of differences. All these hopes were dashed.

When, after the death of George VI in 1952, the Duke saw no letting-up in the antagonism towards him which emanated from Buckingham Palace but seemed to pervade the whole British official scene, he finally and unhappily resigned himself to spending the rest of his life outside his own country, contentedly married to a devoted wife, yet suffering from the longing and dissatisfaction which, according to poets, is the lot of exiles.

The story of the reign of Edward VIII is beyond the scope of this book. But there are two fundamental facts about it which are essential to an understanding of what happened afterwards. The first is that he came to the throne filled with the intention of re-forming the image and style of the monarchy. Under his father, George V, the Court and the royal way of life had made few con-cessions to rapidly changing social ideas and conditions. The new King sought to simplify and modernize. He disliked courtiers, palaces, débutantes, large official receptions, wasteful expenditure, superfluous paperwork, elaborate ceremonies and the Established Church. He regarded the whole world of his father with distaste – the stultifying routine, the unvarying traditions, the extravagance, the ancient hierarchical apparatus, the attendant bishops, the seasonal peregrinations between the royal palaces and estates. As the Arch-bishop of Canterbury, Dr C. G. Lang, ruefully noted in his diary on the old King's death, the new reign also promised to be a new *régime*.

In his memoirs, the Duke of Windsor tended to play down his reforming efforts as King. As he wrote in the late forties, a time of drabness in England when the people were on the whole glad that the monarchy had retained its old-fashioned panoply and style:

> I had no desire to go down in history as Edward the Reformer. Edward the Innovator – that might have been more to the point. Yet I had no notion of tinkering with the fundamental rules of the Monarchy, nor of upsetting the proud traditions of the Court. In truth, all I ever had in mind was to throw open the windows a little and to let into the venerable institution some of the fresh air that I had become accustomed to as Prince of Wales. My modest ambition was to broaden the base of the Monarchy a little more: to make it more responsive to the changed circumstances of my times. . . .

Though the practical changes introduced during so short a reign were comparatively few, its informal style and insistence on simpli-city and economy were enough to cause a conservative Court estab-lishment to regard the departing sovereign, whose good intentions were arguably mixed with a lack of tact and wisdom, as something of a dangerous threat of which they hoped they had seen the end.

The second essential fact about the reign is that, by the time he came to the throne on 20 January 1936, the King was passionately determined to marry Mrs Simpson, without whom he felt that he simply could not survive as a well-balanced human being. There is a letter from him to Mrs Simpson, written on the first day of 1936, in which he prays that they will become 'one' that year. It was not enough for him to keep her as a mistress. As Walter Monckton, who was to be his principal adviser during the Abdication crisis, later wrote:

> No one will ever really understand the story of the King's life . . . who does not appreciate . . . the intensity and depth of his devotion to Mrs Simpson. To him she was the perfect woman. She insisted that he should be at his best and do his best at all times, and he regarded her as his inspiration. It is a great mistake to assume that he was merely in love with her in the ordinary physical sense of the term. There was an intellectual companionship, and there is no doubt that his lonely nature found in her a spiritual comradeship. . . . He felt that he and Mrs Simpson were made for each other and that there was no other honest way of meeting the situation than marrying her.

The problem in the way of marriage was that Mrs Simpson remained the wife of Ernest Simpson. The marriage had ceased to mean very much, for Ernest in the light of his wife's association with the King had sought and found consolation with other women. But it still existed; and Mrs Simpson was inclined to hold on to it, feeling it was something safe and dignified whereas the King's feelings for her would not last. The King therefore set out to achieve three things. First, he needed finally to break up the Simpson marriage, and secure Ernest's compliance to being divorced as the guilty party. Second, he had to persuade Mrs Simpson to begin the proceedings against Ernest. Third, he had to ensure that those proceedings, to which some of those who knew about them would doubtless be opposed, were brought to a successful conclusion, and that Mrs Simpson would receive her divorce decree. Each stage in this process involved the King in great difficulties and anxiety; but in the end, on 27 October 1936, Mrs Simpson was awarded her decree *nisi* at Ipswich.

This was the key date of the reign, and for the King a moment of triumph and relief. If we examine his mood and behaviour before

27 October, and in particular during the immediately preceding weeks, we find him nervous, impatient, unpunctual and abstracted. It is to this period that belong the worst indiscretions of the reign – the *Nahlin* cruise, which exposed his relationship with Mrs Simpson to the gaze of the world's press, and his decision to include her in his September house party at Balmoral, which offended Scottish feeling. After 27 October, however, he was a changed man. Almost a month remained to him of active kingship, and during that time all who dealt with him found him efficient, courteous and serene. November saw the most notable successes of the reign, which recalled his best days as Prince of Wales: the visit to the Home Fleet at Portland, and the tour of the distressed areas of Wales. Even during the last days of the crisis, those around him were astonished at his calmness of spirit.

Before 27 October, the King refused to talk about Mrs Simpson or admit to any man his desire to marry her.[1] Even old friends who were out to help him, such as Winston Churchill and his trusted old private secretary Godfrey Thomas, tried in vain to warn him of the problems bound to arise from the obsession of his private life. On 20 October, when Baldwin came to see him as Prime Minister to ask if he could induce Mrs Simpson to give up her divorce, he evaded the issue by insisting that it was her personal affair, that as King he could not interfere with the private life of a subject. Once the decree *nisi* had been obtained, however, his attitude changed completely. He now wished to a frank admission of his marriage plans at the first convenient opportunity. The opportunity was provided by a letter from his Private Secretary Hardinge which stated, tactlessly and untruthfully, that the Cabinet were meeting in a crisis atmosphere to discuss his relations with Mrs Simpson. That letter was delivered on Friday, 13 November; and on Monday the 16th he summoned Baldwin to tell him, with absolute frankness,

> . . . that marriage had become an indispensable condition to my continued existence, whether as King or as man. 'I intend to marry Mrs Simpson as soon as she is free to marry,' I said. If I could marry her as King, all well and good: I would be happy and in consequence a better King. But if, on the other hand, the Government opposed the marriage . . . *then I was prepared to go.*

[1] Except perhaps his brothers the Dukes of York and Kent.

Men close to the King who wished to save him – Churchill, Monckton, Beaverbrook, Duff Cooper – urged him to delay. So long as Mrs Simpson remained in the background, there was nothing the Government could do to force the issue; and after the Coronation, due to take place on 12 May 1937, his prestige would make him impregnable. This advice he refused to follow, believing it would be tantamount to 'being crowned with a lie on my lips'. Still less did he wish to encourage the rise of a 'King's party', which in supporting his cause politically would have split the country.

It has been alleged – and was always vigorously denied by the Duke of Windsor – that he did not really wish to be King, that he came to the throne with the intention of giving it up, that Mrs Simpson was, perhaps unconsciously, a way out of responsibilities that irked him. This is too simple a way of looking at things; but it is certainly true that there are striking indications during his reign that he never believed it was going to last very long. When discussing his pro-gramme as King, he was always hesitant to commit himself to anything very far in the future; he seemed extraordinarily reluctant in particular to discuss his Coronation. When he moved into Buckingham Palace at the beginning of October, he took only a modest set of rooms, filled them with few of his personal effects, and made no changes to them except to install a shower and an extra telephone switchboard, because, as he tells us in his memoirs, he had a 'curious presentiment' that his occupancy of them would be a temporary one. Most astonishing of all was the appointment of his Household in July. The Court was filled with men of another generation, arch-conservatives who had been in sympathy with George V and were hostile to Edward VIII's desire for change. It would have been natural for the new sovereign to make a clean sweep. Not only did he fail to do so, but also many of the key positions were left in enemy hands.

It was not so much that he did not wish to be King, rather that he always realized that the difficulties in the way of marrying Mrs Simpson while on the throne might prove insuperable. We know from his own memoirs, as well as from independent sources, that he had talked to his brothers in the autumn of 1935 about the possibility of giving up his rights to the throne in order to marry. His decision to pay the price for marriage, even if it meant losing kingship, was not one that he made in December 1936. It was made before he came to the throne; and the whole of his reign was pervaded by it.

It is true that attempts were made, following the King's dramatic announcement to Baldwin on 16 November, to find some solution to the problem other than abdication. There was the proposal that he might marry Mrs Simpson morganatically, without her becoming Queen; and there was an idea that he might broadcast to the nation about his dilemma and then go abroad for a period, to allow public opinion to manifest itself on the subject of his marriage. Both of these proposals were firmly rejected by the Government. The King pursued them diligently but, studying the events of the three weeks preceding the Abdication, one is tempted towards the conclusion that his heart was not really in them, that he always believed it could only end one way. He investigated these alternatives, one feels, not with any realistic hope of remaining on the throne, but for the sake of history – and perhaps also for the sake of Mrs Simpson.

For Mrs Simpson, throughout the autumn of 1936, struggled to escape from him and thus save his crown. On 16 September she wrote to him from Paris attempting to break off their relationship. 'I really must return to Ernest. . . . I am sure you and I would only create disaster together. . . .' But he enticed her back with passionate entreaties. On 14 October she wrote of abandoning her divorce. 'Do you still feel you want me to go ahead as I feel it will hurt your popularity in the country . . . if I hurt you to this extent isn't it best for me to steal quietly away. . . . I can't help but feel you will have trouble in the House of Commons etc. and may be forced to go. I can't put you in that position. . . .' He was deaf to these suggestions. On 3 December, after the press had broken silence and the country had learned of her existence, she fled abroad – with the King's reluctant agreement and under the protection of his trusted courtier Lord Brownlow – to seek sanctuary at Lou Viei, the villa of her friends Herman and Kitty Rogers at Cannes. From there she telephoned and wrote to the King begging him not to abdicate, issuing a public statement in which she expressed her willingness 'to withdraw from a situation which has become both unhappy and untenable'. But by this time he had already made his decision.

As the crisis reached its culmination, the King did nothing to delay the final issue, which arrived with amazing suddenness. On 2 December, Baldwin told him of the Cabinet's refusal to accept on the morganatic marriage proposal, which left him (in the Prime Minister's submission) with only three choices – renunciation of Mrs Simpson (which was unthinkable to him), marriage contrary to the advice of his Ministers (who would resign) or abdication. On the night of Thursday, 3 December – after Mrs Simpson had set out for Cannes – he left Buckingham Palace for the last time and retreated to Fort Belvedere, not wishing to remain in London where his presence might encourage his partisans. It was there, on 7 December, that he communicated to the Government his irrevocable decision to give up the throne; and it was there three days later, on 10 December, that he signed the Instrument of Abdication, which became law the following day.

Baldwin praised the King's conduct during the crisis. Speaking to the House of Commons in the debate on the Abdication Bill on 10 December, he stressed that the King had constantly, in their discussions, repeated the following points:

> That if he went he would go with dignity. He would not allow a situation to arise in which he could not do that. He wanted to go with as little disturbance to his Ministers and his people as possible. He wished to go in circumstances that would make the succession of his brother as little difficult for his brother as possible; and I may say that any idea of what might be called a King's party was abhorrent. He stayed down at Fort Belvedere because he said that he was not coming to London while these things were in dispute, because of the cheering crowds. I honour and respect him for the way in which he behaved at that time.

'Through all that time', Baldwin wrote afterwards to the Duke of Windsor, 'you ran dead straight with me and you accomplished what you said you would do. You maintained your own dignity throughout: you did nothing to embarrass your successor, nor anything, as might so easily have happened, to shake the monarchy more than inevitable in the circumstances.' The Duke did not seek praise or gratitude; but he had cause to feel that, given his view that he had no alternative to leaving the throne, nothing in his reign had become him like the ending of it.

During the last hectic days of the crisis, the King – preoccupied with the business of abdication – gave remarkably little thought to his own future. There were only four things he wished to obtain for himself before giving up the throne and going abroad: an arrangement whereby Mrs Simpson's final divorce decree might be granted immediately, so that he could rejoin and marry her as soon as he left England; the right to live at Fort Belvedere when in future he returned to his country; a financial agreement, whereby he would be guaranteed a pension in return for giving up all that he had inherited from his father; and some provision for the titles of himself and his future wife. But amidst the haste and strain he was only able to give these questions a small part of his attention.

His most urgent concern was for the divorce; and he asked the Government if, simultaneously with the Abdication Bill, they would present another piece of legislation to the House of Commons which would make Mrs Simpson's divorce absolute immediately. He wanted this not just because he was in a hurry to marry Mrs Simpson, but because there was every prospect that the divorce, if not complete at the time of the Abdication, would be attacked and run into difficulties. It is hard now to remember how harsh and absurd were the English divorce laws in the 1930s. The normal reasons for divorce are that the marriage is no longer working, and at least one of the parties wishes to marry someone else. However, at the time of which we speak, not only did these constitute insufficient grounds for seeking a divorce, but also if any hint of such a situation became known to the Court, divorce became almost impossible. It was in fact possible only where it could be shown that the petitioner had behaved impeccably, while the respondent had committed some grave crime against the marriage – in most cases, that of adultery. Thus perfectly blameless couples (such as the Ernest Simpsons), who for some reason mutually wished to put an end to their marriage, had to go through the motions of a ludicrous charade. The husband being divorced, in order to establish his own 'guilt', would theatrically check into a hotel with a lady other than his wife (and usually hired for the purpose), and there proceed to 'cohabit' with her in circumstances which might be witnessed by the hotel staff. If it could be proved – during the six-month interval between decree *nisi* and decree absolute – that the wife had 'colluded' with the husband in condoning this ritual performance in order to 'set up' the divorce (as in reality happened in the vast majority of cases), or if it could be successfully suggested that the wife had been engaging in a relationship with another which inferred adultery, then the whole proceeding failed. It was open to absolutely anyone to 'intervene' in the divorce by coming forward to claim that they possessed evidence of collusion or adultery; and it was open to the authorities, through an official known as the King's Proctor, to examine these claims, or indeed to conduct a full investigation of the case, to establish whether there had in fact been collusion or adultery.

While Edward VIII reigned, it was not constitutionally possible for the King's Proctor to examine his relationship with Mrs Simpson; and to the end of his life the Duke of Windsor was to maintain with some passion that this relationship before marriage had never been of a physical nature. But once he became a private citizen he was in the same uncertain position as any subject wishing to marry a woman awaiting divorce; and he was warned that 'it was not unlikely that some muddle-headed busybody would seek to delay the proceedings by an unjustified intervention'. Hence the request for the special bill. Baldwin supported the King's desire for this, and presented it to the Cabinet on 6 December, feeling 'sure I could carry it through' and that he could 'not be responsible for any other policy'. But after some argument the Cabinet turned it down. Many feared that the King would use this pretext to delay his final decision; but in the end he contented himself with an assurance from his brother, who would succeed him, that he would do everything in his power to promote the smooth passage of the divorce. Such reassurance was needed: for on 10 December, the very day that the King abdicated, the event which had been feared occurred, when a 'muddle-headed busybody' appeared in the person of Francis Stephenson, an elderly solicitor's clerk of Ilford, Essex, who intervened in the divorce, claiming to be able to 'show cause' as to why it should not be made absolute.

In the chaos of the moment, the other matters affecting the future of the departing sovereign were but hastily discussed. In addition to the assurance about the divorce, his successor gave an oral promise that Fort Belvedere would be his to live in whenever he returned to England; but there was no discussion of exactly when this might be. An agreement was worked out concerning the financial consequences of the Abdication in relation to family property and family money, and this was signed at Fort Belvedere between Edward VIII and the future George VI on the evening of 10 December (several hours after the Abdication Instrument itself), as discussed in Chapter 2.

The question as to what the ex-King should be called was not answered until the last moment – on the evening of 11 December, after the Abdication had become law. It was then that George VI, as he had now become, told his brother that he was creating him Duke of Windsor, with the rank of prince. This had been the new King's personal decision – probably the only one which he made in the immediate process of assuming the Crown – and in a note which he wrote at the time he explained that his reason for making his predecessor a royal duke was to leave him with all the honour due to royalty (including his honorary positions in the armed forces), while depriving him of the right he might have had as an ordinary citizen of playing a possible future role in British public life. The question of the rank of Mrs Simpson after her marriage to the ex-King appears to have been the subject of only cursory discussion and no decision.

On the night of Friday, 11 December – the Duke of Windsor's last night in England – he dined with his family at Royal Lodge, George VI's country house in Windsor Great Park. The atmosphere was one of mourning: sadness and not hostility was the attitude towards the former sovereign. From there he drove to Windsor Castle to deliver his famous broadcast, a simple expression of his motives and feelings which he had written with the help of Walter Monckton and Winston Churchill. Announced by Sir John Reith as 'His Royal Highness Prince Edward', he declared, in words that lose nothing by their repetition:

> At long last I am able to say a few words of my own.
>
> I have never wanted to withhold anything from my people, but until now it has not been constitutionally possible for me to speak.
>
> A few hours ago I discharged my last duty as King and Emperor, and now that I have been succeeded by my brother, the Duke of York, my first words must be to declare my allegiance to him. This I do with all my heart.
>
> You all know the reasons which have impelled me to renounce the throne. But I want you to understand that in making up my mind I did not forget the country or the Empire which, as Prince of Wales, and lately as King, I have for twenty-five years tried to serve.
>
> But you must believe me when I tell you that I have found it impossible to carry the heavy burden of responsibility and to discharge my duties as King as I would wish to do without the help and support of the woman I love.

And I want you to know that the decision I have made has been mine and mine alone. The other person most nearly concerned has tried up to the last to persuade me to take a different course.

I have made this, the most serious decision of my whole life, upon a single thought of what would, in the end, be best for all.

This decision has been made less difficult for me by the sure knowledge that my Brother, with his long training in the public affairs of this country and with his fine qualities, will be able to take my place forthwith, without interruption or injury to the life and progress of the Empire. And he has one matchless blessing, enjoyed by so many of you and not bestowed on me – a happy home with a wife and children.

During these hard days I have been comforted by my Mother and by my Family. The Ministers of the Crown, and in particular Mr Baldwin, the Prime Minister, have always treated me with full consideration. There has never been any constitutional difference between me and them and between me and Parliament. Bred in the constitutional tradition of my Father, I would never have allowed any such issue to arise.

Ever since I was Prince of Wales, and later on when I occupied the Throne, I have been treated with the greatest kindness by all classes, wherever I have lived or journeyed throughout the Empire. For that I am very grateful.

I now quit altogether public affairs, and I lay down my burden. It may be some time before I return to my native land, but I shall always follow the fortunes of the British race and Empire with profound interest, and if at any time in the future I can be found of service to His Majesty in a private station, I shall not fail.

And now we have a new King. I wish him, and you, his people, happiness and prosperity with all my heart. God bless you all.

God Save the King.

When the Duke returned to Royal Lodge to take his leave of his family after the broadcast, he felt that what he had said had 'to some extent eased the tension between us'. His farewells with his successor were affectionate; in the words of George VI's diary, 'we kissed, parted as freemasons, & he bowed to me as his King'.

The Duke then drove to Portsmouth, where the destroyer *Fury* was waiting to take him to the Continent. One matter to which he had given virtually no thought during the preceding days was of where exactly he would be going. He could not join Mrs Simpson in France until her divorce was granted; he had vaguely planned to make for a hotel he knew near Zurich; but at the last moment Mrs Simpson prevailed upon him to accept the hospitality of Baron Eugen de Rothschild at Schloss Enzesfeld near Vienna, where she herself had been invited to spend Christmas. It was therefore to Austria that the former King proceeded when he left England, and there that he was to spend the following months.

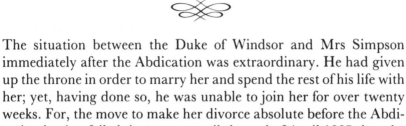

The situation between the Duke of Windsor and Mrs Simpson immediately after the Abdication was extraordinary. He had given up the throne in order to marry her and spend the rest of his life with her; yet, having done so, he was unable to join her for over twenty weeks. For, the move to make her divorce absolute before the Abdication having failed, it was not until the end of April 1937 that she would be able to apply for her final decree; and any association between them (or even rumours of such association) before that time was liable to lead to charges of collusion and rumours of adultery which might well prejudice the proceedings. So he remained in Austria and she in France. During March 1937, after Mrs Simpson had moved from the Riviera to the Château de Candé in Touraine, the Duke of Windsor planned to leave Austria and install himself on the Duke of Westminster's estate in Normandy, so as to be able to join her the instant her decree absolute was granted. But his legal advisers warned him that he could not even risk being in the same country as Mrs Simpson, separated from her though he would be by some three hundred miles; and so he remained where he was until the divorce was finally granted at the beginning of May.

During their long separation, the Duke and Mrs Simpson exchanged some three dozen intimate letters;[2] and, reading these, one is struck first of all by the remarkable difference in mood between the two correspondents. The Duke was in a dazed condition, and distressed at the thought of being parted for so long from the woman he wanted to marry. Yet his general frame of mind was not only contented, but also positively euphoric. By abdicating, he felt he had removed the great obstacle in the way of his heart's desire: what lay

---

[2] These are published in Part III of my edition of *Wallis & Edward, Letters 1931–1937: The Intimate Correspondence of the Duke and Duchess of Windsor* (London, Toronto and New York, 1986).

ahead (after a brief but agonizing interval) was a lifetime of happiness with Mrs Simpson. For Mrs Simpson, however, what had happened was a nightmare. She had tried desperately to disappear from his life and stop him abdicating; having failed, she realized that she would be blamed all her life for what had happened, that she had become, indeed, the most hated woman in the world. Though wretched, however, she had little time for self-pity, for it was now her duty to devote herself to the man who (against her will) had made such a terrible sacrifice for her, to assure him of her love and to try to stir him out of the state of dreamy unreality in which he was living. On 18 December 1936 she wrote to him:

> I have decided to sit in the villa walking in the garden – an occasional drive. So much scandal has been whispered about me even that I am a spy that I am shunned by people so until I have the protection of your name I must remain hidden. Nothing but scandal talk and bitter looks follow me. So this is my 4 months of exile and I must face it. The Rogers are nearly exiles as nobody asks them on account of me. Never mind. If we keep our poor heads and our health everything will be ours. So my darling please be more than careful in everything and the less we are seen the better. That England could have turned on the Prince of Wales has been a cruel blow to my faith in mankind. However we will find a new strong life built on our lonely love which has stood a test to prove its greatness. The anguish and loneliness of these months will be terrifying but we must take it and use our last remaining strength to endure it. I love you my own dear David.

To sensible and affectionate letters of this kind the Duke replied with such passionate effusions as the following, dispatched on New Year's Day 1937.

> Hello! my sweetheart. Such a very happy New Year I wish for WE[3] from the fastness of my 'exile' – my exile from you and not from England my darling and although it is still a matter of weary *months* to wait it is lovely to have 1936 behind us and only this and many

[3] The capitals 'WE', representing the initials of Wallis and Edward, had long been used by the Duke in his intimate letters to Mrs Simpson as a symbol of their union in love.

more happy years to look forward to. . . . God! how I love you love
you my Wallis my beloved sweetheart more and more and more.
I'm holding so tight all the time until that dear lovely precious day.
oh! God make it come quickly and bless WE this year and always.

In spite of the unpopularity of Mrs Simpson, there was little
indication, in the immediate wake of the Abdication, that the ex-
King would become a virtual outcast from his country. It is true that
many sycophants who had formerly made up to him and Mrs
Simpson suddenly pretended never to have known them; but they
were better off without such so-called friends, and the spectacle of
the 'ratting' of such people as Lady Cunard and Sir Philip Sassoon
succeeded in arousing the revulsion even of such stern critics of Mrs
Simpson as Stanley Baldwin, Queen Mary and Mrs Winston
Churchill. The general feeling towards the Duke in England, as the
fan mail he received at Schloss Enzesfeld showed, was one of sympathy. The whole nation had been moved by his broadcast, in which
he had stated his reasons for giving up the throne with such
frankness and simplicity. On the other hand, the harsh and ill-
judged broadcast of the Archbishop of Canterbury on the night of
Sunday, 13 December – which accused the ex-King of 'surrendering
a trust' on account of 'a craving for private happiness', and attacked
his friends for being 'alien to all the best instincts and traditions' of
the British people – aroused great national anger, increasing yet
further the general sympathy for the Duke.

Nor did the Duke's relations with his family seem at all disharm-
onious during the first days of George VI's reign. As we have seen, he
had parted from them in an atmosphere which was deeply
melancholy but not unaffectionate; and several of them (including
the new Queen Consort, who had been absent from the family
gathering on the evening of 11 December because of a cold) wrote
letters to him on his departure from England, wishing him well. The
new King and the old had kissed goodbye and 'parted as freemasons'; and George VI had gone out of his way to announce, in his
accession speech on the first full day of his reign, that his 'first act'
would be to confer a royal dukedom on his predecessor.[4] During the
following few weeks, the two brothers spoke 'every few days' on the

---

[4] This was no doubt the King's intention at that moment; but in fact the dukedom was not
formally created until the following March. See p. 70.

telephone; and their conversations, in December 1936, do not appear to have been in the least acrimonious. 'I would call him to see how he was getting along,' wrote the Duke thirty years later. 'Sometimes he would call me to find out if I needed something or to consult with me on some point of business with which I had been involved.'

During those early days, there was only one cloud on the horizon as far as the Duke was concerned, and that remained the divorce. The possibility of Mrs Simpson being denied this, and of the Duke thus being unable to marry her in spite of his enormous sacrifice, was nightmarish; but, as we have seen, it was a possibility which always existed under the divorce laws of the time. On 10 December, the 'muddle-headed busybody' Francis Stephenson had intervened to try to stop the divorce. When Mrs Simpson heard of this, she was almost frantic. 'It is practically the last straw the intervention. I didn't think the world could put more on two people whose only sin is to love. . . . It is despair for me to have been so badly treated.' Stephenson's 'evidence' amounted to no more than gossip, and he apologetically withdrew his intervention after hearing the Duke's abdication broadcast the following evening. But others might come forward, and if all their 'claims' were examined the divorce might at least be seriously delayed. The Duke relied, however, on George VI's promise to do all in his power to smooth the path of the divorce. Having seen the King, Walter Monckton wrote to reassure the Duke on 22 December that 'I am perfectly satisfied that Your Brother is anxious to help You in any way He properly can. I do not think He can do more at present than let it be known to the Ministers most nearly concerned that He is anxious for the right result. And I am sure that they understand what His view is.'

If this was the only serious worry of the Duke during the month following the Abdication, Mrs Simpson had a more general sense of foreboding. To some extent her feelings were paranoid and hysterical: she had naturally been deeply affected by the hatred which had been unleashed against her, and was inclined to see enemies everywhere. Though she knew better than anyone that the main cause of the Abdication had been the King's own obstinacy, she now persuaded herself (and set out to persuade the Duke) that he had been the victim of a 'conspiracy' led by Baldwin. Yet her sensitive antennae quickly picked up the true fact that a new official regime was arising in England which was frankly hostile to herself, the Duke, and their forthcoming marriage. She perceptively realized that the basic reasons for this hostility were political – in official eyes, it was no doubt desirable that (*a*) she rather than he should be blamed for what had happened, and (*b*) everyone should be encouraged to forget about Edward VIII in order to establish George VI with his somewhat dim personality – but that this official policy seemed to be reinforced and magnified by a strong personal animosity towards them coming from Palace quarters. As she wrote to the Duke on 3 January, only three weeks after the Abdication:

I am so distressed over the way your brother has behaved from the first and [he] is certainly giving the impression to the world at large that your family as well as Baldwin and his ministers do not approve of me. I do think now that the deed is done your family should not give out such an impression. Even in the speech he took the opportunity to convey that idea. I realise it is put there by the politicians whose game it is to have you forgotten and to build up the puppet they have placed on the throne. And they can succeed, because just as they had for months an organised campaign to remove you – and how cleverly they worked – so they have one to prove they were right in what they did and the first step is to eliminate you from the minds of the people. I was the convenient tool in their hands to use to get rid of you and how they used it! Naturally we have to build up a position but how hard it is going to be with no signs of support from your family. One realises now the impossibility of getting the marriage announced in the Court Circular and of the HRH.[5] It is all a great pity because I loathe being undignified and also of joining the countless titles that roam around Europe meaning nothing. To set off on our journey with a proper backing would mean so much – but whatever happens we shall make something of our lives. But since you have been so trusting all along perhaps now you are beginning to realise that you can't go on being and then have praise after you are dead. You must employ their means to accomplish your ends – and after Feb I should write your brother a straightforward letter setting forth the reasons for him not to treat you as a outcast and to do something for me so that we have a dignified and correct position as certainly befits an ex-King of England who really only left to get what the present one was lucky enough to have. Up to the present the only person who has made a big gesture is you. Frankly I am disgusted with them all. . . .

[5] That is, a royal title for herself after her marriage to the Duke.

The Duke did not seem to take these warnings very seriously, merely replying: 'I'll have to watch our interests in England like the dickens although I still have loyal friends like Walter [Monckton] and Ulick [Alexander] and of course E R Peacock and [George] Allen.'

Something must now be said about these 'loyal friends', all of whom had been at the ex-King's side during the days preceding the Abdication, and upon whose support he so greatly relied during the difficult months and years to come. Walter Monckton (1891–1964) was a successful barrister of outstanding intelligence and charm whom the Duke had first got to know at Oxford before the First World War. In 1932 he had been made Attorney-General to the Duchy of Cornwall, a minor court appointment which made him the principal legal adviser to the then Prince of Wales. In this post, Monckton rapidly won the close friendship and trust of his master; and in the middle of November 1936 it was to Monckton that King Edward VIII, having lost all confidence in his own Private Secretary Hardinge, turned in order to conduct his relations with Baldwin and the Government during the constitutional crisis. Monckton served the King faithfully[6] and won golden opinions from all sides for the tactful manner in which he accomplished his difficult mission. He was knighted by George VI as one of the first acts of his reign; and, being respected both by the new King and the old, he continued to be the main 'link' between the Duke of Windsor and the powers that be in England. However, though he undoubtedly had a strong personal sympathy with the Duke, Monckton was far from being his unconditional partisan. He was by nature a 'fixer', a man who smoothed over troubled waters, an impartial go-between. He also had his own career to think of, both at the Bar and eventually in British politics: significantly, he was destined politically to become the 'conciliatory' Minister of Labour under Churchill in the 1950s. In the difficult relations and acrimonious disputes that were to develop between the Duke and the Court, Monckton's advice to the Duke, invariably presented with great tact, was generally to do nothing, to make no protest, and to bide his time, advice which helped the British royal establishment while bringing no ultimate advantage to the ex-King. They nevertheless remained close friends until Monckton's death;

---

[6] Though he was responsible for one possibly thoughtless action that was to have serious consequences for the Duke after the Abdication. See p. 60.

and Monckton's notes of the many affairs concerning the Duke in which he was involved are an important historical source.

Major Ulick Alexander (1889–1973) was probably the only active senior courtier with whom the Duke could claim to be on terms of close personal friendship. A soldier who had been wounded in the First World War, he had long been involved in the royal scene, having been Political Secretary to the Duke's uncle, Lord Athlone, as Governor-General of South Africa in the early twenties, and Comptroller to the Duke of Kent (the brother to whom the Duke of Windsor was closest) from 1928 to 1936. He had been appointed Keeper of the Privy Purse by Edward VIII, and maintained this position under George VI; indeed, he seems to have been very popular with all the Royal Family. The Duke seems to have hoped that he would be able to represent his interests at Court, or at least act as his mouthpiece by the King's ear; but, however much he would have liked to help, Alexander was never in a position to intercede for the Duke: with the general feeling so hostile, it would have meant the end for him. He did what little he could for his former sovereign; he scrupulously looked after his personal possessions in England, and such of his financial interests as were within Alexander's province; and an official of his department, Thomas Carter, who had previously been Chief Clerk to the Prince of Wales, continued to act as the Duke's secretary in London. Alas for Alexander, it was also his baleful fate to be the constant bearer of bad tidings to the Duke; for whenever the latter received a snub from the Court – be it on the subject of money, the Duchess's status, or the Duke's right to live at Fort Belvedere – it was delivered, more often than not, in the form of an embarrassed letter from the Keeper of the Privy Purse, writing on the King's instructions.

Sir Edward Peacock (1871–1962) was a Canadian banker who had made a successful career on both sides of the Atlantic. He held the rank of Receiver-General to the Duchy of Cornwall and had for some years been the Duke's private financial adviser. He was a conservative City man and a Director of the Bank of England, and his notes on the Abdication crisis (in which he assisted Monckton) show him to have been both critical of the King and hostile to Mrs Simpson. Perhaps fortunately, in the years that followed the Duke seems to have relied upon him for advice only in matters of financial investment.

A. George Allen (1888–1956) was the Duke's solicitor, a co-founder in 1930 of the firm of Allen & Overy, which was destined to become one of the most famous and successful in the City. He had been recommended to the then Prince of Wales by Walter Monckton. In doing this favour to the partner of an as yet little-known new firm, Monckton was repaying an old debt, for Allen had saved his life in the trenches during the First World War; but he was also performing a signal service to his master, for no man was ever better served than was the Duke of Windsor by Allen. A taciturn, unspectacular personality, he defended the Duke's interests during the troubled years that followed with a steadfastness which never wavered; no trouble was ever too great for him. This book is largely based on his correspondence with the Duke; and in a sense he is its hero.

If, during the month following the Abdication, the Duke (in spite of Mrs Simpson's warnings) had no great cause to feel that a hostile attitude towards himself was developing in official and royal circles in England, his eyes were opened by three unpleasant shocks which descended upon him between mid-January and mid-February 1937.

The first concerned the divorce. On 21 January, Mrs Simpson's solicitor, Theodore Goddard, wrote to her to say that the President of the Divorce Court had ordered the King's Proctor to 'investigate' Francis Stephenson's intervention in her divorce suit – notwithstanding the fact that Stephenson had sought to withdraw his 'appearance' just one day after entering it. Goddard tried to reassure his client. 'I do not think you need be worried by this. . . . I propose to give the King's Proctor every facility in the matter, as after all we have nothing to hide. . . . My own view of the matter is that the President, having had cognisance of the intervention, feels that he ought to have the matter investigated because he has had this notice, and to allay public criticism.' All that would happen, he thought, was that the King's Proctor would see Stephenson to hear his 'evidence'; and once it was established there was none 'we shall hear no more about it'.

This was wishful thinking. The astonishing fact was that the authorities had decided to order the King's Proctor to conduct a full inquiry into the circumstances of King Edward's relations with Mrs Simpson, with a view to discovering whether the divorce had been tainted with collusion or adultery. In a curious memoir, Sir Donald Somervell, who as Attorney-General controlled the King's Proctor, touched on the motives behind their decision. He himself was not keen on an inquiry: if it uncovered some evidence of adultery, both the Duke and Mrs Simpson 'might well return to the country to give evidence to deny it. . . . Result a first-rate and squalid sensation. . . .' And it was widely felt that 'it would be outrageous if the King having abdicated to marry was prevented from doing so'. On the other hand, there was an influential lobby that 'felt it essential in the public interest that the divorce should be stopped'. Somervell bowed to this pressure. He 'decided we'd go ahead as if this was an A.B. [i.e. an ordinary] case'. The King's Proctor 'as a result interviewed countless people, members of the crew of the yacht, servants, hall porters, etc.'

Both the Duke and Mrs Simpson were aghast at this development. It indicated that there was a current of opinion in high circles hoping to stop their marriage; and there was always a chance that the King's Proctor might turn up some evidence, true or false, which would persuade the court to refuse the divorce. King George VI had promised his brother that he would use his personal influence to try to prevent such complications occurring: had he in fact done anything? Mrs Simpson begged the Duke to write to the King 'telling him what a good thing it would be if he saw Somervell and simply let him know that anything in the way of holding up my decree absolute would be most objectionable to him'. Her letters indicate that her anxiety on the subject was driving her, that February, to the verge of a nervous breakdown:

> Here is the thing about the divorce from the U.S. papers. . . . I have never had a word said in our defence or a kind word in the press. Surely your brother can protect me a bit – not to be the butt of musical comedy jokes on the radio, etc. If they knew your family approved our marriage when free, things would be so different for me. I do feel utterly down. It has always been such a lone game against the world for me and a woman always pays the most – and you my sweet haven't been able to protect me. You can see how worried I am. There must be a way to find out what the King's Proctor is going to do. . . . Surely he has finished his investigation by now?

The investigation discovered nothing. The many eager witnesses who came forward, wrote Somervell, were found to have 'no evidence but were merely repeating the gossip of the Clubs and the Temple'. Nothing was found to indicate that the Duke and Mrs Simpson had 'indulged in the familiarities which normally indicate cohabitation'; and 'our inquiries also confirmed the view that the divorce . . . was not a collusive divorce in . . . any provable sense'. The investigation of the King's Proctor was formally brought to an end in special proceedings before the President of the Divorce Court on 19 March, but not before the ex-King and the woman he wished to marry had undergone two months of acute worry, and been profoundly disillusioned by indications of official hostility as well as the possible bad faith of the King.

In the first half of February, while the divorce investigation was continuing, the Duke received the second shock, which concerned the fate of the financial assurances which had been made to him at the time of the Abdication. This matter will be explained in detail in Chapter 2. In short, the Government had promised that they would recommend his inclusion in the Civil List, the parliamentary vote of pensions to members of the Royal Family which takes place early in each reign; and George VI (in return for the Duke agreeing to give up everything he had inherited from their father) had promised that, in the event of the House of Commons refusing to vote anything to the Duke in spite of the Government's recommendation, he himself would pay his brother an allowance of £25,000 a year. The Duke was now amazed to receive a letter from Allen, dated 10 February, telling him that the Government, as Allen had been told during a heated meeting with officials, 'could not support your inclusion in the Civil List. Nor could they countenance Your Royal Highness receiving an annual payment from the King. . . .' This was followed by a letter from George VI effectively repudiating his agreement to pay the Duke a pension, on account of the mood of Parliament who were 'still a little sore with you for having given up being King'. The Duke, appalled at these developments, replied holding his brother to his word. 'I must tell you frankly that I am relying on you to honour your promise.' But it was to be a year before the King finally did so (in a somewhat reduced form); and that time saw the development of a bitter quarrel between the two brothers on the financial question, described by Winston Churchill as 'a disaster of the first magnitude to the monarchy'. What distressed the Duke in February 1937 was not so much that the promised financial help was being withheld from him (for he knew that it would take the new sovereign time to organize his own finances), but that both the King and the Government, in a striking demonstration of unfriendly feeling towards him, appeared to have broken their word.

The third revealing shock that the Duke experienced was of a symbolic rather than a substantive nature, but none the less painful for that. Now that the air was filled with the vexed and contentious issues of the divorce investigation and the money trouble, the Duke's regular fraternal telephone conversations with the King became more heated and difficult. The Duke recalled in 1966:

> Then one day quite without warning he ended our conversation with the enigmatic remark: 'I'm afraid, David, that I can't go on telephoning to you any more.'
> 'Are you serious?' I asked.
> 'Yes, I'm sorry to say that I am,' was the answer. 'The reason must be clear to you.'
> It never was. . . .

Monckton, visiting the Duke at Enzesfeld towards the end of February, tried to explain some of the reasons for the King's disinclination to talk to him. The Duke was offering advice which sometimes 'ran counter to the advice which the King was getting from . . . the Government'. (This no doubt included the Duke's advice that the King should keep his word on the matters of the divorce and the money.) And 'telephone conversations, especially when they ranged into questions affecting Mrs Simpson, were especially hard for the new King' who did not have the 'same quickness' as the Duke and 'was troubled by the impediment in his speech'. This latter point, indeed, had also occurred to Mrs Simpson herself, who wrote to the Duke on 6 February: 'I must advise writing to your brother instead of telephone. I think with a slow brain such as his that he doesn't take in ideas as quickly as you speak and then the constant yelling which one has to do is apt to get on the nerves of a highly strung person. . . .'

The Duke resigned himself to the fact that he would be unable, henceforth, to speak to his brother. But in his mind the sudden end of this direct (and hitherto amicable) form of communication took on a symbolic significance. As he wrote in 1966:

. . . I was soon to decide that a graver, far more subtle reason accounted for the withdrawal.

It was that my brother, under pressure from the dourer, less forgiving precincts of the Establishment . . . had been persuaded that his reign would best be served by keeping me out in the cold. I have good reason to believe that those closest to my brother were not displeased with the imposition of this freeze.

No-one ever mentioned this turn in our affairs out loud . . . but there was no mistaking the sharp drop in the temperature. . . .

It is evident that there had been a massive change of attitude in both Palace and Government circles between the time of the Abdication, when the Duke had parted from his family amidst tears and kisses and Baldwin had praised the dignified and constitutional manner of Edward VIII's departure to the House of Commons, and the middle of February, when the Duke detected a 'sharp drop in the temperature'. It is tempting to speculate on the reasons for this change, the exact nature of the new positions that were taken up, and the persons or groups of people who were principally responsible. Such speculation, however, must remain unprofitable until detailed and reliable documentary evidence from royal and governmental sources is available on the subject of the offical treatment of the Duke of Windsor; and up to now there has been a conspiracy of silence on this subject, all relevant public archives being closed at the personal request of the sovereign until the year 2037. What is possible here, however, is to attempt to explain whom it was that the Duke himself, and the woman he married, regarded as the main architects of the campaign to exclude and (as they saw it) persecute them. When the Duke wrote in 1966 that he had 'good reason to believe' that 'those closest' to George VI were 'not displeased' with the imposition of a 'freeze', whom exactly did he have in mind?

One thing is clear – that the Duke, who had been close to his brother during their early lives, never imagined the King to be personally responsible for his own and the Duchess's unhappy fate. That is to say, he believed that, left to himself, George VI would never have treated them in the manner he did. And there is much trustworthy evidence to support this view. It will be seen in the course of this book, as substantiated by reliable witnesses, that King

George (*a*) did not at first intend to ignore the Duke's wedding;[7] (*b*) would not, left to his own devices, have offended his brother by denying a royal title to the Duchess of Windsor;[8] (*c*) was in 1938 'not fundamentally against the view' that the Duke should eventually return to England to 'take some of the royal functions off [the King's] hands';[9] (*d*) at first seemed quite happy, when the Duke returned to England in 1939 to discuss his war work, that he should remain in the country in a civil defence post.[10] But on each of these occasions the King was swiftly and firmly induced to change his mind. That he did not do so happily is suggested by his letters to the Duke early in his reign on those sensitive issues (money, title) where the Duke was being thwarted, which are written in a tone of painful embarrassment, with constant expressions of regret.[11] But George VI was not a man of strong personality or independent will. Like Nicholas II of Russia (his first cousin once removed), he was a well-intentioned and devout individual but without much stuffing, mostly the product of influences around him, inclined to agree with the last person he had talked to. Feeling inadequate to the role that had quite suddenly been thrust on him, he relied completely on the guidance and support of a small group of people, with wills and characters far stronger than his own, who surrounded and dominated him. And foremost among these were his own wife and mother.

The attitude of Queen Mary is well known. In the words of her official biographer James Pope-Hennessy, she regarded her eldest son's decision to abdicate in order to marry Mrs Simpson 'with consternation, with anger and with pain'. To her it was an unforgivable dereliction of duty, which had brought shame and dishonour on the British royal house. As she wrote to the Duke in July 1938, it had seemed 'inconceivable to those who had made such sacrifices during the war' that he, 'as their King, had refused a lesser sacrifice'. In his memoirs, the Duke of Windsor recalled the painful scene when, in November 1936, he had told his mother – in

---

[7] See pp. 37–9.

[8] See p. 68.

[9] See p. 133.

[10] See p. 144.

[11] See pp. 50–1, 67.

the presence of his sister, Princess Mary – of his intention to marry Mrs Simpson.

> . . . My mother had been schooled to put duty, in the stoic Victorian sense, before everything else in life. From her invincible virtue and correctness she looked out on life as from a fortress upon the rest of humanity, with all its tremulous uncertainties and distractions. . . .
>
> All the while I was waiting for the right moment to make a request I did not believe would be refused. 'Please won't you let me bring Wallis Simpson to see you?' I asked. 'If you were to meet her you would understand what she means to me, and why I cannot give her up. I have waited a long time to find the person whom I wished to marry. For me the question now is not whether she is acceptable but whether I am worthy of her.' But they [Queen Mary and Princess Mary] could not bring themselves to unbend even this much. It was not, I am sure, because they were wanting in understanding: it was rather because the iron grip of royal convention would not release them. . . .

These careful words were published, in 1951, while Queen Mary was still alive. Two years later, at the time of her final illness and death, he was to write about her in letters to his wife, which will be quoted in Chapter 11 of this book, in terms almost of hatred. 'My sadness was mixed with incredulity that any mother could have been so hard and cruel towards her eldest son for so many years. . . . I'm afraid the fluids in her veins have always been as icy cold as they now are in death. . . . I've been boiling mad the whole time that you haven't been here in your rightful place as a daughter-in-law at my side.'

Not only did Queen Mary refuse to receive Mrs Simpson in 1936, but after the Abdication she also took the unusual step of issuing a statement affirming that, contrary to rumour, she had never done so – a declaration which amounted to a public condemnation of her future daughter-in-law. As Mrs Simpson wrote despairingly to the Duke on 14 December 1936:

> . . . your mother has placed me in a worse position than ever and practically says she would not receive me. It is plain that York [i.e.

King George VI, formerly Duke of York] guided by her would not
give us the extra chic of creating me HRH – the only thing to bring
me back in the eyes of the world. . . .

It seems a reasonable supposition that the King allowed himself to
be 'guided' generally by Queen Mary in matters concerning the
treatment of his brother and sister-in-law: she is known to have
exercised a formidable matriarchal influence in the new reign.
Throughout the first sixteen years of his married life, the Duke of
Windsor regularly implored his mother to meet his wife: always she
refused.

We know that the new Queen Consort was equally adamant in her
refusal to receive the Duchess of Windsor; and she too is known to
have wielded a powerful influence over her husband. She is also said
to have nurtured intense feelings against the Windsors on very
personal grounds: this, at any rate, was what they themselves (and
particularly the Duchess) believed. 'Really David the pleased
expression on the Duchess of York's [*sic*] face is funny to see,' wrote
Mrs Simpson to the Duke at the end of December 1936. 'How she is
loving it all. There will be no support there.' And again in February,
referring to the torment of the divorce investigation: 'I blame it all on
the wife – who hates us both.' Queen Elizabeth did not have better
things to say about the Duchess. 'With all her charity', wrote Sir
Ronald Lindsay on discussing the Duke's desire to visit America
with her at Balmoral in October 1937, 'she had not a word to say for
"that woman".'

Both queens seem to have felt that the Duke of Windsor represented some kind of threat to George VI. Shortly after the Abdication Queen Mary was 'furious and outraged' when Lord Salisbury
expressed his sympathy for the ex-King, proclaiming with 'indignation': 'The person who needs sympathy is my second son. He is the
one who is making the sacrifice.' Walter Monckton, who had conversations with Queen Elizabeth at various times on the subject of the
Duke's future, always found her adamant that the Duke should not
return to England or be given 'any effective sphere of work . . .
because the Duke of Windsor, to whom the other brothers had
always looked up, was an attractive, vital creature who might be a
rallying point for any who might be critical of the new King who was
less superficially endowed with the arts and graces that please'.

The animosity towards the Windsors on the part of the two queens was reinforced by that of powerful courtiers. We have seen that Edward VIII had disliked the existing court apparatus and during his short reign had made vague moves in the direction of dismantling it. With the accession of the conservative George VI, who was happy to leave things as they were, the Court breathed a sigh of relief and closed ranks, determined to exclude the man who had tried to interfere with their settled ways. In the ordinary course of things, the Duke could not therefore expect much support or understanding from the senior figures of the Royal Household, now more powerful than before in that they virtually ran the whole business of monarchy on behalf of an inarticulate and indecisive sovereign. But it also happened that the two men who occupied the key position of royal Private Secretary during George VI's reign – Alexander ('Alec') Hardinge and Alan ('Tommy') Lascelles – regarded the Duke of Windsor with an intense and irrational personal loathing. It is an almost incredible fact that the Duke had maintained these two officials in their posts during his own reign, though it must have been obvious to him how entirely out of sympathy they were with his personality and ideas. Certainly they never afterwards showed the slightest loyalty or even pity towards the man who had once been their sovereign and master. It is known, incidentally, that neither Hardinge nor Lascelles got on particularly well with the Queen Consort; but on one subject at least the three of them were of the same mind.

Hardinge (1894–1960), the son of a Viceroy of India, had been George V's Assistant Private Secretary from 1920 until 1936. In December 1935 'Chips' Channon thought him, 'though quite young', the very embodiment of a Court that was 'dead and out of date'. He had, wrote Channon, 'very much criticised the Prince of Wales and his entourage. It is high time such dreary narrow-minded fogies were sacked, as, indeed, they will be, in the next reign.' Yet Edward VIII, coming to the throne only a month after these words were written, not only kept him on, but promoted him (on the advice of the retiring occupant of the post, Lord Wigram) to be his Principal Private Secretary. Hardinge's first act on acceding to this high position was to quarrel with the King on the subject of his salary. Hardinge will go down in history as the man who set the constitutional crisis moving in November 1936, by writing a letter to the King which stated – untruthfully – that the Cabinet were meeting to discuss the King's relations with Mrs Simpson. The King was 'shocked and angry': he did not question Hardinge's right to address him on such a subject (indeed, he immediately acted by making a frank confession of his intentions to the Prime Minister), but 'what hurt was the cold formality with which so personal a matter affecting my whole happiness had been broached'. He now lost all confidence in Hardinge, and for the brief remainder of his reign conducted his official relations through Monckton. Hardinge was maintained in his post by George VI, who immediately knighted him. One of his colleagues later recorded that he 'disliked Edward VIII so much that he was overjoyed at the Abdication'. He seems all the same to have been somewhat exhausted by it, for he was on leave for most of the following winter; but as soon as he returned to the Palace he proved himself (to quote Channon again) 'ever the late King's relentless foe'. A powerful but generally unattractive figure – Harold Macmillan described him as 'idle, supercilious, without a spark of imagination or vitality' – he became increasingly high-handed as Private Secretary until he was effectively sacked in the summer of 1943 as the result of an incident which occurred during the King's visit to North Africa. The Duke is said to have written subsequently to his brother: 'What did I tell you and warn you?'

Hardinge was succeeded by his deputy Lascelles (1887–1981), a man of stronger character and greater intellectual gifts, but like him the very embodiment of the old Court establishment. He had been appointed Assistant Private Secretary by George V in 1935 and maintained this post under Edward VIII and George VI. Previously, in the 1920s, he had been Assistant Private Secretary to the Prince of Wales, but had quarrelled with his master, and finally resigned, on account of his disapproval of the Prince's life-style. Again one can only wonder that Edward VIII, finding his old critic installed at Buckingham Palace in 1936, did not get rid of him at once. That Lascelles' almost pathological dislike of the sovereign had only intensified with the years is shown by the following entry from Harold Nicolson's diary for 14 December 1936, three days after the Abdication.

> I lunched at the [Travellers] Club with Tommy Lascelles, who is so relieved at the fall of his master that he was almost indiscreet. . . . He says that the King was like the child in the fairy stories who

had been given every gift except a soul. He said there was nothing in him which understood the intellectual or artistic sides of life, and that all art, poetry, music etc were dead to him. Even nature meant nothing to him . . . and his gardening at the Fort meant nothing beyond a form of exercise. He had no friends in this country, nobody whom he would ever wish to see again. . . . I really believe that Tommy is glad he is gone. He said: 'He was without a soul, and this made him a trifle mad. He will probably be quite happy in Austria. . . . There is no need to be sorry for him. He will be quite happy wearing his silly Tyrolean costume' – there was a note of real fury at that – 'and he never cared for England or the English. He hated his country since he had no soul and did not like being reminded of his duties.'

Lascelles' aim with regard to the Duke of Windsor, as he wrote to a friend at the end of 1937, was to ensure that 'the public should cease to take him seriously', to make them realize that 'his mental and moral development stopped dead when he was about 15', and to establish the view that 'though a sad figure, he is no longer a particularly interesting one'. We may assume that, throughout his long years in the royal secretariat, Lascelles – 'that evil snake', as the Duke was eventually to call him – worked relentlessly and cunningly to realize his aim of keeping the ex-King away and diminishing his public stature. In the 1950s, Lascelles (whose own preferences were homosexual) was to be the man principally responsible for frustrating Princess Margaret's desire to marry Group-Captain Peter Townsend.

If it is necessary to discover yet further influences upon King George VI which effectively turned him, and the whole of British royal policy, so violently against the Duke of Windsor, one can find them in the upper echelons of the Church of England. By seeking to marry a divorced woman, the Duke had offended against a sacred canon of the Church at a time when it was in the midst of a campaign to reassert its moral authority. The new sovereigns were devout churchgoers and (again like the last Russian sovereigns) surrounded by religious advisers. The Archbishop of Canterbury had expressed his attitude in his bitter (and bitterly resented) broadcast attack on the ex-King after the Abdication; and, although the tone of this broadside (which included a reference to George VI's stammer) somewhat embarrassed the Royal Family, Dr Lang was on terms of close personal friendship with the King and particularly the Queen, the latter of whom certainly seems not to have dissented from the views expressed.

Did the Duke have any allies in powerful positions in England? Most of his friends at Court were thrown out early in the new reign, in what can only be described as a Palace purge. Sir Godfrey Thomas, his faithful old aide since the First World War, was removed from the post of Assistant Private Secretary, in which he had been the colleague of Hardinge and Lascelles but had failed to share their hysterical view of Edward VIII. Lord Brownlow – who had been the King's faithful friend during the crisis and Mrs Simpson's protector during her terrible journey to Cannes, and who had afterwards provided useful information to Baldwin on the state of mind of the ex-King and his future wife in their respective places of refuge – found himself sacked ignominiously from his post as Lord-in-Waiting before Christmas 1936, learning of his dismissal from the newspapers.[12] 'Am I to be turned away', he protested to Lord Cromer, the Lord Chamberlain, 'like a dishonest servant with no notice, no warning, no thanks, when all I did was to obey my late Master, the King?' 'Yes,' came the reply.[13] Eventually there were only two courtiers of stature whom the Duke could look upon as close friends – Ulick Alexander (who remained as Keeper of the Privy Purse) and Walter Monckton (who retained his post as Attorney-General to the Duchy of Cornwall), neither of whom exercised much influence or was ever able effectively to help him.

In British politics, the Duke could count on the loyal friendship of Winston Churchill and David Lloyd George – both at this time 'in the wilderness' but nevertheless possessing considerable personal followings in the House of Commons – and at least two members of the Cabinet: the Transport Minister Leslie Hore-Belisha and the War Minister Alfred Duff Cooper.[14] But these men – along with a not inconsiderable number of senior officials who retained an affection

---

[12] This was especially humiliating in that, by custom, all courtiers are normally retained in their posts for six months at the beginning of a new reign.

[13] The purge continued down to lower levels: René Legros, probably the greatest living French chef, who had been engaged in the Royal Household by Edward VIII in the summer of 1936, found himself dismissed shortly before the Coronation on the grounds, he imagined, that he had been 'found' by Mrs Simpson.

[14] In May 1937, when Neville Chamberlain succeeded Baldwin as premier, Cooper became First Lord of the Admiralty and Hore-Belisha went to the War Office.

for the ex-King – were able to do little more than offer moral support. Such was the popular sympathy for George VI in the position in which he so suddenly found himself, and such the desire of politicians to establish him firmly on the throne, that it was impossible for the Duke's supporters to move against the overwhelming feeling, and the various relentless measures, which emanated from the Palace on the subject of the Duke of Windsor.

Under these circumstances, the Duke came to see himself as the victim of a conspiracy on the part of leading members of his family and of the Court. In his mind, the cold attitude towards him of successive British governments and of officialdom was no more than a natural and inevitable consequence of the Palace campaign of exclusion and persecution. As he wrote from the Bahamas in 1941,[15] where he found his attempts at reform and good government impeded and sometimes frustrated by Whitehall: 'The world being composed of snobs and satellites, any serious efforts of mine are handicapped from the outset. . . . The royal ostracism of me is condoned by the Government and reflects universally, as everyone has the impression that a good word for me or my work might close the doors of Buckingham Palace against them. . . .' In the Foreign Office and Colonial Office – whose governors and ambassadors were the sovereign's personal representatives – royal influence, and hence the sentiment against him, seemed particularly strong.

What is clear, in any case, is that George VI, who on coming to the throne may have been somewhat intimidated by his unsought elevation but nevertheless seems then to have retained a warm-hearted and fraternal attitude towards his predecessor, was within three months brought to regard his brother as his enemy. On 17 March, when Lloyd George dined at the Palace for the first time during the new reign, his confidante Frances Stevenson noted in her diary:

> H.M. is most anxious that the Duke should not return to this country, but D. [David Lloyd George] told him that he did not take that view & thought H.M. would be wiser not to oppose it. '*She* would never dare to come back here,' said H.M. 'There you are wrong,' replied D. 'She would have no friends here,' said H.M. D. did not agree. 'But not you or me?' said the King anxiously.

---

[15] In a letter to Lord Beaverbrook, which appears to have been drafted but not sent.

And a visitor to Balmoral the following October noted that the King did 'not yet feel safe on his throne', being 'like the mediaeval monarch who has a hated rival claimant living in exile'.[16]

The harsh new attitude manifested by the Palace raised the question of how far the Royal Family would be concerning themselves with the Duke of Windsor's marriage – if, that is, Mrs Simpson succeeded in obtaining her divorce and it took place at all. Which (if any) of them would be attending the ceremony? Would it be officially announced? As always, Mrs Simpson took a realistically cynical view of the prospects. In late December she wrote to the Duke: 'I am getting rather worked up about what support we are going to get from your family for our wedding. It is so important – everyone around me realises the importance of the announcement etc.' And on 3 January: 'One realises now the impossibility of getting the marriage announced in the Court Circular. . . .'

The Duke, however, found it impossible to accept that his family would simply dissociate themselves from his marriage to Mrs Simpson, the great event, so crucial to his personal well-being, for which he had waited and struggled for so long and given up so much. Even the disillusioning factors which had brought home to him the 'drop in the temperature' – the divorce investigation, the money difficulties, the end of telephone talks with his brother – could not bring him to believe that his wedding, if and when it finally took place, would not be a royal wedding. And, indeed, it would appear that, throughout the winter, the King fully intended at least to be represented at the occasion. In the course of February 1937 the Duke received two family visits at Enzesfeld – first from his sister Princess Mary and her husband Lord Harewood (from the 7th to the 13th), then from his youngest and favourite brother Prince George, Duke of Kent (from the 24th to the 28th) – and from none of these did he receive any hint that there would be a royal boycott of his marriage; in fact, they all seem to have expressed their intention of attending, and carried messages from the Duke to the King about the arrangements he had in mind. 'My sister and Harewood will be arriving in a fortnight', wrote the Duke to Mrs Simpson on 26 January, 'and I'll

[16] See p. 116.

be able to give them a lot to say and arrange for our wedding when they return. And then of course I'll write and explain myself too. . . .'

The most important decisions to make with regard to the wedding were as to where it would take place and when; and on both of these questions the Duke – firmly imagining that it would be a royal occasion – consulted the King, who seems to have been quite happy to offer his advice.

As concerned the matter of venue, the King approved the Duke's decision to be married at a private house in France. Two suitable houses had been offered – La Cröe, an enormous shorefront villa at Cap d'Antibes on the Côte d'Azur, and Candé, a modernized castle in Touraine belonging to the French-American time-and-motion tycoon Charles Bedaux, a friend of Mrs Simpson's hosts the Rogers. According to the Duchess of Windsor's memoirs:

> David then asked his brother for his reactions. The King was not enthusiastic about the Riviera, because of its reputation as a playground, and he favoured the old château in the centre of France as the more dignified setting. That was how Candé came to be chosen.

This choice was approved by the Duchess, who wrote to her aunt at the time: 'I don't regret for a moment the decision to go to Candé. The Riviera has a cheap air about it no doubt and the reputation for being the world's playground. It will be more dignified to be in the country. . . .' In the second week of March, Mrs Simpson and her friends the Rogers left Cannes, and, skilfully eluding the press, installed themselves at Candé, where they awaited the moment when the divorce would be granted and the Duke be able to join them.

The Duke's original idea was to marry Mrs Simpson the moment she was free, which (if all went well) would be at the end of April or the beginning of May; but she wisely refused to countenance their marrying before the Coronation, which was due to take place on 12 May. As she wrote to him on 7 March:

> I have come to what I think is a very wise decision from every-body's point of view. . . . I have decided that we must not be married until after the Coronation. . . . We are unimportant com-

pared with the show they are trying to bring off. Once [the Coronation is] successfully accomplished they will turn their attention to you and the whole atmosphere will be cleared. . . . It also proves there was no great hurry for the marriage, Mr B wrong, and it is more dignified. . . . You must believe in this – it is all intuitive, but I know right. . . . Also whoever [from the Royal Family] is coming [to the wedding] can then arrange their engagements accordingly. I mean Kent etc. . . . I'm quite sure you'll agree that this is the dignified and better method . . . and I am keen to let them have their show. . . .

The Duke accepted this sensible advice, and then proceeded to consult the King as to which post-Coronation date would suit him best for the marriage. This he did through the intermediary of his cousin and old shipmate Lord Louis Mountbatten, who visited him at Enzesfeld from 11 to 13 March. Mountbatten seems to have wasted little time, on his return to England, in seeing the King and getting him to name a date; for, on 22 March, Mrs Simpson wrote to her aunt from Candé:

> . . . the Duke and myself decided it would be more politic to have the wedding after the Coronation, and as May is very booked for all members of the family George VI has suggested June 4th as a convenient time for him to send a member to the wedding. . . .

For some reason Mrs Simpson was unhappy about 4 June since it was a Friday, and in the end the wedding was fixed for 3 June – possibly a slightly tactless choice, since it had been the birthday of King George V.

On 3 May, Mrs Simpson's divorce was finally made absolute. That night, the Duke of Windsor left Austria on the Orient Express, and the following day he joined her at Candé. 'It was wonderful to be together again,' wrote the Duchess of Windsor in her memoirs. 'Before, we had been alone in the face of overwhelming trouble. Now we could meet it side by side.'

New trouble came almost immediately, for no sooner had the Duke been joyously reunited with Mrs Simpson than he received the shattering news that none of his family would be attending his wedding after all. This came in a letter from Mountbatten dated 5 May – the day after the Duke's arrival in France. Mountbatten explained that, although he had succeeded in fixing a date for the marriage 'that suited Bertie, Georgie, etc.', other people had 'stepped in' and created a state of affairs which had made all the Duke's friends 'very unhappy'. Mountbatten had made 'several attempts' to try to change the situation, but in the event he was not even in a position to accept the Duke's 'kind invitation' himself.[17] He had not 'given up all hope' of coming, but the chances of his doing so did not 'look too good'.

Not only would no member of the Royal Family be coming, but – an equally bitter blow – the royal ban seems to have been extended to include any person who held office under the Crown. That is to say, no courtier, officer, diplomat, civil servant or member of the Government was authorized to be there. This put those officials who were friends of the Duke in a terrible position. If they went, they would be incurring the displeasure of the King and ruining their careers; if they did not, it would cause pain to the Duke and expose them to the charge of 'ratting' on him. An extraordinary account of this situation – unpublished up to now – is that of Lord Brownlow (known to his friends as 'Perry'), who had been so closely involved in the personal lives of the Duke and Mrs Simpson at the time of the Abdication. As we have seen, he had been abruptly sacked at the end of December from his position in the Royal Household as a Lord-in-Waiting; now he was told that, if he attended the wedding, he would also lose the post (which he cherished) of Lord Lieutenant of Lincolnshire. On 20 May he confided the details of his dilemma to his cousin and close friend Sir Ronald Storrs, who recorded in his diary:

> I found Perry sallow, nervy & unhealthy-looking: not without reason for he is indeed far from the end of his troubles. . . . The Bishop [of Lincoln] said that this news [of the association of Brownlow and his wife with the Duke and Mrs Simpson after the Abdication] had had a bad effect and that if, as rumoured, Perry attended the Duke of Windsor's wedding, feeling in the County would be so strong that P. would have to resign the Lord Lieuten-

---

[17] In his later years, Lord Mountbatten alleged that the Duke had never invited him to his wedding at all – but in this, as in so many other things, he was suffering from a lapse of memory.

antship. This, & identical advice from Cruikshank, Minister of Mines, was duly confirmed in writing. . . . He was (& to date is) in the delicate position of having to resign his post or be branded by the hostile in London as one of the most egregious of rats. Ulick Alexander had asked the King whether he could go [to the wedding] & the King after much humming and hawing had said that as Ulick was representing him (the King) he had perhaps better not. . . . The situation now was that the Royal Family had set themselves definitely against the wedding & would neither attend themselves or be represented there. The only man going was Walter Monckton the legal adviser to the Duchy of Cornwall, who as P. elegantly said only drew £150 a year from his position and didn't care a —— whether he lost it or not. Perry . . . had written a very short letter to the King which would be delivered that evening on the yacht asking for a definite yes or no. He was by no means hopeful of getting this because he said that A. Hardinge was his greatest enemy & would almost certainly advise the King not to give Perry definite instructions so as to force him to take the necessarily unpopular decision himself. Naturally he was worried. . . . He showed me the D of W's rather pathetic invitation letter . . . saying that he relied so much on P's assistance. . . .

In the end the Duke absolved those of his friends who held public posts from attending, lest it harm their careers. He nevertheless hoped that the King would relent to the extent of permitting some diplomatic representative to come. Sir Walford Selby, who as British Minister to Vienna had looked after him during his long sojourn in Austria after the Abdication, had to refuse for himself but sent his wife. In the end, the only diplomats present at the marriage abroad of their former sovereign were his old friend and aide Hugh Lloyd Thomas, who was Counsellor at the British Embassy in Paris and whose attendance must be counted an act of personal courage, and His Majesty's Consul in Tours, who was obliged to be present at the local marriage of a British subject as part of his ordinary consular functions.

Under the circumstances, it was hardly surprising that the authorities of the Church of England refused to allow the ex-King to be married according to the rites of the faith in which he had been confirmed and of which, so short a time before, he had been Supreme Defender. But the Vicar of St Paul's, Darlington, the Reverend R.

Anderson Jardine, defied his bishop and offered to come to Candé to perform the religious ceremony – an offer which the Duke gratefully accepted.

There was a further blow in store. On 27 May, exactly one week before the wedding, the Duke received a letter from the King informing him that his rank of Royal Highness would not, following his marriage, be shared by his wife; and the next day it was officially announced that Letters Patent had been issued by the King to this effect. The circumstances which surrounded this unprecedented act, the enormous offence which it caused to the Duke, and his numerous but futile efforts over the years to have it reversed, will be explained in detail in Chapter 3.

These were the circumstances in which the Duke and the woman he loved, in the presence of a small group of friends, were married at Candé on 3 June 1937. It was in one sense the happiest day of the Duke's life, the moment of which he had dreamt and for which he had waited, planned and conspired over the course of three years, in order to realize which he had given up kingship. But in the period of less than six months since the Abdication he had been snubbed and humiliated and effectively excluded from the royal fold. He was, quite literally, no longer on speaking terms with his brother, from whom he had parted affectionately at Windsor in December 1936. Two raging quarrels – over the money and over the title – guaranteed that a feuding relationship with his family and the Court would continue for the immediate future. 'The drawbridges are going up behind me,' he told his wife shortly before their marriage. 'I have taken you into a void.' Yet it did not occur to him that these unhappy circumstances would last for ever; that he would be spending the rest of his life as an outcast and exile from England, permanently prevented from returning to his own country by every kind of political, social and financial pressure.

We must now examine the two matters which, in the period following the marriage, did most to place obstacles in the way of return – those of the Duke's allowance and the Duchess's status.

Chapter Two

The Financial Settlement
and Quarrel

*I*t has often been alleged that Edward VIII was paid an enormous sum to abdicate – that he had to be bribed, as it were, into agreeing to renounce the throne. Frances Donaldson quotes 'informed sources' as saying that he exacted a cash settlement from his successor of £2 million in addition to a pension of £60,000 a year; and A. L. Rowse has written in a widely syndicated article that he 'dunned the Royal Family'. The truth is very different but not less startling. When Edward VIII signed the Instrument of Abdication on the morning of 10 December 1936, no financial provision had yet been made for his future. On the evening of the same day, however, he signed an agreement with his successor whereby he would receive an annual sum of £25,000 for the rest of his life in return for giving up everything he had inherited at the time of his father's death. This legally binding agreement was later repudiated by George VI, who offered instead a lesser sum – to cease on George VI's death – on condition that the Duke of Windsor agreed never to return to his country except by the consent of the authorities. This breach of faith, and the humiliating nature of the condition, embittered the Duke and did much to fuel the flames of the family quarrel and estrange the ex-King from his country and successor.

On the evening of Thursday, 10 December, the Abdication having been signed but not yet taken effect, Edward VIII and his brother the Duke of York, who was to succeed him as King the following afternoon, met at Fort Belvedere with six of their advisers to settle the financial questions arising out of the Abdication – 'a terrible lawyer interview which terminated quietly and harmoniously', as George VI later described it in his diary. It was a private family meeting to discuss family money; the property of the Crown was not at issue, for this passed automatically from one sovereign to the next. There were no politicians or officials present, only lawyers and courtiers. These were Sir Ulick Alexander, Keeper of the Privy Purse; Sir Edward Peacock, in his capacity as the King's private financial adviser; Lord Wigram, the former royal Private Secretary, who was at this time advising the Duke of York; Walter Monckton, who had been the King's principal adviser in all matters since 14 November and effectively discharging the functions of his private secretary; the King's solicitor, George Allen; and the Duke of York's solicitor, Sir Bernard Bircham. The main questions were two. How were the private estates and their contents and the heirlooms of the House of Windsor to pass from Edward VIII to George VI? And how was the ex-King to be provided for after the Abdication?

An agreement had already been reached in principle. This was that, in return for surrendering the estates and the heirlooms, the Duke of Windsor should receive an annual allowance of £25,000. This was the sum which the younger sons of George V, the Dukes of Gloucester and Kent, each received under the Civil List of 1911; and there was a general idea that the Duke of Windsor should henceforth be treated as if a younger brother of the sovereign. There were, however, two further problems to be resolved.

First, who was going to pay the £25,000? At that moment, it seemed not improbable that Parliament would agree to allow this sum to the Duke of Windsor in the Civil List which was to be voted early in the new reign – provided he had not offended public opinion by any of his post-Abdication actions, in particular by seeing Mrs Simpson before her divorce decree was made absolute. This was what the King's agents, Monckton and Allen, had been assured by the Home Secretary, Sir John Simon, and the Chancellor of the Exchequer, Neville Chamberlain. At the meeting of 10 December, therefore, the Duke of York promised to pay his brother £25,000 a year if Parliament failed to do so, 'unless the reason for such action is due to His Majesty's conduct from this date [*sic*]'; and the King promised 'not to see Mrs Simpson until the Civil List becomes law'.

The second problem arose out of the private estates of Sandringham and Balmoral, which were owned by royal trustees from whom Edward VIII held a life tenancy. It would have been possible for him simply to assign his life interest to his successor; but upon his death the estates would then revert to his next-of-kin, and in the event of the Duke of Windsor having children by his forthcoming marriage – a prospect which still seemed not impossible[1] and which must have been a nightmare for the Royal Family and British officialdom – Sandringham and Balmoral would pass out of the hands of George VI and his descendants and into the hands of Edward VIII's descendants. The solution proposed at the Fort Belvedere meeting was that Edward VIII should direct the royal trustees to sell the two estates to George VI; the new King would then be legal owner, and the ex-King would henceforth have a life interest not in the properties but in the sale money, which interest he would surrender to his successor in consideration for the promise to guarantee him an income of £25,000.

Once these matters had been settled, the following agreement was signed:

1. His Royal Highness[2] will provide His Majesty[3] with an income at the rate of twenty-five thousand pounds a year if Parliament does not make provision for His Majesty in the new Civil List, unless the reason for such action on the part of Parliament is due to His Majesty's conduct from this date.

2. His Majesty undertakes not to see Mrs Simpson until the Civil List becomes law.

3. His Majesty agrees to sell and His Royal Highness to buy the Sandringham Estate at fair value. . . .

4. If Balmoral does not pass to the Crown under Scotch Law, His Majesty agrees to sell and His Royal Highness to buy the Estate at fair value. . . .

---

[1] Edward VIII was forty-two and Mrs Simpson forty years of age.

[2] The future George VI.

[3] The abdicating Edward VIII.

5. In consideration of the above guaranteed provision for His Majesty, His Majesty agrees to surrender to His Royal Highness His life interest in the proceeds of sale of Sandringham and Balmoral.

6. For the same consideration, His Majesty agrees to make a gift of all the contents of Sandringham and Balmoral belonging to him, the live and dead stock at Windsor . . . and any other effects that he inherited on King George's death.

7. His Royal Highness will assume His Majesty's liability for the pensions at present shared by all four brothers.

8. As head of the Royal House of Windsor which His Royal Highness will assume on succeeding to the Crown, His Majesty agrees that the heirlooms will pass into His Royal Highness's possession.

EDWARD R.I.
ALBERT

In order that one may understand what the guarantee of £25,000 a year meant to the abdicating Edward VIII, something must be said about the state of his personal finances.

As heir to the throne from 1910 to 1936, he had been entitled to the revenues of the Duchy of Cornwall. These were substantial – they came to £70,941 in 1936, and had been higher before the Depression. During the twenties and early thirties he had required these revenues to pay for his busy official and social life and his large staff;[4] but in the early years, and particularly before coming of age in 1915, he had been able to save most of them. These savings had been increased by inheritances and prudent investment, and by the time he came to the throne amounted to almost a million pounds (worth about £25,000,000 in the values of fifty years later); and in his will, George V left no money to his heir, who seemed to have no need of it, but bequeathed his private fortune to his widow and younger children.

In the course of his reign Edward VIII spent large sums out of his own pocket, notably on buying jewellery for Mrs Simpson and

---

[4] In 1934 he spent some £15,000 on salaries and a further sum in pensions.

improving Fort Belvedere. This was partially compensated for by the fact that he managed to save £12,704 out of his Privy Purse Account.[5] He also settled the enormous sum of £300,000 on Mrs Simpson; but she did not wish to accept this and returned most of it to him before the Abdication. At the time he abdicated, the King possessed investments worth not less than £800,000; he also had his personal possessions, which were stored at Windsor[6] awaiting his eventual return to England; but he owned no real property anywhere except for a ranch in Alberta, Canada, which regularly lost money.

In the late 1930s, £800,000 shrewdly invested would have brought in an income of something over £25,000. As Prince of Wales and sovereign, Edward VIII had paid no income tax; but, if and when he returned to England after the Abdication, this substantial personal income would have been liable to income tax and a high rate of 'surtax' which would have reduced it by more than half.[7] The receipt of an additional tax-free allowance of £25,000, therefore, promised to represent an enormous increase in the ex-King's means.

Did the Duke of Windsor, having abdicated, deserve to receive what was, in effect, a large tax-free pension? He had served his country strenuously and faithfully for a quarter of a century; and he had stepped down for constitutional reasons, accepting the advice of his ministers that he could not marry and remain on the throne. Abroad, he would have to live in a manner befitting a former sovereign and entertain and travel in a certain style; and for the first time in his life he would be absolutely on his own, with no royal residence to live in, no royal retainers to serve him, and no royal machine to protect him. Very few people seem to have disputed his right to be supported in principle. Anyway, it was what he was promised.

---

[5] Nevertheless, Edward VIII was in debt when he abdicated, because the revenues of the Duchy of Cornwall and Lancaster for 1936 were only due to come in towards the middle of 1937, and meanwhile he had been obliged to borrow money from Baring Brothers in order to pay his current Privy Purse expenses. These loans were repaid by him with interest shortly after his marriage in June 1937, after his receipt of the greater part of the Duchy revenues.

[6] They were later moved to Frogmore on George VI's orders. See note on p. 132.

[7] The standard rate of income tax at this time was 22.5 per cent, and the top rate of 'surtax' – payable on income over £20,000 – was an additional 47.5 per cent.

The Duke of Windsor had not been out of England long when it began to look doubtful whether he would receive a grant from Parliament. Before the Abdication, Simon and Chamberlain had assured Monckton and Allen that the new Civil List Act would provide for the Duke so long as he had not been associating with the as yet undivorced Mrs Simpson; and, as late as 16 December 1936, Churchill could write to the ex-King: 'From some words I had with Neville . . . I gathered that what he attached great importance to was your living absolutely separate until everything is settled and the Civil List is voted.' But, just after Christmas, Monckton wrote to him that, despite the sympathy evoked by his broadcast and the national anger at the Archbishop of Canterbury's attack on him, 'a hardening of opinion has nevertheless continued in some not unimportant quarters [*sic*], and in the result I expect there will be a real dispute and conflict about the question of a money provision for Your Royal Highness in the Civil List Bill'.

Monckton was not mistaken. The usual procedure at the start of a reign is that the sovereign, within a month of his accession, sends a 'message' to the House of Commons requesting a Civil List vote: the House then appoints a select committee which deliberates in secret and presents its final recommendations in a report which is laid before the House as a white paper. But two months after the Abdication no message had yet been received from George VI. Early in February 1937 the lobby correspondents reported that it was the question of an annuity for the Duke of Windsor which was holding things up. According to Reuters, the Government wanted 'to secure as near an approach to unanimity as possible', and feared that there might be some opposition to the outright inclusion of the Duke in the List; they were therefore examining the possibility of 'making the Civil List of such dimensions that the Royal Family would make direct provision for the Duke' although 'it is known that at least a section of the Cabinet dislikes the idea of indirect provision'.

On 10 February, a new development occurred. George Allen received a telephone call from Sir Ulick Alexander, Keeper of the Privy Purse, asking if they might meet in the office of Sir Warren Fisher, the Permanent Secretary to the Treasury and thus Neville Chamberlain's principal civil servant. Allen took Monckton with him, and they arrived to find a considerable meeting in progress. Apart from Alexander and Fisher there were Wigram, the King's solicitor Bircham, and Sir Horace Wilson, the mysterious mandarin who was later to run Neville Chamberlain's foreign policy, and who had been involved in the Government's curious efforts to get Mrs Simpson to give up her divorce in the days before the Abdication.

To Allen's amazement, the meeting was freely discussing the Fort Belvedere Agreement, which was supposed to be a private and secret family affair. He felt that Wigram must have revealed this to the Government. 'I think the reason for doing so', he wrote afterwards to the Duke, 'must have been to try to bring pressure on the Government to include you in the Civil List and thus relieve the King of his obligation.' But, if this had indeed been the object, it had failed. As Allen continued:

> It soon became obvious that the real purpose of the meeting was to convey to us [Monckton and Allen] the conclusion of the Government that they could *not* support your inclusion in the Civil List. *Neither* could they countenance Your Royal Highness receiving an annual payment from the King. . . .

Allen protested, pointing out that, if the King defaulted on his promise to guarantee the Duke an income of £25,000, then the Duke would no longer be bound by his promise to convey Sandringham and Balmoral to the King. Fisher replied that perhaps the Duke could lease the estates to the King 'for a rent of around £10,000 per annum'. As Allen wrote to the Duke: 'Sir Warren Fisher, while objecting to your receiving £25,000, does not apparently object to your receiving £10,000.' When Allen continued to insist that the Fort Belvedere Agreement was a legally binding contract, Fisher pointed out that, at the time the agreement was signed, the Duke of Windsor had failed to make full disclosure of what his means were and who had control of them.

> It was quite evident [wrote Allen] that he [Fisher] had advised the King that, as you had not disclosed the extent of your private fortune to the King when he signed the document at Fort Belvedere, the King was entitled to repudiate what he had signed. . . . What Sir Warren Fisher really wants is that the Fort Belvedere Agreement shall be cancelled so that there is no promise by the King to make any payment to you. . . .

The day after this strange meeting, George VI wrote his brother a letter from Buckingham Palace, the tone of which was one of embarrassment. He was 'very disturbed' that the Fort Belvedere Agreement had somehow got into the hands of the Government and even into the popular newspapers, which threatened to complicate the forthcoming discussions of the Select Committee on the Civil List. Having had notice of the Agreement, the Committee would probably insist on a full disclosure both of the Duke's private means (which had not been divulged at the time the Agreement was signed) and any sum the King proposed to pay him. They might well try to reduce the Civil List by such a sum, being still 'a little sore with you for having given up being King'. It was all 'very difficult' and 'so complicated'; Monckton would go out to Austria to explain things, and the King hoped 'for both our sakes' that they would 'hit on a solution'.

Having seen Monckton, the Duke replied from Schloss Enzesfeld on 21 February.

[11 February 1936]

My dear Bertie,

. . . I am sorry there seems to be some misunderstanding about the document which you and I signed at the Fort on the 10th December in what I thought was the most amicable spirit and after full consultation with our legal advisers.

You now infer that I misled you at that time as to my private financial position. While naturally not mentioning what I have been able to save as Prince of Wales, I did tell you that I was very badly off, which indeed I am considering the position I shall have to maintain and what I have given up. . . .

You now ask me to tell you what my private means are, but I prefer not to do so for two reasons. Firstly because the figure of £25,000 . . . was in no way arrived at by reference to my private means, but solely as being the lowest provision that would be appropriate in the circumstances. We all thought at that time that Parliament would make at least that provision, and after all it is through no fault of mine that they are now going to fail us.

Secondly I am certain that it would be a grave mistake if the private means of any member of the Royal Family were to be disclosed to the Select Committee and that it would only

embarrass you and your advisers if I were to put you in a position
of being able to answer questions on this subject.

I have kept my side of the bargain[8] and I am sure you will keep
yours. . . .

Having consulted Monckton, the Duke now suggested a new agreement. This omitted all reference to the King's promise to pay
£25,000 if Parliament failed to do so, and proposed instead an annual
rent for Sandringham and Balmoral of the same sum. As a gesture of
goodwill, the Duke made a financially important concession: he
offered to pay his quarter share of the pensions granted by his father,
from which he had been absolved under clause 7 of the Fort
Belvedere Agreement. This liability would cost him £4,000 in 1937.
'I should be very sorry and it seems quite unnecessary that there
should be any disagreement between us,' the Duke concluded; 'but I
must tell you quite frankly that I am relying on you to honour your
promise.'

The King replied to this with some agitation on 9 March. It was
essential, he said, that there be no financial agreement whatever in
existence between them when the Civil List came before Parliament;
otherwise the House of Commons would feel they were providing for
the Duke indirectly. The King did not 'want to let you down', but
owing to 'unforeseen changes' which had occurred since the Abdication he needed 'a free hand' to deal with the Select Committee, and
it would be 'to your advantage as well as my own' to say there was no
family arrangement. The only solution was for the old agreement to
be scrapped and an entirely new one drawn up after the Civil List
Act. The whole matter had been 'a great worry' to the King and it
would be 'a great pity' if the Duke could not agree with him.

On 13 March, the Duke sent George Allen copies of the King's
letters

. . . which if ever published would become world famous for their
sheer naivety! I have never posed as super intelligent, but even on
my own I could always have produced better arguments for my
case than these efforts.

It really does make it very difficult to deal with my brother,

[8] Isolation from Mrs Simpson.

because he makes it so clear that he refuses to see my point of view, or that I should say that his advisors [*sic*] won't let him. You know the last thing in the world I want is a family row, but they are heading the right way for the finest ever, and I am anxious to avoid that if possible.

One thing I am absolutely determined not to do, and this is to destroy the original signed document until I get another in its place. I have already given my brother the loophole of the estates agreement, and if he won't accept that, why then everyone will suffer in the Civil List.

At any rate, I have what I inherited, and nothing can alter that, or prevent me disposing of it all as I care to, should the necessity arise. I wonder if they realise that? Maybe it's better not to remind them. Or maybe they think I will never use that stick? Well, I sincerely hope it will never come to that, but I won't hesitate, if needs must be. . . .

I realise the urgency of the settlement of this private controversy in view of the imminent debate on the Civil List, but I will not move a yard from the strong position I am lucky enough, thanks to you, to find myself in.

Yours sincerely,

EDWARD

On 16 March 1937, King George VI at last issued 'His Majesty's Most Gracious Message relating to the Civil List and to Provision for Her Majesty the Queen and for Members of the Royal Family and other matters connected therewith'. The following day the Select Committee was appointed under the chairmanship of the Chancellor of the Exchequer, Neville Chamberlain. It was virtually identical to the Committee which had discussed Edward VIII's Civil List the year before, and consisted of twenty-one Members of Parliament from the main political parties in proportion to their parliamentary strength. Among them were two steadfast friends of the Duke of Windsor who were determined to keep an eye on his interests – Lloyd George and Winston Churchill.[9]

[9] Lloyd George does not seem to have been very active – he only attended one of the Committee's four meetings, probably for reasons of health – but he appears to have authorized Churchill to speak for him in the matter of the Duke of Windsor. Dining at Buckingham Palace on 16 March, he told the King 'quite bluntly that it would be wisdom to see that [the Duke of Windsor] got a generous allowance'. (Frances Stevenson, *Lloyd George: A Diary*, London, 1971, p. 326.)

Churchill had been in touch with Monckton about the Duke's circumstances; he knew about the Fort Belvedere Agreement and the King's attempt to repudiate it. On 24 March, two weeks before the Select Committee was due to meet for the first time, he wrote to Chamberlain on behalf of Lloyd George and himself. What they proposed was a deal. Provided Chamberlain could assure them that 'proper and satisfactory provision' would be made privately for the Duke of Windsor, then they would do all in their power, as friends of the Duke, to ensure that the Duke's name be kept out of the discussion both on the Committee and during the House of Commons debate, which was what the Government anxiously desired. But if Chamberlain could not give this assurance, then the Duke's friends would insist on his inclusion in the Civil List. The purpose of the List was 'the maintenance of the honour and the dignity of the Crown', and 'a proper establishment for the Duke with the formalities due to royalty' was in Churchill's view 'an essential part' of this. He knew there was a signed agreement between the brothers for an allowance of £25,000, but that there had 'lately been some discussion about this'. If the signed agreement held good and the allowance was free of tax, this would, taking into account the Duke's other means, 'constitute a satisfactory and proper provision'.

On 1 April, Churchill reported to Lloyd George that he had received a reply from Chamberlain which was 'satisfactory, so far as it goes', and that he was seeing Monckton to discover 'the Duke's latest wishes'. Churchill does not appear to have received all the assurances that he was seeking, but nevertheless fulfilled his side of the bargain by contriving to keep the Duke out of the Civil List discussions and quieten his partisans.

On 8 April, Churchill reported to Lloyd George on the first meeting of the Select Committee which had taken place that day. Attlee, Leader of the Labour Party, had tried to ask about the private fortunes of the Royal Family, but they had managed to shut him up. Then, 'quite unexpectedly', the matter of the Duke of Windsor had been raised by Leo Amery,[10] one of the Conservatives on the Committee, who had said that the ex-King

---

[10] L. S. Amery (1873–1955), MP for Birmingham South 1911–45, First Lord of the Admiralty 1922–24, Colonial Secretary 1924–29, the articulate and forceful leader of the imperialist wing of the Conservative Party.

... ought to be treated like one of the King's sons. His marriage might unfit him for the position of Sovereign, but we could not adopt an attitude of unctuous rectitude and pretend that thereby he was cast out altogether from the Royal Family and from our society. ...

Churchill had succeeded in quietening Amery for the time being. But he wrote to Chamberlain that the intervention 'shows how easily we might find ourselves immersed in awkward topics. The best solution would surely be that the King should honour his signature about the £25,000 a year. ... The idea of a dispute between the brothers upon the question of good faith ... would of course be a disaster of the first order to the monarchy.'

On 25 April, Churchill was visited by Lord Wigram, George V's old Private Secretary who was seeing the new King through his early months, and who (as Churchill wrote to the Duke) 'brought me privately the King's assurance about the financial affair, that I could be sure he would not let you down. I told Wigram that he ought to talk to Lloyd George also, which he did. In consequence of this assurance, which I felt bound to accept, coming as it did directly from His Majesty, neither of us raised the matter on the Civil List Committee. ...'

The Select Committee reported on 28 April. It did not mention the Duke; and the total sum it proposed for a married sovereign, at £410,000, was £36,000 less than that granted in the Civil List of 1936. But, in Edward VIII's List, £50,000 had been earmarked for the Duke of York; George VI was therefore making an overall saving of £14,000. As Duke of York in 1936 he had also received a grant of over £17,000 from the Duchy of Cornwall; the new reign therefore disposed of over £30,000 more annual revenue than the last, and Churchill was right in suggesting to Chamberlain that, under these conditions, 'it would not be a hardship for the King to pay the £25,000'.

In the House of Commons, there was a small party of the Duke's supporters which looked upon the absence of his name with dismay. Michael Beaumont, the thirty-four-year-old Member for Aylesbury, wrote to Churchill that

... the omission is of the utmost gravity. ... Both on the grounds of equity, in that a man who has done so much for his country as the Duke should not be allowed to pass out without some form of recognition, and on those of policy, in that the omission of any specific provision for the Duke will give a tremendous lever to those who desire, against his will, to use his name as a rallying point against the existing form of Government. . . . My present wish is to object to the passage of the Civil List on the grounds that it makes no provision for the Duke of Windsor. . . .

But Churchill was able to assure this and other malcontents that 'satisfactory provision has been made for the Duke within the Royal Family'. This fact was also announced in the editorial of *The Times* (then a mouthpiece of government policy) on 4 May: 'No controversy should be aroused by the omission of any public provision for the Duke of Windsor. It is understood that the private means of which he disposes will be augmented by a provision from sources with which the taxpayer has no concern. . . .'

The Duke had been told by his brother that Parliament would never tolerate the idea of his receiving a family allowance. What had in fact happened was exactly the opposite: trouble was threatened by the idea that he might not be receiving an allowance, and the Government had been obliged to let it be publicly known that he would indeed be supported from family sources.

The Civil List Bill was laid before the House of Commons on 24 May. It was the last legislative measure presented to Parliament by the Baldwin government, which resigned two days later. It merely remained for the King to honour his promise (so recently confirmed by Wigram to Churchill) and pay his brother the agreed allowance.

During the course of April 1937, while in the midst of the Civil List affair, Churchill received some news which he found shocking and extraordinary: that the Government had recently advised the King to make any payment to his brother dependent on the Duke of Windsor's agreeing never to return to England unless invited to do so by the authorities. Wigram confirmed confidentially that this was the case; and Churchill told him bluntly that such ministerial advice was unconstitutional, and that the King should refuse to have anything to do with it. Churchill noted down the remarks he made to Wigram in this connection on 25 April.

I understood that the allowance . . . was a matter of family affection arising out of the King's promise to the Duke before the latter's abdication. It is altogether a personal and brotherly affair. It would not be right for Ministers to advise the King to make the payment of this allowance contingent on the Duke's not returning to England without the King's permission. . . . Above all, Ministers should not advise that such a condition should be presented to the Duke through the lawyers. The Duke would have no option but to refuse to receive such a communication; for otherwise he would put himself in the position of bartering his right to return to his native land for a pecuniary advantage. . . .

It was stated by the Attorney-General during the passage of the Abdication Bill that no condition of exile followed a voluntary abdication. As this declaration preceded the Abdication, it must stand as a solemn pledge both to Parliament and the late King. It would therefore be all the more undesirable that Ministers, especially those personally involved in the said pledge, should advise the King to take the burden of preventing the return of the Duke upon himself and to use the allowance given in family affection for that purpose. If for any grave public reason Ministers considered that the return of the Duke of Windsor to England could not be allowed, their only course is to pass an Act of Parliament forbidding or regulating his return. This they could no doubt do. But it would . . . cause much pain and scandal throughout the British Dominions and the world. . . .

It remained to be seen whether the King would follow this advice, and resist the ministerial pressure which Churchill considered so improper. Meanwhile the Duke knew nothing of these proceedings.

On 3 June 1937 the Duke of Windsor married the woman he loved at Candé, and left to spend the summer honeymooning with her in Austria. Since the signing of the Fort Belvedere Agreement six months earlier, he had received no funds or financial assurances from his brother; and he began married life in exile without knowing for certain what his future means would be. He was angry at what he considered to be a breach of faith, and relied on his two trusted advisers, Walter Monckton and George Allen, to obtain satisfaction from the King.

When Monckton returned to England after attending the wedding in France he went to see the King, who 'said he would want to see Allen soon on the question of money'. Allen then wrote to Ulick Alexander to say that he would have to go to Newfoundland on business on 17 June, but would be at the King's disposal until that date. On the eve of his departure, however, Allen wrote to the Duke that he had received no summons from Court.

The Duke wrote to Alexander:

> I have purposely not worried my brother . . . for some months, first because the Civil List had not been passed . . . and secondly because I have been reassured from several reliable sources, which include no less important people than yourself, Winston Churchill and Walter Monckton, that the King intends to stand by the agreement we both signed at the Fort on December tenth.
>
> Now I am amazed to hear from Allen, who tells me that despite receiving a message that the King would want to see him on this soon, in spite of having telephoned you that he was about to go abroad and would be available until a certain date and you having said you would convey that message to the King, he received no communication either from my brother or his solicitor before he sailed for America.
>
> I ask you quite frankly – is this business like behaviour on the part of my brother, and is it any encouragement to me to believe that he intends to keep his word of December as a gentleman?

The Duke did not require immediate payment of the money owing to him – he knew royal revenues take time to come in at the start of a reign – but he wanted 'a more concrete assurance of a speedy settlement than mere vague messages that The King does intend to do the right thing by me'.

By the end of June the Duke had still received no such assurances. On 2 July he wrote to Allen in Newfoundland:

> I shall be very glad when you are back in London, and able to deal with Buckingham Palace who really are behaving abominably. . . .
>
> I have heard from Ulick that the valuations of Sandringham and

Balmoral are not yet complete, and that, since the Agreement was signed at the Fort, 'some difficulties were not realised, amongst others the peculiar status of Balmoral under Queen Victoria's will'.

I have no idea what 'difficulties' they are trying to 'trump up' in your absence, and I am sure you know of none, and that all my brother is trying to do is to wriggle out of the Agreement, which I am absolutely determined he shall not.

When I wrote to Ulick yesterday I stressed that it was high time somebody told the King very plainly of the embarrassing position his delay puts me in as regards the future . . . that it was impossible for me to forecast where and on what scale I was going to live without knowing what my resources were going to be . . . that I was confident that the King would be the first to realise the importance of having a home, and the inconvenience and impossibility of an indefinite period of rented houses.

Personally I feel very strongly that the only way we will get a speedy settlement is to force the King's hand now in the most dignified and expedient way in our power. There might be legal objections to the following plan; but if you were in London now I would instruct you to inform the King that, if he does not fulfil his part of the bargain by the end of July, I will take steps to prevent 'the Court' moving to Balmoral in August. . . .

This dramatic threat proved unnecessary, for within a few days Allen's partner Thomas Overy, looking after the Duke's affairs in London in Allen's absence, was invited to call on the man who was now the King's private solicitor. Their meeting took place on 19 July.

The King now put forward an entirely new set of proposals. He offered the Duke a pension of £20,000 a year. Part of this would come out of the Duke's life interest in the sale money of Sandringham and Balmoral, and for this purpose a very low value had been put on the estates by the Crown Surveyors – £146,000 for Sandringham, £90,000 for the Scottish properties. The annual return from these sums would be about £8,500. The remainder of the Duke's payment would arise under clause (ix) of the new Draft Proposals, which read:

The King to make a voluntary allowance to the Duke for their joint lives of such a sum as would . . . make up £20,000 in all, to be continued so long as neither H.R.H. nor the Duchess came to this country without The King's previous consent.

These terms were infinitely less favourable to the Duke than those agreed at Fort Belvedere. He was to receive £20,000 instead of £25,000; he was to receive most of it, not as a matter of legal right, but by way of a mere 'voluntary allowance'; and this allowance was only to be for the joint lives of the Duke and the King – and would thus be terminated in the event of the King predeceasing the Duke. But the shocking surprise was that the Duke would get nothing at all unless he remained abroad so long as the King wished him to – a condition, indeed, which at this stage even included the Duchess.

It was explained to Overy that the Duke, at the time of the Abdication, had promised not to return to England save by the permission of his successor. 'I objected straight away,' Overy wrote afterwards to Allen. 'I said that, if there had been any promise, it was not in connection with the financial agreement. It was quite plain that the Fort Agreement contained no such condition. I did not take it that the Duke would want to come here necessarily but that if [the King] . . . wanted a real fuss, that was the best way to create it.'

From Newfoundland, Allen, who had been at the King's side throughout the Abdication crisis, telegraphed:

> Client never made promise and no promise was ever asked for in any shape or form and we should advise him to reserve full freedom of action for the future. He would always play game.

The following months saw endless and acrimonious negotiations on the subject of the financial contract. Back in London, Allen pursued his client's interests with great tenacity, contesting every point which was in violation of the original agreement. He insisted that the Duke receive more than a mere £20,000; that the estates (from which the Duke would receive the only fully guaranteed part of his income) be revalued; and that the allowance be obligatory and for the whole of the Duke's life, as had clearly been envisaged by the Fort Belvedere Agreement. Letters filled file after file, and Allen twice went to Paris to consult the Duke, who upon his return from Austria in September had moved into the Hôtel Meurice until he knew of his financial future. Eventually, after much resistance, the King agreed to the revaluations and to increase the total sum from £20,000 to £21,000.[11]

But the most contentious point was the exile condition. Following Overy's protest, this had been dropped from the King's proposals in late July; but in November – just when it seemed that the new agreement was about to be signed – the King's solicitors again insisted that, as part of the financial deal, the Duke must give an undertaking never to return without consent. On 24 November, Allen wrote in a private handwritten letter to the Duke:

> . . . I feel we must take adequate time to consider afresh the whole subject of the financial settlement on the one hand, and your right to return to the land of your birth on the other.
>
> I can see no justification for linking them together.
>
> It seems to me that you must now make a determined stand, or for ever, to speak plainly, become a remittance man. I scarcely think the King and his advisers can realise the humiliating and insulting nature of their proposals. . . .

The King's advisers continued to insist that the Duke had promised to remain in exile unless invited to return; but this was vigorously denied by Allen and the Duke. After long enquiries, it transpired that the idea had arisen from an unauthorized remark of Monckton on the day before the Abdication. On 9 December 1936 Monckton, together with Peacock, had gone to see the Duke of York at his London residence, 145 Piccadilly, to discuss such matters as the abdicating monarch's future title and his desire to live at Fort Belvedere 'if and when he should be allowed to return to England'. (These words are from Peacock's diary.) By implying that the Duke of Windsor would be willing to remain in exile at the pleasure of his successor, Monckton now accepted that, in the tension of the moment and his sympathy for the heir apparent, he had gone far beyond what he had been instructed to say.

Nevertheless, the King continued to insist on the condition; and it

---

[11] This sum was supposed to represent the original £25,000 minus the Duke's share of the royal pensions which he had offered to bear in February. However, although a quarter-share of the pensions amounted to about £4,000 in 1937, it would have declined over the years as the pensioners died off, so the fixing of the Duke's allowance at the permanent figure of £21,000 again left him at a disadvantage.

was now that he revealed that he had been advised by his Ministers the previous April to make any financial arrangement dependent on exile. As we have seen, Churchill had got wind of this at the time, and had urged the King to reject such advice on the grounds that it was unconstitutional and improper. But in spite of these wise warnings the King had accepted the notion that financial pressure should be used to keep his brother abroad. Indeed, as with the ministerial advice to deny a royal title to the Duchess of Windsor, one cannot resist the suspicion that it had been prompted in the first place by the King's own courtiers.

Learning that November of the involvement of the Government, Allen commissioned a brilliant junior barrister, Colin (later Lord) Pearson, to prepare an opinion on the subject of the English law relating to exile.[12] This was categorical. Neither the King nor his Ministers had any power to banish a British subject. The right of an Englishman to remain on his native soil was one of the fundamental liberties laid down in 1215 by Magna Carta, which had declared:

> No freeman shall be taken or imprisoned, or be disseised of his freehold, or liberties, or free customs, or be outlawed, *or exiled*, or any other wise destroyed nor will we not pass upon him nor condemn him but by the lawful judgment of his peers, or by the law of the land. We will sell to no man, we will not deny or defer to any man either justice or right.

The Crown might under certain circumstances prevent its subjects going abroad; but nothing short of an Act of Parliament could rob a British subject of his right to return to England. All the old, authoritative textbooks of English law had considered this axiomatic (except for the old punishments of abjuration and outlawry, long since abolished); and the matter was so well settled that modern works of constitutional law did not even bother to mention the subject.

To find out what was in the official mind, Monckton and Allen went to see Sir Horace Wilson, the powerful and secretive civil servant who was known to be the Prime Minister's closest adminis-

---

[12] Reproduced in Appendix I.

trative confidant.[13] Wilson was vague, but said that the only real worry as far as the Government was concerned was that the Duke's return might be exploited by extremist political groups. Monckton made the point that if the Duke were minded to return, and felt that there was no grave public reason why he should not do so, he would never be deterred by the fear that this allowance would be docked.

The Duke expressed his own feelings in a letter which he wrote from the South of France to Neville Chamberlain on 22 December 1937:

When I decided to give up the throne last December, I realised that the only dignified and sensible course for me to follow was to leave the country for a period, the length of which was naturally to be determined by a number of considerations. But I never intended, nor would I ever have agreed, to renounce my native land and my right to return to it – for all time.

If my understanding of the present situation is correct, it is now proposed that my personal freedom in this respect be linked with a private family arrangement on financial matters which my brother, the present King, made with me the day before I abdicated, in such a way that he would be permitted to break his private agreement with me if I were to exercise my right to visit my country, without at first obtaining his approval under the advice of his ministers.

I regard such a proposal as both unfair and intolerable, as it would be tantamount to my accepting payment for remaining in exile.

I should have thought that my record as Prince of Wales and as King was sufficient to convince anyone that I am a man of my word, and that there was no necessity to seek to impose financial sanctions on me. I have already intimated to the King that whenever I contemplated going to England, I would inform him of my plans a reasonable time ahead, and during any visit would scrupulously avoid doing anything which might in any way cause

---

[13] Sir Horace Wilson (1882–1972) held at this time the unassuming title of 'Chief Industrial Adviser to H.M. Government seconded to the Treasury for service with the Prime Minister'; but his position was one of immense power owing to the total reliance on him of Neville Chamberlain, who consulted him even in matters of foreign policy of which Wilson knew nothing. He had made his reputation during the General Strike in 1926, and was renowned as a 'fixer' who knew how to smooth over difficult problems. Among the many strange events in which he had been involved was the Cabinet's attempt to get Mrs Simpson to give up her divorce proceedings in the days just before the Abdication.

embarrassment to him or the Government, and that I had no present thought of taking up residence in Great Britain. An undertaking of this kind surely carries conviction as to its intentions. Further, having always been very sensitive to public opinion, I could never remain long in any country where I felt my presence was unwelcome.

It is hardly necessary for me to repeat to you my loyalty to my brother the King; nor as a patriotic Englishman could I countenance any disruptive action in others. But I cannot refrain from saying, with the frankness you would expect of me, that the treatment which has been meted out to my wife and myself since last December, both by the Royal Family and the Government, has caused us acute pain. . . .

The Duke's protest to the Prime Minister produced a soothing response. Chamberlain replied on 7 January 1938 that he was 'exceedingly sorry to learn that any advice which the Government have thought it their duty to tender to His Majesty has caused you pain'; that it was 'the earnest desire of the Government to see an end to the discussions which have been proceeding between the representatives of Your Royal Highness and His Majesty in a manner which will avoid all feelings of bitterness or resentment'; and that it was not the case 'that the Government is actuated by motives unfriendly to Your Royal Highness or indeed by any other motives than those dictated by its inevitable responsibilities'. A compromise was suggested. The Duke would no longer be required to give an 'undertaking' not to return without consent, but he would 'take note' of an 'aide-mémoire' summarizing the Government's attitude. This document, drafted by the ubiquitous Sir Horace Wilson, read as follows:

It is recognised that if H.R.H. desired to come to this country or, being here, wished to stay, in circumstances which (in the view of the Government of the day) would make his presence contrary to the public interest (e.g. if it created or seemed likely to create a state of feeling that might lead to public demonstrations or disorder), Ministers would, if they thought it necessary, advise His Majesty to suggest to his brother that he should not come, or should not remain.

If, notwithstanding this, H.R.H. should elect to disregard this suggestion – which all concerned agree is most unlikely – it must be assumed that the House of Commons and public opinion would insist upon discussion of the circumstances; this would very likely bring about a disclosure of financial arrangements in which public money would be thought to be concerned, directly or indirectly. Ministers might well feel that there was a risk that His Majesty would become involved in public controversy if he continued the payment, and in order to prevent that, they would then doubtless feel obliged to advise His Majesty to suspend it; they could not do otherwise while the circumstances were such as to adversely affect the public interest.

Replying to Chamberlain on 12 January, the Duke agreed to 'take note' of this text. He had protested against what appeared to be a general decree of banishment, and honour had been satisfied. He was anxious to conclude the financial negotiations with the King without delay, and thus draw the income which would enable him to set up his own establishment in France.

In the course of February 1938, all was settled. The total value of the royal estates was set at £300,000 – an increase of £64,000 on the original Crown Valuation; this was duly paid by the King to the Royal Trustees, who invested it in British Government War Loan stock;[14] the income from this came to £10,144 17s 2d per annum, to which the Duke would be entitled for the rest of his life. The balance of £21,000, £10,855 2s 10d, would be paid to the Duke annually by the King in the form of a voluntary allowance, to be discontinued in the event of the Duke coming to or remaining in England against the advice of the Government. Having finally been assured as to their financial future, the Windsors moved out of the Hôtel Meurice, where they had been living since their return to France the previous September, and took the leases, in the early weeks of 1938, of two substantial properties – the Château de la Maye at Versailles, and the Villa La Cröe at Cap d'Antibes.

The Duke wrote to Peacock from Versailles that April:

---

[14] The dividends from War Loan, unlike other forms of British Government stock, were not liable to surtax in the case of British subjects resident overseas.

You will no doubt have heard that the year-old and rather unpleasant negotiations regarding the King's payment to me in lieu of the Civil List grant have at last been brought to a satisfactory conclusion. This is almost entirely due to Allen, who has not only shown himself to be very astute but has kept up a magnificent front in the face of every kind of odds and intrigue.

Allen suggested that the Duke write a friendly letter to his brother acknowledging his gratitude and relief at the settlement, but the Duke could not bring himself to use such generous wording. 'After the insulting way I have been handled, I feel neither grateful, appreciative nor relieved,' he wrote to Allen. 'I can merely express satisfaction!'[15]

There was one occasion on which it was hinted that the threat to cancel the allowance might be invoked. In January 1940 the Duke, then serving as a British liaison officer at French General Headquarters with the rank of major-general, spent two nights in London for discussions at the War Office. Two weeks later he heard from Allen:

I think I should let Your Royal Highness know . . . that there may conceivably be some idea of action being taken with regard to your voluntary allowance. . . . A day or two ago one of my partners was seeing a prominent chancery counsel who advised the King in connection with his arrangement with you, who said: 'Oh, I notice

[15] Any note of reconciliation which might have been engendered by the settlement was dissipated when George VI insisted on deducting from the Duke's allowance the cost of three pensions which the Duke, as Prince of Wales, had granted out of Duchy of Cornwall revenues – to his steward Frederick Finch, his footman William Young, and Mrs Burt, the widow of one of his detectives. Though the burden was not enormous (about £400 in 1938), the Duke resented being made to pay royal pensions when no longer in receipt of royal revenues. There was also some discussion as to whether he ought to be made to pay the salary of Thomas Carter, his former Chief Clerk as Prince of Wales, who was now an official of the Privy Purse Office but still spent part of his time looking after the Duke's possessions and business interests in England.

Another cause of acrimony was that the Duke found himself required to pay surtax on his and the Duchess's investment income arising in England. Allen went to see the Commissioners of Inland Revenue in June 1938 and told them (as he wrote to the Duke) that 'it seemed . . . very unfair that you should be asked to pay any taxes in this country at all, seeing that . . . you were in a less fortunate position than a foreigner who had English income because the foreigner was free to visit this country at any time and to remain here a substantial part of the year without incurring taxation liability, whereas you, an Englishman, by the peculiar circumstances which existed, were precluded from enjoying the liberties to which your birth would normally entitle you'. The Commissioners concluded, however, that 'a departure from the normal procedure would not be justified'.

that your client has been in England recently. Has he had his allowance stopped yet? Of course, that can be done, you know.' My partner made a non-committal reply to this most injudicious utterance. . . .

The King would not, of course, be justified in stopping your voluntary allowance. . . . I imagine that you duly warned the authorities in advance of your visit to England, and it is, I think, important to be scrupulous in these preliminaries so that no-one would be justified in tendering advice of a hostile character. . . .

The Duke had indeed informed Buckingham Palace in advance of his visit, as he always would. 'You should be more than ever on your guard', urged Allen, 'so that there is no excuse for action of this sort.'

The years passed. On 6 February 1952, King George VI died. The Duke was informed that his allowance would be discontinued. Allen waged a long battle with the Court and its lawyers, arguing, with overwhelming documentary evidence, that an allowance for the Duke's life was what had definitely been agreed, that since he had given up his inheritance for all time his corresponding annuity must be for life. Eventually this was accepted, and the Duke continued to be paid an annual pension of £10,855 2s 10d until his death in 1972. In the 1960s he had asked whether the Duchess might be given half of this sum if he predeceased her; this was agreed to by the Queen, and the Duchess received a yearly income of some £5,000 from the Palace throughout her widowhood.

Chapter Three

The Duchess's Status and Title

On the evening of Thursday, 27 May 1937 – fifteen days after the Coronation of George VI, and exactly one week before the Duke of Windsor was due to marry Mrs Simpson at Candé – Walter Monckton arrived on a special mission at that French castle with a letter for the Duke from the King. Dated the same morning from Buckingham Palace, occupying three octavo sheets engraved with the Royal Arms, written in a painful jerky copperplate, probably the last of many drafts, it consisted half of formal legalistic phrases, half of personal expressions of embarrassment and regret. Its essence was as follows. The King had been advised that, when his predecessor had abdicated, he had given up not only the throne but also his royal status, since such status, according to Letters Patent of Queen Victoria, could only be held by 'near relations of the sovereign who are in succession to the throne'. The King was now pleased to restore the Duke's royal rank – but he was unable to confer the title of Royal Highness on the future Duchess of Windsor. To do so would be unconstitutional, for the Prime Ministers both of Great Britain and the Dominions had advised against it. The matter had caused the King endless worry; to have to write about it made him 'unhappy & sad'; he was 'sorry'; he hoped the Duke would 'understand' and not regard the move as 'an insult' or let it affect their relations 'in any way'. Monckton would explain all these matters to the Duke, and would be able to bring back a reply.

The following day, the news was announced officially in the *London Gazette*:

The KING has been pleased by Letters Patent under the Great Seal of the Realm bearing date the 27th day of May, 1937, to declare that the Duke of Windsor shall, notwithstanding his Instrument of Abdication, executed on the 10th day of December, 1936, and His Majesty's Declaration of Abdication Act, 1936, whereby effect was given to the said Instrument, be entitled to hold and enjoy for himself only the title style and attribute of Royal Highness so however that his wife and descendants if any shall not hold the said title style or attribute.

By an unfortunate coincidence, the same page of the same publication announced that the King intended to confer an earldom on Baldwin, who was resigning the premiership that day.

The Duke's immediate reactions to his brother's letter were those of shock and rage. 'This is a fine wedding present!' he remarked to Monckton, who recalled that the King's comment on handing him the letter that morning had been much the same: 'This isn't going to make a nice wedding present for my brother. . . .' To Mrs Simpson he said: 'I know Bertie – I know he couldn't have written this letter on his own.[1] Why in God's name would they do this to me at this time!' The reference to 'them' indicated the Duke's feeling that the Letters Patent were the outcome of a conspiracy involving members of the Royal Family, the Court and the Government; and, rightly or wrongly, he believed he knew the identity of the person principally responsible. In a letter to Winston Churchill of October 1940 he referred to 'the famous Court ruling . . . whereby the King (or shall we say the Queen?) decreed that the Duchess shall not hold Royal Rank. . . .'[2]

---

[1] This was also the view of Monckton, who wrote: 'If the King had been left to himself, I feel confident that he would not have assented to this course because he knew the effect it would have on his brother.' (Quoted in Lord Birkenhead, *Walter Monckton*, London, 1969, p. 166.)

[2] In creating titles by Letters Patent, the King was constitutionally obliged to follow the advice of his Ministers; but in this case we happen to know that George VI – probably in the form of a letter from Hardinge to Baldwin – took care to let the Government know what advice he wished and expected to receive. (See H. Montgomery Hyde, *Baldwin*, p. 518, who tells us that the Letters Patent as issued were 'in the form desired by the King'. Mr Montgomery Hyde – who had privileged access to Baldwin's papers on the Abdication and its aftermath – was allowed to see and refer to the document in which the King expressed his views to the Prime Minister, whose given reference in the Baldwin Papers is 176 f. 21, but not apparently to quote from it.)

In fact, the news ought not to have come to the Duke as a total surprise. The day before the Abdication – 9 December 1936 – he had sent Monckton and Peacock to see the then Duke of York at 145 Piccadilly to discuss (amongst other matters) the future titles of himself and his wife-to-be; and it is not certain that he received any guarantee on that occasion about the status of the future Duchess of Windsor. Mrs Simpson, however, was realistic enough to foresee trouble on this front. On 12 December 1936 – the day that the ex-King left England for Austria – she wrote to him from her retreat at Cannes:

> I don't know your name but rather hoped it would be The Prince [*sic*] of Windsor. I suppose we will have difficulty about a name for poor me as York [*sic*] I don't suppose will make me H.R.H. Above all we want to have a dignified position no matter where we are. That is also important to the throne. . . .

Two days later she wrote again:

> . . . your mother has placed me in a worse position than ever and practically said she would not accept me. It is plain that York guided by her would not give us the extra chic of creating me H.R.H. – the only thing to bring me back in the eyes of the world . . .

and on 3 January she wrote:

> One realises now the impossibility of getting the marriage announced in the Court Circular and of the H.R.H. It is all a great pity because I loathe being undignified and also of joining the countless titles that roam around Europe meaning nothing. To set off on our journey with proper backing would mean so much – but whatever happens we will make something of our lives. . . .

The Duke paid little attention to these warnings. Such was his state of euphoria that he had convinced himself that all would be well in all things upon his marriage.[3] The problem which then worried and obsessed him was not his future wife's title, but whether he would be able to marry her at all. For at that moment she had not yet received her divorce, which appeared to be running into nightmarish difficulties. These, as we have seen, were finally resolved towards the end of March 1937.

It was only then that the Duke asked Allen to investigate the legal possibilities of Mrs Simpson, upon her marriage to him, being denied a royal title. Allen wrote on 19 April that there was nothing to suggest this might happen: as a matter of immemorial custom, his wife would share his rank. To reassure the Duke, he enclosed a cutting from *The Times* at the time of the marriage of the Duke and Duchess of York in 1923, stating: 'It is officially announced that, in accordance with the settled general rule that a wife takes the status of her husband, Lady Elizabeth Bowes-Lyon on her marriage has become Her Royal Highness the Duchess of York, with the status of a Princess.'

At this time neither Monckton nor Allen had picked up any hint of what was in store, and in fact the matter had not yet been finally decided.[4] The first inkling that something was amiss came early in May, when Allen discovered that the Letters Patent creating the Dukedom of Windsor had passed the Great Seal in March. It was odd that the Duke had not been informed of this or sent a copy of the document, and when examined it was found to contain a surprising fact. Unprecedentedly for the creation of a royal or any dukedom, it contained no subsidiary titles which might be borne during the Duke's lifetime by the heir (if any) to his ducal title. This seemed to indicate an official desire to confine the dignities of honour as much as possible to the Duke himself, to the exclusion of his wife and descendants.

It was only in the middle of May that Allen heard rumours of the

---

[3] He did in fact ask Monckton to raise the matter with George VI, but Monckton replied on 22 December 1936 that 'I feel it would be a mistake to urge Him too much at the moment about the question of the Royal title. I am afraid that He might feel that He was being unduly troubled and too soon. It must be the hardest thing in the world to be patient at such a time as this but it really is the right course. We at this end will constantly keep in mind the importance of securing what You want. . . .'

[4] On 2 September 1937, Hardinge at Balmoral wrote to Vansittart at the Foreign Office apologizing for not having replied earlier to a letter from Vansittart of 4 May on the subject of how the Windsors were to be treated abroad, 'but the Royal Highness issue had not then been settled'. (Anthony Eden's papers in Public Record Office, FO 954/33 f. 36.)

impending issue of Letters Patent on the subject of the royal title. On 25 May, in accordance with the Duke's wishes, he wrote urgently to Sir Ulick Alexander, now the last remaining link with the upper echelons of the Court:

> I think I should let you know that, when I was at the Château de Candé last week-end, I found the Duke of Windsor very deeply concerned about the right of his wife, on marriage, to assume the title of 'Her Royal Highness'.
>
> You know my view of the legal position, and I received from the Duke instructions to consult the highest legal opinion in the country, which I have done, and my view has been confirmed.
>
> I should be failing in my duty to the Duke of Windsor as my client, and indeed to His Majesty and his family, if I did not record in the most serious terms my belief that any positive discrimination against the Duke's wife will lead to a grave and unhappy position, and I hope this course will not be contemplated.
>
> I shall be glad to come and see you as I am sure you will realise that you are my only source of communication in this matter.

But Alexander, however much he may have sympathized with the Duke, did not dare intercede for him on this or any of the many other occasions when he was approached. As the only high official remaining at Court who had been on terms of personal friendship with the former King, his position was precarious: that he survived as Keeper of the Privy Purse throughout the whole of George VI's reign is a tribute to his circumspection. He replied the same day, briefly, that all he could do was pass the letter on to the Private Secretaries' Office; and Allen found the letter returned to him by Hardinge with a curt note that the King would only act on the advice of his legal counsellors and five Prime Ministers.

While Allen had been trying to intercede with the Court, Monckton had been in touch with the Government. He wrote to the Home Secretary, Sir John Simon, saying that to deprive the future Duchess of her husband's rank 'would create an intense bitterness in the Duke that should not be underestimated'. This plea too proved ineffective, though Monckton later expressed the view that 'had it been left to the Cabinet alone his advice would have been accepted'. Sending the Duke a copy of his letter to Alexander, Allen added ominously:

'Walter is ringing you up tonight to tell you the present position regarding the title, which I am afraid is serious. . . .'

The Duchess of Windsor is unique in being the only wife of an Englishman in recent centuries not to have shared the status of a husband to whom she was legally married.[5] The Duke of Windsor's reactions to this fact are well known. It was a permanent wound, the thing that caused him more pain than anything else in the whole of his life. Writing in 1966, he described it as 'this cold-blooded act', a 'kind of Berlin wall' which had cut him off from country and family. There were three reasons for the intensity of his feelings.

First, there was the simple fact that he worshipped his wife, and considered that nothing was too good for her. As Walter Monckton wrote: 'To him she was the perfect woman. . . . He felt that he and Mrs Simpson were made for each other and there was no other way of meeting the situation than marrying her.' Under these circumstances, it was natural that he should feel that his union with her, the sacred goal for which he had waited so long and made such sacrifices, had been tarnished by the unprecedented decision to deprive her of his rank. The Letters Patent seemed in effect to be a public declaration that she was not good enough for him. 'Titles count for less and less nowadays,' he wrote to Winston Churchill on 30 June 1941, 'and I am sure you do not think for one moment that I want the "H.R.H." for the Duchess for snobbish reasons. I would not hesitate to drop mine for that matter if the occasion arose. But it is to protect her from the world being able to say, and indeed they do, that she has not really got my name.'

Second, he felt cheated. During the Abdication Crisis, one of the solutions considered had been a morganatic union, whereby Mrs Simpson might marry Edward VIII without sharing his royal rank; but the King had been informed by the Government at that time that unequal unions of this type were unknown to English law, and that only an Act of Parliament could make them possible. As the editor of

[5]The wives of the Dukes of Sussex and Cambridge in the nineteenth century had not shared either the ducal or the royal titles of their husbands, but their cases were quite different from the Duchess of Windsor's in that, under the terms of the Royal Marriages Act, they were not legally married to their husbands at all.

Debrett's Peerage has written: 'As was made perfectly clear by Mr Baldwin to the former King during his reign, we have no system of morganatic marriages in Britain. A wife, whether the illegitimate daughter of a milliner, as was the Duchess of Gloucester, sister-in-law of George III, or an Emperor's daughter, as was the Duchess of Edinburgh, daughter-in-law of Queen Victoria, takes her style from her husband.' But a morganatic status was precisely what the Letters Patent purported to confer on the Duchess.

Third, the difference in rank between the Duke and his wife was a recipe for endless social embarrassment. Anyone encountering the Windsors for the first time had to make a choice between disobeying the King or offending the Duke; in the event of their choosing the second course (which official persons were generally obliged to do irrespective of their feelings), they had to be on their guard as to which of their interlocutors was entitled to a bow or curtsy and a royal form of address. Under these circumstances, ordinary social intercourse became difficult and many people for this reason alone chose not to associate with them at all.

The person who suffered most from the Duchess's inferior status was the Duke, who had been brought up to regard matters of title and precedence as being of high importance and who had given up so much in order to be married to her. The Duchess regretted the matter for his sake, but for herself was never much bothered by it. In so far as she resented it, it was because (as her post-Abdication letters show) she feared it would affect the dignity of their marriage; in so far as she craved a royal title, it was because (to quote from her memoirs) she 'dreaded being condemned to spending the rest of our lives together as the woman who had come between David and his family'. It will be seen that her role was always to restrain the Duke in his angry efforts to obtain 'justice' for her. As she wrote to him when he was attending the funeral of George VI in England in 1952: '*Do not mention or ask for anything regarding recognition of me.*' It is notable that, whereas the Duke made it a rule never to be present at receptions in France except where his wife was recognized as his equal, the Duchess during her brief period of active widowhood cheerfully attended a number of charitable and semi-official occasions to which she had been invited as a non-royal person.

The rights and wrongs of the Letters Patent of 27 May 1937 have been endlessly debated, and it is important to separate the political question from the legal question. In the first place, it was decided as a matter of policy that the Duchess of Windsor should not be recognized as a member of the British Royal Family, that she should not be entitled to any royal dignities, and that she should be permanently regarded as being in a status inferior to that of her husband. To know exactly who were the persons responsible for this decision, and what their roles and motives, one would need to have complete access to the Royal Archives and the Public Records of the British and Dominion Governments. The political merits must therefore remain for the time being a matter of opinion based on limited evidence; but the legal merits have been the subject of exhaustive investigation, beginning in May 1937 when the Duke instructed Allen to consult 'the highest legal opinion in the country' on the validity of the Letters Patent. Allen approached Sir William Jowitt, K.C., acknowledged as one of the most brilliant senior counsel of his day, who had been Attorney-General and thus official head of his profession from 1929 to 1932 and was also a close friend of Walter Monckton. With the aid of an equally brilliant junior barrister, Patrick Devlin (now Lord Devlin), he produced an opinion which may be regarded as a classic of lucidity and brevity.[6]

The central point of Jowitt's argument was that Letters Patent under the Great Seal, being an act of the Prerogative, could only be used to create rights. They could not abolish rights which already existed by virtue of customary law or statute. All therefore depended on whether, at the time of abdicating, Edward VIII had given up not only his sovereignty but also his royal rank. If this were indeed so, then it was quite possible for Letters Patent to restore him to a limited form of royalty which could not be transmitted to his wife or children. If, on the other hand, he remained by right a full Royal Highness after the Abdication, then Letters Patent could do nothing to restrict this rank by denying it to his wife who would normally enjoy it by reason of immemorial custom.

The official argument – contained in the King's letter to the Duke, the Letters Patent themselves, and the officially inspired commentary which accompanied the publication of the Letters Patent in *The*

---

[6] The original opinion drafted by Jowitt and Devlin is reproduced in Appendix II.

Times and elsewhere – was that the Duke in abdicating had ceased to be a Royal Highness since this attribute was only due by right to persons who were 'in line of succession to the throne'. The only legal precedents cited in support of this view were previous Letters Patent on the subject of royal titles which had been issued by Queen Victoria in 1864 and King George V in 1917. When examined, however, these previous Letters Patent were found to say nothing which might be interpreted as meaning that a royal title was confined to those in line of succession: they merely confirmed that the attribute of Royal Highness was due to all sons, and sons of sons, of a sovereign.

The Duke of Windsor had ceased to be King but he had not ceased to be the son of a King. He had thus never lost his right to be a Royal Highness, which was his for life both under customary law and a statute of Henry VIII. Indeed, there was ample evidence that he had been officially recognized as a Royal Highness from the moment of his Abdication. That was how he had been announced in the famous radio broadcast on the night of 11 December 1936; and George VI, during his Accession Council the following day, had confirmed that his brother would henceforth be known as 'His Royal Highness the Duke of Windsor'.[7]

Jowitt therefore concluded that the Letters Patent were legally ineffective as a means of restricting the Duke's royal title to himself only, and might be challenged by having them referred to the Lords of the Council.

It is possible to argue that the denial of royal dignities to the Duchess of Windsor was a politically necessary act. (All that will be said here is that the necessities which might have been argued in 1937 – to satisfy public opinion, to punish the Duke for abdicating, to discourage him from returning to England, and to guard against the possibility of his marriage being a failure – became progressively less arguable as the years passed and ceased to have any validity after the mid-1950s, when the discrimination against the Duchess could only be explained either as the continuation of a vendetta or reflecting a complacent view that it was too late to do anything about it.) On the question of the legality of the act, however, the overwhelming weight

---

[7] The Letters Patent creating the Dukedom of Windsor, which antedated by almost three months the Letters Patent of 27 May 1937, also carried the superscription 'H.R.H. the Duke of Windsor'.

of independent opinion has now come down on the side of the view expressed by Jowitt and Devlin in 1937. As the editor of *Debrett's Peerage* wrote in 1972: 'It is doubtful how knowledgeable the British and Commonwealth Ministers of the Crown were on constitutional and legal issues, whether they consulted eminent authorities for advice before the May statement was issued, or if they did do so, whether they took that advice.' And in 1967 *Burke's Peerage*, affirming that 'immediately upon his abdication and without any special act of the Prerogative, the former sovereign became . . . a Prince of the United Kingdom of Great Britain and Ireland', went so far as to describe the Letters Patent as 'the last act of triumph of an outraged and hypocritical establishment . . . the most flagrant act of discrimination in the whole history of our dynasty'.

Lord Devlin recalls his own view of the matter at the time:

> Legally the only way of depriving the Duchess of royal status was to deprive the Duke first. If that had been done, a large body of opinion in Great Britain would have resented it. On the other hand, there would also have been some resentment at having to treat the former Mrs Simpson as royalty. The clever solution to appease both sides was to 'restore' royalty to the Duke without 'conferring' it on the Duchess. It was in its way a good political solution; but it banked on the willingness of the public to overlook a technical illegality, and it was mean and ungenerous and absurd. It was mean in that it was a poor return for Edward VIII's decision not to fight for his crown in 1936. It was absurd in that a government which had advised the King that he could not make a morganatic marriage was now legislating to make morganatic the marriage which he did make. This was my view and I am sure Jowitt would not have disagreed with it, though it was only on the legal aspect that we were asked to advise.

In his letter of 27 May 1937, the King had told the Duke that he might send a reply by hand of Monckton. In the event the Duke charged Monckton with sending two oral messages to his brother, which Monckton did in writing as soon as he returned to London the following day. First, the Duke wanted the King to know 'that He had taken the highest legal advice – that of Sir William Jowitt, K.C. – and had been firmly advised that no Letters Patent were necessary to create Him a Royal Highness but that, on the contrary, He was at His birth and had always been entitled to that style'. It was 'a matter for the lawyers to work out', and the Duke 'wished an opportunity to be given to Sir William to discuss it with those who had advised the Government'. Second, the Duke 'could not regard the action proposed to be taken as other than an insult to the lady who in a few days will become his wife and, therefore, an insult through her to himself'.

The Duke wrote to the King himself a few days later. His letter was purely formal, its purpose being to place his point of view on the official record before he married Mrs Simpson, at which moment the question of her title would arise. Unlike the King's letter of 27 May, it contained no brotherly expressions.

Candé
2nd June 1937

Dear Bertie,

On the eve of my marriage, I wish to refer to the Letters Patent of 27th May 1937, and the announcement (which I presume was official) which was published at the same time.

I am advised that both the Letters Patent and the announcement are based on fallacious premises in that the title of Royal Highness is not either by usage or any Letters Patent which have been issued by previous Sovereigns confined to those who are 'in succession to the throne' and in that my renunciation of the Throne did not abolish my right to use the title but was the natural occasion for my resuming the use of it.

In these circumstances I wish to place on record to you that I do not deem myself to be bound by the Letters Patent of 27th May 1937, and that I claim the right to hold the title of Royal Highness by virtue of the Letters Patent which were issued by Queen Victoria and King George V and the claim is fortified by the fact that in your speech of 12th December 1936 on your accession you referred to me as His Royal Highness.

Yours ever,

DAVID

The following day the Duke and Mrs Simpson were married at Candé, and went off to spend their honeymoon at Schloss Wasserleonburg in Austria. The Duke, however, was unable to get the Letters Patent out of his mind. Jowitt had expressed the opinion that their legality might be challenged; but the Duke had another plan. He had decided that the only honourable course was to give up the use of his own royal title, and become an ordinary duke. In doing so, he would both make an effective protest against what he regarded as an injustice, and solve the problem of the inequality between his own and the Duchess's rank. His papers contain the following draft of a letter he intended to send the King, dated 12 June 1937 and the product of long international telephone conversations with George Allen.

Dear Bertie,

Since writing to you on the 2nd of the month, I have had time to give further thought to the position which has been brought about by the issue of the Letters Patent of the 27th May.

My Wife and I have decided that, although according to the advice which I have received, the Letters Patent were unnecessary and have achieved no purpose, yet my Wife could never wish to adopt the style to which by the immemorial usage of our country she would otherwise have been entitled unless the right were freely accorded to her.

Consequently an impossible situation has been created, since you will appreciate that it would only lead to difficulty and embarrassment both in our household and in public if in the above circumstances I were to continue to use the style of Royal Highness.

I have come to the conclusion, therefore, that I cannot for the future use the title and I am now writing to you for the purpose of informing you of my decision and of sending you a copy of the formal announcement which it will be necessary for me to issue to the Press in a few days.

Yours ever . . .

But this letter was never sent, and no statement was issued. The Duke was deflected in his purpose by Monckton, who wrote to Allen on 9 June to say how disturbed he was at the course the Duke proposed to adopt, which would lose him public sympathy and be seen as offensive to the King. At the moment of his marriage the Duke had been deluged by letters of good wishes from his former subjects, but Monckton felt it would be 'very dangerous' to judge English public opinion by this. Although the Duke theoretically would be attacking the Government and not his brother by making his protest, the public would regard it as an attack upon the sovereign in whose name the Letters Patent had been issued. Monckton was 'desperately anxious for the sake of H.R.H.' that nothing should be done at that moment to cause controversy. 'His patience and forbearance in very difficult circumstances are having their effect and I am sure the tide is slowly beginning to turn in his favour.' If the Duke wanted to return to England eventually, it was 'essential to do nothing to spoil this result and not to make one unnecessary enemy'. One could not afford to give the press 'the chance of embittering the relations between H.R.H. and the powers that be'. The Duke would be accused of putting his brother into a position he never wanted and then increasing his troubles.

On 7 August, Monckton came out to Wasserleonburg to urge his views personally on the Duke, who reluctantly agreed to let the matter rest for the time being, to keep his own royal style and not to make any sort of protest or statement. The whole problem could be cleared up within a few years after his return to England. It is clear from Monckton's notes that he found the Duchess an effective ally in the task of restraining her husband.

The Duchess of Windsor's unique and anomalous position led to a complex problem in the realm of precedence – the detailed body of rules laying down the relative importance of the King's subjects to one another. Was she to be regarded, in spite of the absence of a royal title, as the most junior of the King's sisters-in-law, and thus the eighth woman of the realm? Or was she to be considered as the last-ranking (because the most recently created) of the twenty-nine non-royal duchesses? The rules of precedence laid down in the 1938 editions of *Burke* and *Debrett*, the authoritative annual reference works, tended by implication to support the first of these two views. They did not specifically mention the Duchess of Windsor at all, but the general category of 'wives of the sovereign's brothers' preceded the wives of all non-royal persons, and it was stated categorically that 'precedence of ladies is always derived from the father or husband, except in the case of a Peeress in her own right'. In December 1937, however, newspaper articles appeared in the popular press announcing that the Court would make a ruling in the New Year on the Duchess of Windsor's precedence, putting her in effect in a special class of her own. The source of this story was the editor of *Burke*, who said that in his own view the Duchess of Windsor ought to rank as the twenty-ninth duchess.

Allen, who confirmed the existence of these rumours by ringing up the offices of *Burke* anonymously from a public telephone box, was deeply disturbed. On 4 January 1938 he wrote a letter of warning to the Prime Minister's right-hand man Sir Horace Wilson:[8]

> I have hesitated very much in writing to you on this subject but I feel that it is my duty to do so, knowing as I do the intensity of the Duke's feelings on the delicate matter of his wife's title. I want to give expression to my conviction that if, at this critical stage, the Duke and Duchess should receive a further rebuff of a personal nature, I would be quite helpless and would not be answerable for the consequences.

The Duke's correspondence with Allen reveals that, had a ruling been given in 1938 laying down the Duchess of Windsor's inferior precedence, the Duke would at once have published the statement which had been drafted the previous summer but which he had then refrained from issuing, challenging the Letters Patent and renouncing his own royal title. In fact, Allen and Jowitt made a special trip to Paris in January 1938 to discuss this matter with the Duke and draft the necessary documents. But Allen's warning seems to have had its effect, for in the event no formal ruling on the matter was ever given at all.

The doubt as to where the Duchess of Windsor stood in relation to ordinary non-royal duchesses was bound, sooner or later, to result in an absurd situation of embarrassment; and it is a source of wonder that the situation did not arise until February 1948, when the Windsors were in Palm Beach. Another visitor there was the Duch-

---

[8] Allen had been closely in touch with Wilson over the preceding weeks in connection with the financial settlement between the King and the Duke. See Chapter 2 pp. 61 ff.

ess of Sutherland,[9] who was offended at finding herself seated below the Duchess of Windsor at dinner parties and made her feelings known to her hostesses. The story was quickly picked up by the scandal columnist Cholly Knickerbocker, and soon filled the newspapers. On 23 February the Duchess of Windsor wrote a letter to Allen, the tone of which suggests that she herself took a somewhat light-hearted view of the matter:

> The point to my mind seems to be, do I as the wife of a royal duke sit ahead of the wife of a non-royal duke? I am sure you can get an opinion or ruling from the Lord Chamberlain's Office or whoever knows the correct precedence. This is the first time this particular question has arisen and I would like to have the correct answer. What a pity it was not all settled in 1936. Will you if tactfully possible wire ruling and then send a statement. I am convinced that the Lord Chamberlain's Office would prefer not to have me at the table at all! Anyway we will all know where we stand or rather where we sit. I am writing to you tomorrow on more important and vital subjects. . . .

Allen replied four days later with a cryptic but reassuring telegram: 'Happy to report that notwithstanding power politics Motherland comes twentieth whereas Princess America stands ninth. Question is decided without peradventure by affinity with Number One.' In a letter of 1 March he explained further that the Duchess of Windsor, as the wife of a brother of the sovereign, belonged (quite apart from any question of royal title) to the top category of duchesses, whereas the Duchess of Sutherland, whose husband held a mere United Kingdom dukedom created in the nineteenth century, belonged to the bottom category. These facts were evident from the general tables of precedence laid down in *Burke* and *Debrett*, and Allen did not think it necessary to seek a formal ruling: doubtless he was apprehensive of what the result might be.

[9] She was Clare Josephine Dunkerly, daughter of Herbert O'Brien of Calcutta, who had married the fifth Duke of Sutherland (1888–1963) in 1944 as his second wife.

With a great effort of restraint, but with encouragement from the Duchess, the Duke followed Monckton's advice to remain silent on the subject of the title up to the outbreak of war in September 1939. This was the first of many occasions on which he believed that he would be welcomed back to his country and accepted, together with his wife, back into the royal fold: but he was to be bitterly disappointed. Though he did briefly return to England with the Duchess to resolve the matter of a war job, he was ignored entirely by the Court and all of his relations. He was unable to see any of them except for a single meeting with the King – and even this had only been arranged with the greatest difficulty, and on the condition that wives were not to be present and that such controversial matters as the subject of the Duchess's status should not be mentioned. Having at first been told that he might remain in Great Britain in a civil defence job, he was eventually left with no choice but to take up a military liaison post in France, where he returned determined to do his best in this sphere, but filled with shock and anger at the manner in which he had been cold-shouldered.

With the Duke abroad and the war in full progress, the ruling regarding the inferior status of the Duchess continued to be rigorously enforced, even in extraordinary situations. On 22 June 1940 it became known to the War Cabinet that the Windsors, who had fled from France following the military defeat, had arrived in Spain. The Foreign Office telegraphed to the British Embassy in Madrid: 'Please invite Their Royal Highnesses to proceed to Lisbon.' This was the most critical moment of the war, the day that France signed an armistice with the Germans and left Britain to fight alone. Yet Hardinge, the King's Private Secretary, could find time to write to the Foreign Office reprimanding the official who had used the forbidden words 'Their Royal Highnesses', and expressing the King's desire that steps be taken to ensure that such an error never occur again.[10]

Arriving in Madrid, the Duke hesitated to return to England: he was still smarting from the emotional scars of his ostracism in September 1939. As he wrote in 1966: 'The year before, while we had been in England, the presence of the Duchess at my side had never been acknowledged, even perfunctorily. Before going back I wanted an assurance that simple courtesies would be forthcoming.'

[10] Sir Alexander Hardinge to W. I. Mallet, 24 June 1940, FO 800/326 f. 195.

He did not choose this moment to ask that the Duchess be granted her royal title, but he did make his return conditional on the King and Queen agreeing to receive them together just once, by way of a gesture to end the public scandal which resulted from the Duchess's inferior status. In her memoirs, the Duchess admitted that the episode

> . . . now seems fantastic and perhaps even a little silly. But David's pride was engaged, and he was deadly serious. When, after some time, he felt it necessary to tell me what was going on, he put the situation to me in approximately these terms: 'I won't have them push us into a bottom drawer. It must be the two of us together – man and wife with the same position. Now, I am only too well aware of the risk of my being misunderstood in pressing for this at such a time. Some people will probably say that, with a war on, these trifles should be forgotten. But they are not trifles to me. Whatever I am to be I must be with you; any position I am called upon to fill I can only fill with you.'
>
> It was characteristic of him to hold such a view. . . . I tried as hard as I could to make him see the matter in another light: the importance above everything else of his not allowing his gallantry towards me to interfere with his returning to England in a war job. The question of my position as his wife, I said, could be dealt with later, if it had to be dealt with at all. But . . . David turned a deaf ear to my argument. And in truth, all that he ever specifically asked for was a fairly simple thing: that I be received, just once, by the King, his brother, and the Queen, in order to erase by that single gesture of hospitality the stigma attaching to my never having been received since our marriage by the Royal Family, his family.

The British Ambassador to Madrid, Sir Samuel Hoare, tended to take the Duke's side in the request, urging Churchill to get the King to agree to it. 'I am certain that this is the moment to end the trouble and if it is not ended now, the rift between them and the rest of the family will become deeper and more dangerous.' All the Duke wanted, Hoare stressed, was a 'once only' meeting 'of a quarter of an hour'. The request was refused, however, and the Duke, who had offered to serve anywhere in the Empire in the event of his not returning home, accepted the post of Governor of the Bahamas.

If the Windsors' difference in rank had been embarrassing enough among the French and such English people as they encountered abroad, in Nassau, where the Duke now became the King's representative and had to deal with a parochial and bigoted local white ruling class, it became intolerably so. 'I will admit to being apprehensive', the Duke wrote to Churchill in October 1940, 'of the possible effect of this difference in our official status on our position in a small community like this British Colony; but somehow I felt that in view of the war situation, this chronic insult to my wife might well be overcome, if not entirely lost, in the vast changes that are taking place before our eyes.' But he had been shocked to discover on his arrival that a telegram from the Lord Chamberlain had preceded him with the following urgent instructions to his officials: 'You are no doubt aware that a lady when presented to H.R.H. the Duke of Windsor should make a half-curtsey. The Duchess of Windsor is not entitled to this. The Duke should be addressed as "Your Royal Highness" and the Duchess as "Your Grace".' The Duke can hardly be blamed for using his authority as Governor to insist that his wife be treated with full royal honours in the Bahamas, and there were few (among both officials and non-officials) who resisted this, out of both respect for the Duke and liking for the Duchess.

The Duchess was successful and popular in Nassau. Apart from her ordinary duties as the Governor's wife and her direction of war charities, she displayed her talent for organization by running two infant welfare clinics; and in 1942, when Nassau was about to become an important war station, she worked hard to set up a forces' club and canteen. On 10 November that year, having submitted the Colony's New Year's Honours List to London, the Duke could not resist writing to Churchill asking him

. . . to submit to the King that he restore the Duchess's royal rank at the coming New Year's, not only as an act of justice and courtesy to his sister-in-law, but also as a gesture in recognition of her two years public service in the Bahamas.

The occasion would seem opportune from all angles for correcting an unwarranted step, taken, I will admit, at a time when feeling was still running high with regard to my Abdication, and in Coronation Year, when any action calculated to build up the King's position was considered justifiable, even to the extent of hitting me where I was most vulnerable, which was to insult the lady who had consented to become my wife. I will be grateful, therefore, if you will make this submission to the King personally on my behalf, and inform me of His pleasure in the matter.

Churchill duly laid the matter before the King; and the King replied to the Prime Minister on 8 December, not by a personal letter but in a formal minute which was almost certainly drafted by Hardinge. This document, published in 1987 in Patrick Howarth's biography of George VI, is the only official record so far to have been released in which the King explains the reasons behind his attitude. It also makes clear that, although the King had told the Duke in 1937 that this was a matter in which he sought and was bound by ministerial advice, he in reality regarded it as a personal decision entirely for himself and his family.

The King had read his brother's letter 'with great care', but after 'much thought' he did not feel he could 'alter a decision which I made [*sic*] with considerable reluctance' before the Duke's marriage. In abdicating, the Duke had renounced the succession for himself and his descendants – and this had also meant renouncing the title of Royal Highness for himself and his wife. There was therefore no possibility of 'restoring' the title to the Duchess, who had never possessed it in the first place. There were still many people in England and the Empire 'to whom it would be most distasteful to have to do honour to the Duchess as a member of our family'. The whole affair had settled down 'so well', and to bring everything up again would be 'a tragedy'. The King had consulted his family, 'who share these views': he was sure Churchill did too. It pained him to have to reply in this way, but country and family came first.

Churchill telegraphed the Duke with the bad news on 22 December 1942, in such a way as not entirely to extinguish the ex-King's hopes.

I laid Your Royal Highness's wish before the King. His Majesty is willing to let question remain in abeyance but not to take action in sense desired. . . . I am sorry not to have more agreeable news but I hope Your Royal Highness will not attach undue importance to this point after the immense renunciations you have made.

Two years later, the Duke made another appeal to Churchill. He and the Duchess planned to pass through England on their return to Europe in 1945, and he revived his old plea of June 1940 that he and the Duchess be received at Court just once, for the sake of public appearances. As he wrote to the Prime Minister on 3 October 1944:

> Were the King and Queen to behave normally to the Duchess and myself when we pass by England, and invite us merely to tea at one of their residences, a formality which as a matter of fact is prescribed by Court protocol in the case of Colonial Governors and their wives, it would avoid any division of feeling being manifested. . . . It could never be a very happy meeting, but on the other hand it would be quite painless, and would have the merit of silencing, once and for all, those malicious circles who delight in keeping open an eight-year-old wound that ought to have been healed officially, if not privately, ages ago.

Churchill did his best for the Duke, but had to write that he saw no possibility of getting the King and Queen to receive the Duchess.

The war years witnessed one ludicrous episode which is worth describing as an example of the anomaly of the Duchess's position. The Duke owned a ranch (known as the E. P. Ranch) in the Pekisko Hills of Alberta, which he had bought on his first visit to Canada in 1919 and on which he had practised stockbreeding for many years. It had always lost money heavily and during the Depression he had wanted to sell it; but the Canadian Government considered it 'a valuable asset in the relations between the Dominion and Great Britain' and, to persuade him to keep it, they had in 1931 granted him control – rare among Canadian landowners – of the mineral rights on his land. This grant suddenly became relevant when, exactly ten years later, oil was struck in the Pekisko Hills. To the Duke, who was then in the Bahamas, it seemed that the ranch might cease to be a drain on his resources and become, indeed, an asset which could restore his overall finances. A survey (which unfortunately proved inaccurate) suggested that oil was present on the ranch in commercial quantities; and in 1943 he began a drilling venture in partnership with two American tycoons, Cushing and Walker.

The sums involved were substantial,[11] and before committing themselves his partners naturally wanted to know what would happen to the venture if the Duke died. Under the grant of 1931, the mineral rights were to go with the land for ninety-nine years so long as the ranch was farmed by the Duke *or a member of the Royal Family*. As the Duke's sole heir was the Duchess, the question of whether the grant would survive him seemed to depend on whether the Duchess was to be regarded as 'a member of the Royal Family'. There was, however, no legal definition of the phrase 'member of the Royal Family'; it therefore appeared to be a personal question of whether the King considered his sister-in-law a member of his family. On 27 October 1943 the Duke wrote to Allen from New York asking him to approach the King about this:

> As the Prime Minister has informed me that The King is not yet inclined to give the Duchess her rightful rank, I do not press for the restoring of the appellage of 'Her Royal Highness' at the present juncture. On the other hand, I do expect The King to make it known . . . through the High Commissioner of the United Kingdom in Canada that, although the Duchess's royal status is not officially recognized, she is, as my wife, to be regarded legally as a member of the Royal Family.

After a brief audience with the King, and interviews with the royal private secretary Sir Alan Lascelles and legal adviser Sir Claud Schuster, Allen was informed that the expression 'member of the Royal Family' probably only included the sovereign and his wife and his close blood relations – in which case it would exclude not only the Duchess of Windsor but also the wives of all princes. In any case, the King refused to make any formal decision on the matter. The Duke's Canadian lawyer Heward then had a new idea. Why not bequeath the ranch in name to someone who was incontestably 'a member of the Royal Family' (such as the Duke of Gloucester), while reserving a life interest (including oil rights) to the Duchess? 'Have carefully considered proposition', Allen replied by telegram on 23 November,

---

[11] The Duke himself lost $100,000 over the affair.

'but judging from my past and recent experience am satisfied perso-nalities involved would refuse.' Doubtless much to the relief of the Palace, who would hardly have welcomed a situation where the Duchess's status was tested in the English courts, this absurd prob-lem was finally sidestepped by a ruling of the Lord Chancellor that, under English law, the reference to the Duke in the grant might be interpreted so as to include his executors and successors.

In July 1945 a Labour government came to power in Great Britain under Clement Attlee. The new Lord Chancellor was the same William Jowitt who had advised the Duke in 1937 that the Letters Patent denying royal honours to the Duchess were legally invalid; and it now naturally occurred to the Duke to ask him to put his advice into practice by having them revoked. For over three years, however, he restrained himself from raising the matter with either his family or the Government: in family discussions, all he pressed was his old demand that the Duchess be received once only for the sake of form. He was hoping that the Government would offer him an important semi-diplomatic job, and that the King would allow him the use of Fort Belvedere for certain months of the year; he (and above all the Duchess) did not want renewed argument about the title to prejudice his chances.

By the end of 1948, however, it was clear that he was going to be offered nothing; and he had been strongly influenced by two recent factors. First, he had begun to write his memoirs, and reminiscence had renewed his sense of grievance. Second, there was the case of Walter Monckton. Monckton had been forced to resign as Attorney-General to the Duchy of Cornwall, the appointment at Court he had held since 1932, when his first wife began divorce proceedings against him in 1946; but in the autumn of 1948, a year after his remarriage, he was reinstated in the post. This was unprecedented in the case of a member of the Royal Household who had been the guilty party in divorce proceedings, and was seen by a hopeful Duke as indicating a possible change in general Palace attitudes. On 7 December 1948 the Duke wrote to the King congratulating him on having made the reappointment, adding with heavy irony: 'Apart from other considerations, one of my main objections to the official attitude towards divorce in Great Britain has always been the regrettable loss of the services of able and experienced men which is not infrequently incurred thereby.' When the Duke next saw his brother he at last raised the matter of the title and, having first obtained the King's permission, had a meeting with Jowitt in London on 13 April 1949.

Jowitt, however, was no longer the Duke's man. A brilliant lawyer, he was also a shrewd and ambitious character who knew when to switch his loyalties: in the previous twenty years he had changed his party allegiance no less than three times in his quest for high office.[12] As an opposition politician in private practice at the Bar before the war, he had been happy to advise the Duke that the Letters Patent were legally ineffective. But now that he was the Crown's most senior servant and the head of the English judiciary he was unlikely to do anything to prejudice his relations with the Court.

This is evident from Jowitt's account of their meeting,[13] which shows him avoiding all commitment. Beginning by pointing out that he had gone to see the Duke at the latter's own request, he continued: 'Any embarrassment I might have felt in view of my present position in discussing this matter with the Duke was allayed when he told me that he had mentioned to The King that he was going to ask me to come and see him to discuss this topic and when he added that The King had expressed no objection.' Jowitt did not deny the substance of the legal opinion he had given in 1937 – that the Duke was a Royal Highness not by virtue of the Letters Patent but by right as the son of a sovereign, that Letters Patent could not take away what had not been created by Letters Patent, and that the Duchess automatically shared the Duke's rank by virtue of being his wife. But he now explained that the law was irrelevant, for 'whatever subtle arguments lawyers might adduce, the fact was that the Letters Patent of 1937, issued by the King on the advice of his responsible Ministers, plainly contemplated that the Duchess should not enjoy this honour'. The marks of respect paid to royalty were 'in no sense a legal obligation' but 'rather a question of good manners'.

---

[12] Elected to Parliament as a Liberal in 1929, he at once switched to the Labour Party in order to become Attorney-General. In order to retain this office, he followed Ramsay Mac-Donald into the National Labour Party in 1931, only to change back to Labour in 1936 after the National Labour Party had been virtually wiped out in the elections of the previous year.

[13] Reproduced in Appendix II.

The question for instance whether ladies should curtsey to the Duchess would depend in practice, not upon the view they formed upon a legal question, but upon their desire to uphold and carry out the intention of His Majesty the King as the fountain of honour.

Jowitt appeared to have forgotten that in 1937 he had advised that the Letters Patent were invalid and might be legally challenged, for he now told the Duke that they could only be revoked by new Letters Patent, and that these could only be issued by the King on the advice of his Ministers. He thus inferred that the matter was not a legal one for himself but a political one for the Prime Minister and the Cabinet.

The Duke, wrote Jowitt, 'expressed his anxiety to end the present situation, which he thought had gone on all too long. It certainly needed tidying up. Its continuance amounted to nothing less than an insult to his wife, to whom he had been happily married for many years past.' The position was exactly as if there had been a morganatic marriage, 'and this was the position which Mr Baldwin had said was impossible in this country, and to which the Duke of Windsor, when King, would never have assented'. The Duke thought he had better go to discuss the matter with Attlee, and asked if Jowitt might at the same time talk to the King, to which Jowitt replied cautiously that he was always available if the King cared to send for him.

Though Jowitt had committed himself to nothing, he had evidently used a sympathetic tone with the Duke,[14] who went to see Attlee in a mood of optimism. On 26 April, however, Attlee wrote to the Duke that he had 'given most careful consideration' to the 'personal matter' which the Duke had drawn to his attention, that he had discussed the matter with the Lord Chancellor, that he was 'very sensible' of the Duke's motives in bringing the matter forward, but that 'I feel bound to say that I do not think it advisable or opportune to take any action at the present time'. On 3 June the Duke wrote to Jowitt:

---

[14] This is apparent from a short handwritten note which the Duke made of the meeting, which read as follows: '*Letters Patent*: although in existence and beside the point must be rescinded by the King *on advice of his Ministers*. No legislation required of Parliament. Ld Chancellor would like to explain it all to Bertie. Advises me to talk to Attlee. Dominion P.M.s here next week. Winston? He is writing Lascelles to report our meeting. Everything above board.'

I cannot attempt to disguise my intense disappointment at Mr Attlee's letter, all the more so as the opinion you gave me in 1937 and your understanding attitude the other day gave me high hopes to believe that your influence in my favour would be considerable.

I have received no communication from my brother; therefore I am uninformed as to whether he ever sent for you so that you might explain the invalidity of the Letters Patent of 27 May 1937.

Embarrassing situations created by the denial to the Duchess of my royal status are not infrequent and always undignified. After twelve years of loyal self-effacement, we should now be spared the social rudeness involved, a source of unnecessary pain to both of us.

The Duke hoped to discuss the problem again with the Lord Chancellor on his next visit to London, but Jowitt scotched such further efforts in a terse letter of 13 June in which he regretted that it was 'not, of course, a matter in which I can in any way help Your Royal Highness'.

Once again, the Duke felt he had been the victim of a game. Jowitt had described the question as a political one for the Prime Minister, the Prime Minister as a personal one for the King. The Duke's anger was now concentrated on his brother, and he resolved upon what he would have called 'a showdown'. This took place in London in December 1949. That the confrontation between the two men was stormy is evident from the letter which the King wrote to the Duke on 15 December and the Duke's subsequent reply. This correspondence is especially interesting in that it casts light on the original motives for the King's decision – the need to satisfy public opinion, the desire for retribution, and the hope that the continuing discrimination against his wife would encourage the Duke to stay abroad.

The King's tone was one of injured innocence. It had been useless to reason with the Duke while he had been 'in that state of emotion', but now the King wished to put his case. It had been 'a very great shock' to him in November 1936 to learn that his brother wished to marry Mrs Simpson, and the subsequent course of events had caused him great anguish and suffering. The Duke's departure (as he had never seemed to understand) had left 'a most ghastly void' in both the Royal Family and the Empire which George VI had been called upon to fill 'with nothing but sympathy for what had happened'. It had been an ordeal for him to go through with the Coronation that had been intended for his brother. In abdicating, the Duke had accepted the view of the British people that the woman he wanted to marry was unfit to be Queen. It therefore followed she was equally unfit to be a member of the Royal Family, and for this decision now to be reversed 'wouldn't make sense of the past'.

It was not until almost six months later, on 6 June 1950, that the Duke replied to the King from Paris.

Dear Bertie,

For some unaccountable reason your letter of December 15th last, together with other mail received around that date, got locked in my filing cabinet here. Having only made this discovery upon my return from America, I write to acknowledge receipt of your communication although its tone is surprising to say the least.

In the first place, I never used the words 'life is not worth living' at our last meeting in London. On the contrary, I could not conceive greater happiness than Wallis has given me these thirteen years of our married life which we celebrated last Saturday.

No more did I get into 'that state of emotion' as you infer. Considering the manner in which you have been temporizing with me ever since I raised this subject almost two years ago, I have remained commendably calm and patient. But having found a normal approach ineffective and unproductive of any response from you, I merely became more frank in stating my case and registering my feelings over what I regard as an injustice to the innocent person, my wife.

Then the 1936 and 1937 skeletons you have now pulled out of the closet are hardly in line with some of the questions you asked me at our last meeting. I refer for example to your wanting to know whether the granting of my rightful request on behalf of Wallis would alter my attitude towards living in Great Britain. You also asked me whether I had ever discussed this subject with Mama.

From the things you and various people have told me since I raised this subject I cannot accept what you call 'the facts of the case' for withholding my request – a tortuous and unconvincing thesis to which you have never so much as hinted in our conversations and which quite frankly I can neither follow nor understand.

Before leaving New York I arranged with Life magazine to send you the four issues in which my articles are being published.[15] I hope you are receiving them.

Yours,

DAVID

During the following years, there were further occasions on which the Duke raised the matter of his wife's status with the British authorities: one such was the return to office of Churchill in 1951. The Court, however, always remained immovable, and the government of the day was always prepared to leave the final decision to them. The Duke was forced to resign himself permanently to a situation where his wife was officially regarded as his social inferior, and every encounter with a stranger was a potential cause for social embarrassment.

In the 1960s there was a slight thaw in relations between the Windsors and the Royal Family in England. When the Duke was in hospital in London in February 1965, the Queen called on him and met the Duchess for the first time since the Abdication; and in June 1967 both the Duke and Duchess were allowed to be present at a brief royal ceremony to dedicate a memorial to Queen Mary. Thus the Duke's request for 'a once only meeting of a quarter of an hour', which he had first made in June 1940 in an effort to 'efface by a single gesture of hospitality' the public notion that his wife was a woman with whom the British Royal Family refused under any circumstances to be associated, was at last satisfied. In August 1970 the Queen agreed that both the Duke and Duchess might ultimately be laid to rest in the royal burial ground at Frogmore. This symbolic decision effectively granted the Duchess a posthumous status as a member of the Royal Family; but it was accompanied by no formal decision granting her a royal title during her lifetime. Even during the early days of her widowhood she received a request from the Lord Chamberlain's Office asking her to destroy all of the Duke's stationery bearing the Royal Arms, and to cease to use any of his

---

[15] See Chapter 9.

effects which bore his crown and cipher. In April 1986 the Duchess died and, after a funeral service in St George's Chapel which was remarkable in that her name was not once mentioned from beginning to end, was buried next to her husband in the graveyard of his family.

Chapter Four

Fort Belvedere

*J*ust after the Abdication, Lady Diana Cooper wrote to the Duke of Windsor: 'I shall pray for your happiness, Sir, and for the day you return to those who love you so and to the Fort you so love.' And, on 16 December, Winston Churchill wrote : 'I suppose, Sir, you saw that the Attorney-General in the debate on the Abdication declared formally that there was no obligation on Your Royal Highness to reside outside the British Dominions; so I earnestly hope that it will not be many months before I shall be paying my respects to you at the Fort.' In the months and years that followed it was made clear to the Duke that he would return to be treated as an outcast; but the one thing which continued to draw him back to England was the house he always thought of as home. In his memoirs (published in 1951) the Duke wrote:

> The Fort laid hold of me in many ways. Soon I came to love it as I loved no other material thing – perhaps because it was so much my own creation. More and more it became for me a peaceful, almost enchanted anchorage, where I found refuge from the cares and turmoil of my life. . . .

It was to Fort Belvedere that the King had withdrawn after the Abdication crisis had become public on 3 December 1936; and it was there that the drama of the final week was enacted. Once he had made the decision to give up the throne, the thing which saddened him most was the thought of leaving his own house; but he never thought he would be leaving it for ever. Indeed, one of the few favours he asked of his brother was that the Fort be kept for him as his English residence. On the afternoon of 9 December, Walter Monckton and Sir Edward Peacock went to see the Duke of York about this matter at his residence, 145 Piccadilly (the other matter discussed was the King's future title, and it was on this occasion that Monckton made his ill-fated remark about return without consent); and the Duke of York gave his promise that the Fort (which was held at the sovereign's grace-and-favour) would be the ex-King's to enjoy whenever he came to England throughout the rest of his life. This assurance eased the abdicating monarch's mind; but when, having abdicated, he drove away from the house two days later it seemed a symbol of all he was giving up. 'The Fort had been more than a home', he wrote; 'it had been a way of life for me. I had created The Fort just as my grandfather had created Sandringham; I loved it in the same way; it was there that I had passed the happiest days of my life.'

It was not strange for such a place to induce nostalgia, for its setting and history were romantic. The Fort's turrets peeped out of a wooded hill near Windsor which rose from the artificial lake of Virginia Water. The lake had been created by George II's soldier son William, Duke of Cumberland, and it was he who had built the original triangular Belvedere Tower in the 1730s. In the 1820s this was expanded by Wyatville, the architect of Windsor Castle, into a miniature fortress for royal tea parties, the lodging of royal favourites, and the housing of a royal collection of guns; a battery of cannon was installed to be fired on royal birthdays by a resident bombadier. 'It was a child's idea of a fort,' wrote Diana Cooper. 'The sentries, one thought, must be of tin.' The last salute was fired in 1907, and in 1910 the house was granted 'at grace and favour' to Sir Malcolm Murray, the Duke of Connaught's comptroller. In the 1920s the Prince of Wales, looking for a place of his own, fell in love with it; and when Murray died in 1929 he asked his father for the 'enjoyment' of it – which George V granted him with the words: 'What could you want that queer old place for? Those damn week-ends I suppose. . . .' Two years later, King George was similarly to grant the Duke and Duchess of York the enjoyment of Royal Lodge, Windsor – still enjoyed by the Duchess, now the Queen Mother.

The Duke of Windsor has written in his memoirs of the passion with which he turned the Fort into his home (which he did with his own money – structural alterations alone cost him £21,000 in 1929–30), and in particular of how he devoted himself to its hundred acres of garden. 'I cleared away acres of dank laurel and replaced them with rare rhododendrons. I cut winding paths through fir and beech trees, revealing the true enchantment of the woodland setting. . . . I found a new contentment in working about the Fort with my own hands. . . . I begrudged as lost a daylight hour that I did not see the work progressing. . . . I pressed my week-end guests into arduous physical labour . . . and presently they began to share my enthusiasm.' It was in these surroundings that the Prince created a private life away from his official duties, and it was here that his friendship with Mrs Simpson developed. Much of the interior decoration, the comfortable atmosphere and the smooth running of weekends was ultimately due to her. 'Mrs Simpson was entitled to considerable respect,' wrote Rebecca West. 'Not many women can pick up the keys of a rented house, raddled by long submission to temporary inmates, and make it look as if a family of cheerful good taste have lived there for centuries.' On 1 January 1935 a new visitors' book in scarlet morocco was inaugurated with the signatures of the Prince and Mrs Simpson.

With the accession of Edward VIII the Fort assumed a special significance as 'the King's independent home' where he could escape from the restrictions of Court life. The atmosphere of palaces made him tense, but at weekends he could be at ease again among friends. He now especially depended upon Mrs Simpson to organize this 'other life'. As she wrote to her Aunt Bessie on 30 January 1936, ten days after the accession: 'The King has lost six pounds and the strain has been tremendous . . . but last week-end we went to the Fort and we go again tomorrow where he will get the needed rest.' Most weekends saw about four guests, generally an English couple and an American couple. In 1936 the King spent further substantial sums from his private fortune improving the Fort. With the aid of Lady Colefax, Lady Mendl, and Jansen of Paris, Mrs Simpson planned the redecoration of the main reception rooms; Sir Giles Gilbert Scott added a guest wing, and central heating was installed. But the King's greatest pride remained his garden, especially the rhododendrons he had planted six years before. When the Prime Minister called on 20 October 1936, to ask the King to induce Mrs Simpson to give up her divorce, he complimented the sovereign 'upon the beauty of the grounds, the arrangement of the garden, the silvery radiance of the birch trees, and the delicacy of the autumn tints'.

The King's withdrawal to the Fort a week before the end (so as not to lend himself to a 'King's Party' which might rally to him in the capital) lent 'an air of mystery to the tense constitutional and dynastic drama enacted amidst its shrubberies and bastions'. On 9 December the Duke of York gave his 'guarantee'; on 10 December the Instrument of Abdication was signed in the Octagonal Drawing Room (where the financial agreement was signed on the evening of the same day); and on the evening of 11 December the Duke of Windsor, as he now was, drove away from the Fort, a symbol of the England to which he hoped one day to return. Among the few personal items he took with him was the visitors' book he had started with Mrs Simpson in 1935. *The Fort* was tooled on its cover; and it would lie on the hall table of all of the many houses they were to live in. It is a curious catalogue of exile. Under little strips of gummed letterhead, visitors signed at Schloss Enzesfeld, Candé (where all their wedding guests signed), Wasserleonburg where they spent their honeymoon, their rented house at Versailles, their rented villa at Cap d'Antibes, their rented *hôtel particulier* on the Boulevard Suchet, the house in Portugal where they spent anxious weeks in the summer of 1940, Government House, Nassau . . . until it finally came to rest in the fifties at the Moulin de la Tuilerie at Gif, their country house near Paris. For it never came home.

But during the first years of exile the Duke never doubted that he would be going back to the Fort: he continued to pay for the gardeners, insurance and upkeep. It was the general expectation, frequently voiced in the popular press, that he would be returning and that the Fort was where he would live. 'I am hoping the Duke of Windsor will be able soon to come back and live quietly as a private gentleman,' Churchill wrote to a prominent friend not long after the Abdication. 'I am sure he has no other wish but to live quietly in his house in England.'

In the spring of 1938 the Duke took the lease of Sir Pomeroy Burton's villa at Cap d'Antibes, La Cröe; and wishing to give it something of the air of the Fort (he called his sitting room 'the Belvedere') he sent for many of his personal possessions from the Fort which since the Abdication had been in store first at Windsor and later at Frogmore. Quantities of furniture, china and glass were carelessly packed, and over half arrived in a damaged condition. 'I am extremely sorry that this should have happened,' wrote Sir Ulick Alexander; 'and I fear it has caused Your Royal Highness considerable loss.'

In July 1939 the historian Philip Guedalla, then writing a book on the reign of Edward VIII, stayed at La Cröe, and later sent his host a set of his books for the villa's library. 'I certainly hope', wrote the Duke in his letter of thanks, 'it will not be too long before we are asking for one for the Fort. . . .'

A few weeks later, war broke out. The Duke, still at Antibes, wanted to return to serve his country. The Fort was at that time uninhabitable, but he hoped to be lodged nearby. In the event, however, he was not put up in any royal residence, and his presence in England was ignored by the Court and his family, none of whom wished to see him except for a banal interview with George VI. He and the Duchess stayed with friends in Sussex until he was speedily packed back to France with a military liaison job. One afternoon before their departure, however, they motored over to see the Fort. The Duchess later remembered it as 'a sad visit. . . . The lawn was overgrown; the garden . . . was a mass of weeds; and the house itself . . . was slowly decaying.' The Duke, however, wrote to a friend at the time that he was 'agreeably surprised at how my plants were doing after three years'. Though he returned to France disillusioned by the way he had been treated in his own country, it was evident that the Fort – for which he still paid the upkeep – was a magnet which would continue to draw him back.

But not for long. On 17 February 1940, during the Phoney War, the hapless Alexander wrote to Major-General the Duke of Windsor in France. He was sure the Duke was anxious to hear 'any news about the Fort', so was writing 'by the wish of the King' to say that the Government wanted to take it over 'to accommodate Crown Lands Headquarters in the event of bombing activity over London' – and that the King had agreed to this. Since the Fort was a folly with small rooms and obviously unsuited to offices, the Duke not unnaturally suspected that behind this apparently reasonable request lay a desire to cheat him of his future right to live there. He therefore had George Allen write to say:

> . . . His Royal Highness has during the course of many years expended large sums of money improving the property both structurally and decoratively. . . . You will therefore appreciate that his interest in the property is substantial, and though he is very willing that his property should be put to good use during the war, he considers that it would be expedient that the general condition of

the property should be placed on record before Crown Lands go into occupation in order that it may not be difficult to reinstate the property into its former condition on the termination of the occupation. . . .

The reply which came from Windsor on 13 March confirmed the Duke's fears. The Fort no longer belonged to the Duke because the present sovereign had never formally confirmed him in possession of it, and 'all warrants [to occupy grace-and-favour residences] are automatically cancelled on the termination of a reign, and unless renewed by the Sovereign, the former occupant has no longer any claim to the premises'. On receiving this news, the Duke – who had also learned that his plants from the Fort's gardens were being moved in mid-winter to the Royal Nurseries at Windsor – wrote bitterly to Allen:

> It is crystal clear that this proposed reserving of the Fort for the use of Crown Lands is nothing more than a piece of bluff, and the first excuse that the King has been able to find to deprive me of my right to occupy the place should I ever desire to do so. . . . Quite apart from the detail of whether the accommodation is sufficient (which I doubt), or whether Crown Lands are bombed out of London, what is Savill's[1] idea of removing my rhododendrons? . . . The whole thing is of course only another example of my brother's failure to keep his word to me of December 1936, when amongst other guarantees it was clearly understood verbally (unfortunately not in writing) that The Fort would be reserved for me until such time as it was considered mutually suitable that I should take up residence in England again. . . .

But there was no appeal. During the war, incidentally, the Fort did not accommodate government offices, but remained shuttered.

The Duke and Duchess would never see the Fort again. But they did not cease to think of it. In the autumn of 1940, when she was devoting her energies to the refurbishment of Government House, Nassau, the Duchess told Adela St Johns:

[1] Sir Eric Savill, Assistant Ranger of Windsor Great Park.

... Don't you see, I must make him a home. That's why I'm doing this place over, so we can live in it with comfort as a home. All his life he's been travelling, and a place to come back to is not always a home. The only one he ever had he made for himself at Fort Belvedere. He had to leave it – you don't know what that meant to him. . . .

In both their memoirs, the Windsors wrote of the Fort and the times they had spent there with some passion; and whenever the Duke in later years was asked by interviewers whether there was anything he missed or regretted, it was of the Fort (and little else) that he invariably spoke.

After the war, they made one attempt to obtain the right to live there. By the beginning of 1947 the Duchess had become disturbed by the prospect of their spending the rest of their lives drifting between the world's hotels. They had not yet managed to construct any suitable existence in France. In February she wrote from Palm Beach to George Allen:

> ... With the Duke's dislike of cold weather we could spend winters in America from . . . November to April if we had a house. If *only* we could have the Fort for the autumn and spring (until July when we could go to France spending a couple of months in hotels) so we could make our home between England and here. Do you see any chance of getting the Fort for this arrangement? We would not be there long enough to upset the powers that be, and we in our old age could have 2 nice houses where we want them. . . . It is a waste of time being homeless on the face of the earth and most disturbing. . . .

The Windsors were evidently hopeful of the granting of this request, for in May and June 1947 they visited England and took a rented house at Sunningdale very close to the Fort. On 29 May 1947, Harold Nicolson met them at Sibyl Colefax's and recorded:

> She [the Duchess] says that they do not know where to live. They would like to live in England, but that is difficult. He retains his old

love of Fort Belvedere. 'We are tired of wandering,' she says. 'We are not as young as we were. We want to settle down and grow our own trees. He likes gardening. But it is no fun gardening in other people's gardens.' . . . I feel really sorry for them. She was so simple and sincere.

A formal request was made to the King that the Duke should be allowed to use the Fort during his visits to England. It was refused.

The Windsors decided to continue living in France, with its hospitable government and protection of privacy. In 1952, now reconciled to permanent exile, they at last bought a property of their own there, a mill in the valley of the Chevreuse which they proceeded to transform and refurbish. The Moulin de la Tuilerie was filled with the surviving contents of the Fort, including some of the fittings which the Duke managed to recover; and it was there that he at last managed to plant his trees and create his garden.

In 1953, while the Duke was working on his new property, it was announced by Buckingham Palace that the Fort would cease to be a grace-and-favour residence and would be offered for sale on a long lease. In the spring of 1955 a ninety-nine-year lease was granted to the Queen's first cousin Gerald Lascelles, the younger son of the Princess Royal. He announced that the house was 'falling to pieces' and that he meant to spend two years 'refashioning it completely' – which he proceeded to do both within and without. When the architectural historian Christopher Hussey visited the refashioned Fort in 1959, he found nothing which might serve as a reminder of its former occupancy, except for the famous 'battlements walk' with its formal garden and swimming-pool terrace where the Duke as Prince of Wales had entertained his guests.

Mr Lascelles lived at the Fort until 1976 when financial pressure caused him to sell the remainder of his lease to a son of the Emir of Dubai. It might have been thought that, after the Duke's death in 1972, the proper destiny of the Fort was as a monument or museum to the penultimate King of England; and something of this sort came to pass. For in 1977 the house was sub-let to a television company (presumably with the approval of the superior landlords, the Crown Estates) for the making of a popular historical film series about the Abdication of Edward VIII; and the Fort was suddenly restored by expert hands into something resembling its former state. Meanwhile the Duke (eventually to be reunited there with the woman he loved) had been laid to rest not far away, in the royal burial ground at Frogmore.

Part Two

Exile – The First
Ten Years

Chapter Five

From Marriage to War
1937–39

*T*he principal causes of conflict between the Duke and his family and the British authorities having been examined, it is now necessary to chart the chronological story.

Following their marriage at Candé on 3 June 1937, the Windsors made their way to Austria, where they were to spend their honeymoon at Schloss Wasserleonburg, Count Munster's spectacular castle in Carinthia. An interesting chronicle of their lives which will be quoted throughout this book consists of the Duchess's regular letters to her aunt, Bessie Merryman, who lived in Washington and was the only member of her family to whom she remained very close. On 13 June she wrote that they were exhausted, having so far spent all their time trying to reply to the many thousands of letters of good wishes they had received; but that they were very happy. 'The situation of the house is ideal and the country lovely, the house itself rather run down at the heels with a combination of Austrian and English comfort. . . . We have decided to treat it as a picnic and not worry until we recover from the last six months.'

Having achieved his heart's desire, the Duke was indeed a happy man. But since the Abdication he had received three severe blows. First, there had been the money problems – his omission from the Civil List, and his brother's repudiation of the Fort Belvedere Agreement; next, his family's boycott of his wedding; finally, the Letters Patent of 27 May purporting to deprive his wife of his royal status. We have seen how the matter of his allowance, and that of the Duchess's title, preyed upon his mind that honeymoon summer, forming the subject of bitter correspondence. The Duchess tells us in her memoirs that they also spent some of their time discussing how the Abdication might have been avoided; and, while they soon made a sensible vow never to talk about this subject amongst themselves again, such speculation undoubtedly intensified the Duke's sense of grievance.

There was also the question of how they were to live and occupy themselves during the years (at most a couple of years, as they then believed) before they returned to England. Here they felt that a solution might be provided by Charles Bedaux, the expansive time-and-motion tycoon who was the proprietor of Candé and had spent some time with them there (as their guest) before the wedding. A subject in which the Duke had always been interested was the living conditions of workers; as Prince of Wales, he had studied model housing developments in Austria and Sweden. At Candé in May, the Duke had asked Bedaux about labour conditions in the various countries served by his international business empire; and there had been an idea that Bedaux might organize something to absorb the interest of the ex-King during his sojourn on the Continent. Bedaux and his wife Fern were due to visit the Windsors at Wasserleonburg in the second half of August.

Bedaux has received a bad press from historians. The fact that he committed suicide in an American prison in 1944, while awaiting trial on charges of wartime collaboration which would probably have resulted in an acquittal,[1] did not assist his subsequent reputation. In November 1937, in circumstances which brought an end to his close association with the Windsors, one of his principal lieutenants, Albert Ramond, wrenched control of the American side of his business organization from his grasp. Henceforth Ramond did everything to discredit his former master, and much of the writing on the subject of Bedaux – notably from the pen of Janet Flanner – is based on doubtful information provided by Ramond.

Bedaux was fifty in the summer of 1937, at the height of his powers. An engineer by training, and an extraordinary inventive genius, while still in his twenties he had perfected the industrial efficiency system which still bears his name: contrary to what was often imagined, it was not based on the principle of getting workers to work harder. He also created a scientific unit of measurement, the

---

[1] In 1961, Bedaux was formally absolved by the French authorities of any treasonable wartime conduct, and posthumously awarded another grade in the Legion of Honour (of which he had already been a *chevalier*) for his work in rebuilding the city of Tours after its bombardment by the Germans in 1940.

'B', representing the amount of work a normal person could do in a minute under normal conditions. The Bedaux system became enormously popular after the First World War, and Bedaux's international business increased during the economic depression as companies looked to him to find a solution to their difficulties. By 1930 he had become immensely rich, and as his business was functioning efficiently in the hands of capable assistants he more or less retired from its active direction in order to devote himself to other projects. He undertook a series of remarkable expeditions to remote parts of the world, some of which lasted for years on end, of which the most celebrated was a much-publicized but unsuccessful attempt to traverse the northern part of British Columbia in 1934. In the seclusion of these far-off places, he began to work out an elaborate political theory which he later called equivalism. This argued that whole countries should be organized on industrial efficiency principles, that the B should be adopted as a standard economic unit, and that the prices of goods and services should be based on the amount of human effort involved in their production or provision. If these tenets were adopted, Bedaux contended, workers would become happy and prosperous, and political tensions (and ultimately boundaries) between nations would disppear. The theory reads oddly today, but with its internationalism and emphasis on planning and organization it was typical of the 1930s when desperate solutions were being sought to the world economic crisis, and it was vaguely related to both Communism and Fascism. Bedaux developed these ideas with a passionate idealism, and there is no doubt that he saw the Duke of Windsor, who also believed in a vague way that the peace of the world depended on the contentment of the working man, as someone who might further them. The Duke did not really understand equivalism, but liked the sound of what he heard.

At Candé during the spring, the Duke had received through Bedaux a letter from Colonel Oscar Solbert of Rochester, New York. Solbert was a friend of Bedaux and the senior executive of the Eastman Kodak Corporation which was one of Bedaux's principal business clients in America; he also knew the Duke, having been Military Attaché at the United States Embassy in London in 1924, in which capacity he had accompanied the Prince of Wales on his tour of America that year. Solbert wanted to suggest that the Duke 'head up and consolidate the many and varied peace movements throughout the world. . . . I am not a pacifist, as you know, but I do believe that the one thing the world needs more than anything else is peace. . . .' On 23 August 1937, Bedaux, following his discussions with the Duke at Wasserleonburg, replied to Solbert on the Duke's behalf. It is clear from this letter that Bedaux had won the Duke over to his way of thinking.

> . . . The Duke of Windsor is very much interested in your proposal that he lead a movement so essentially international. We all know that as Prince of Wales and as King, he has always been keenly interested in the lot of the working man and he has not failed to show both his distress and his resolve to alter things whenever he has encountered injustice. . . . Yet he is not satisfied with the extent of his knowledge. He is determined to continue, with more time at his disposal, his systematic study of this subject and to devote his time to the betterment of the life of the masses. . . . He believes this is the surest way to peace. For himself he proposes to begin soon with a study of housing and working conditions in many countries. . . .

Bedaux concluded with the reflections that the Duke was 'proving to be as great a man as he was as King', and that the Abdication might well have been the work 'of a Superior Will intent on assuring a greater joy on earth'. Sending a copy of the letter to the Duke for approval (which appears to have been given), he wrote: 'It is my fervent hope that this letter may be the first step that will lead to the organisation of a World Movement dedicated to good and wise enough to make, for the first time, full use of all you can give of yourself.'

On a practical level, Bedaux offered to organize for the Windsors a short industrial tour of Germany in October, to be followed by a longer tour of the United States later in the autumn. The Duke expressed great interest in these plans. It was quite easy for Bedaux to fix up these visits at short notice. In America, many of the industrial concerns the Duke would wish to visit were already clients of the Bedaux Corporation. As for Germany, Bedaux had spent much of the previous six months there, attempting to re-establish his German business operations which had been shut down by the Nazis on their coming to power in 1933. He had achieved this in July, before visiting the Duke at Wasserleonburg, but only after paying a large bribe to the authorities, and on condition that his business was henceforth to be under the supervision of the Nazi labour organiz-ation, the Arbeitersfront, which had now declared itself willing to play host to the Windsors in Germany.

It is customary to portray Bedaux as a sinister figure who sought to exploit the Duke for business purposes. But Bedaux, reputedly the fifth-richest man in America at this time, hardly needed to use the Duke from this point of view. In the event, his association with the Duke contributed to his ruin in America, and did him no good in Germany, where his organization was shut down for a second and final time at the beginning of 1938. Rather one must see him as a naïve idealist, who sought sincerely to promote the Duke as a world statesman who might help solve the problems of the Depression and avert war. The Duke went along with what Bedaux proposed partly because he was influenced by the older man's immensely persuasive charm, and partly because he shared to some extent his naïve ideals. It would of course have been much wiser of him to stay out of the limelight so short a time after the Abdication; but one must remem-ber his sense of isolation after, as he saw it, the British authorities and his own family had turned their backs on him. The secretiveness with which he prepared for Bedaux's tours – neither the Foreign Office nor any of the friends who normally advised him was told of them until all had been arranged – suggest that, by doing these things on his own, he may have meant to cock a snook at a British Establishment which had been so unfriendly to him.

On leaving Wasserleonburg at the beginning of September, the Windsors went to spend a week in Hungary with Bedaux and his wife, who had rented a hunting lodge called Borsodivanka from a nephew of the Regent Horthy. 'This is a dirty house and the country full of bugs and mosquitoes,' wrote the Duchess to her aunt on the 13th, 'but the shooting has been good and a wonderful sight to see the cowboys in their quaint costumes, the native dances, the peasants, clothes, and above all the amazing plains that stretch for miles as flat as a pancake.'

Bedaux had gone to Germany after leaving Wasserleonburg, and had now fixed up the proposed tour of the Windsors there through Robert Ley, the head of the *Arbeitsfront*, and Hitler's adjutant

Captain Wiedemann.[2] 'You probably have seen the [press] rumours about Germany,' wrote the Duchess to her aunt. 'We are actually planning to go there to look at [workers'] housing and conditions as the Duke is thinking of taking up some sort of work in that direction. The trip is being arranged by Germany's No. 1 gentleman so should be interesting. It is a secret so say nothing. . . . We are also coming to the U.S. to look at housing etc. and the programme is to be arranged by certain business people. This is all tentative and may not come off. . . .'

The Windsors spent the last days of their honeymoon in Vienna, where they were mobbed by enthusiastic crowds. 'I am not used to it and really become quite dazed,' wrote the Duchess. On 26 September they arrived in Paris, which they intended to make their base, and moved into the Hôtel Meurice in the rue de Rivoli. It was from there, on 3 October, that the Duke issued the following press statement:

> In accordance with the Duke of Windsor's message to the world press last June that he would release any information of interest regarding his plans or movements, His Royal Highness makes it known that he and the Duchess of Windsor are visiting Germany and the United States in the near future for the purpose of studying housing and working conditions in these two countries.

Some of the Duke's friends, including Churchill and Beaverbrook, tried to dissuade him from going to Germany; but after some hesitation he decided not to put off the trip. He had one overriding motive in wishing to make it: to give the Duchess the sensations of a royal progress. Although it proved an error of judgement on the Duke's part, there was nothing unusual about a prominent Englishman visiting Germany in 1937. War was still two years away, curiosity about the Nazis was intense, and many respectable people accepted government invitations. It was fashionable to go to Germany and visit Hitler in the mid-thirties just as it was to go to China

---

[2] Though Bedaux never met Hitler, Wiedemann seems to have become something of a friend. He had been Hitler's commanding officer during the First World War and was never a convinced Nazi. He became disenchanted with Hitler and in 1939 was banished to the German Consular Service, serving first in San Francisco and later in China.

and visit Mao Tse-tung in the mid-sixties; Lloyd George had gone in 1936, and the month after the Duke's visit Lord Halifax, a senior cabinet minister, was to make an extended trip and stay as the personal guest of Goering. Sir Eric Phipps, the British Ambassador to Paris who had previously held the post in Berlin, warned the Duke that 'the Germans were past masters in the art of propaganda and would be quick to turn anything he might do or say to suit their own purposes', to which he replied that he was 'well aware of this' and 'would be very careful and would not make any speeches'.

The tour, which lasted from 11 to 23 October, was not a wholly comfortable experience for the Windsors. Their host and guide, Dr Ley, turned out to be a coarse individual addicted to alcohol and high-speed driving; in his unedifying company, they were raced around Germany on an exhausting programme of visits to industrial complexes and housing developments. The trip was not given an official character and was reported without comment in the German press; but they were entertained privately and enthusiastically by Goebbels, Goering, Hess and Ribbentrop. Like many other visitors to Germany, the Duke seemed to have the view that the Nazi leaders were rough but potentially reasonable men with whom the democracies, with careful handling, might reach some accommodation. Correspondents experienced in German affairs, like William Shirer, felt he had little idea of what his hosts were really like.

On 22 October, the day before their departure, they had tea with Hitler at Berchtesgaten, who kept them waiting for an hour. The Duke and the Führer had an hour-long interview, in which most of the talking was done by the latter. According to the interpreter, Paul Schmidt,

> ... Hitler was evidently making an effort to be as amiable as possible towards the Duke, whom he regarded as Germany's friend, having especially in mind a speech the Duke had made some years before, extending the hand of friendship to Germany's ex-servicemen's associations. In these conversations there was, so far as I could see, nothing whatever to indicate whether the Duke of Windsor really sympathised with the ideology and practices of the Third Reich, as Hitler seemed to assume he did. Apart from some appreciative words for the measures taken in Germany in the field of social welfare, the Duke did not discuss political questions. . . .

But the Duke's equerry, Dudley Forwood, remembers that his master did make some remarks critical of the tendencies of the regime, and that he noticed these remarks were being modified by Schmidt and cried out: *'Falschübersetzt!'* ('wrongly translated').

The Duchess wrote in her memoirs that the Nazi bosses both fascinated and repelled her. She seems to have been exhilarated by the attention they received in Germany, but rather bored with the substance of their tour. On 18 October she wrote to her aunt from Leipzig to say that 'no words can express how interesting this trip is but very strenuous, so many things in a day and miles of walking through factories, housing settlements etc.' That was all she had to say about Germany, and the rest of her letter was about their forthcoming tour of the United States. It was clear that, in her mind, the German trip was no more than an hors-d'œuvre to the main event of the autumn, the American visit.

⚜

During the summer, before anything was known of the Duke's wish to visit Germany and America, Sir Robert Vansittart, the Permanent Secretary at the Foreign Office, and Alexander Hardinge, the Private Secretary at the Palace, considered how the Windsors were to be treated by British representatives abroad. It was a sensitive issue: first, because of the Duke's unique position as a former head of state; second, because of the unique status of his wife as not sharing his royal rank. Were they to be shown the courtesies traditionally extended to royalty in foreign countries? 'The most important point in His Majesty's opinion', wrote Hardinge to Vansittart on 2 September, 'is that His Royal Highness the Duke of Windsor and the Duchess should not be treated by His Majesty's representatives as having any official status in the countries which they visit.' They 'should not be invited to stay as guests in the Embassy or Legation concerned'. If they were met at the railway station, it should only be by a junior member of the staff. Although they might be entertained at the Embassy 'in an absolutely private and informal way . . . care should be taken in the invitation of guests, as the Duchess of Windsor should be placed on the right of His Majesty's representative on every occasion'. That was to say, no woman could be invited who took precedence over the non-royal Duchess of Windsor.

The Duke revealed his intention of visiting Germany and America in private letters dated 20 September – two weeks in advance of the public announcement – addressed to the British Chargé in Berlin, Sir George Ogilvie-Forbes, and the Ambassador to Washington, Sir Ronald Lindsay. The news provoked indignation when communicated to the Foreign Office and the Palace. 'Personally I think these tours, prearranged without a word to us, are a bit too much,' wrote Vansittart to Hardinge on 1 October. 'And I hope our missions abroad will be instructed to have as little as possible to do with them.' Hardinge replied: 'I entirely agree with what you say about these tours, and I feel strongly that nothing should be done to make them appear other than what they are, i.e. private stunts for publicity purposes – they can obviously bring no benefit to the workers themselves.'

When they received their instructions from London, both Ogilvie-Forbes and Lindsay objected strongly. Neither welcomed the Windsors' highly publicized arrival in the countries to which they were accredited, but both believed it would be bad policy to cold-shoulder the ex-King. 'It would be extremely painful and embarrassing for me if I am instructed to ignore His Royal Highness's presence,' wrote Ogilvie-Forbes from Berlin on 2 October, 'for this will not be understood here.' Lindsay, who was on leave in England, wrote to Vansittart on 3 October that, while he personally regarded the Duke's forthcoming trip 'with unmitigated horror', it was in his view essential not to give the impression 'that the visit to America in itself is in any way disapproved, and I think therefore that I ought certainly to put the Duke and Duchess up at the Embassy while they are in Washington; and I think they should be presented at the White House and that I should at least give them a large Belshazzar.' (Lindsay was 'staggered' when he saw the Foreign Office file on how the Windsors were to be treated by British representatives abroad. 'They are *forbidden* to put him up in the house, or to give him a dinner, though they may give him a bite of luncheon, or to present him officially to anyone, or to accept invitations from him, except for a bite of luncheon, or to have him met at the station by anyone bigger than a junior secretary.')

The official attitude, however, was clear. Ogilvie-Forbes was told to have nothing to do with the Windsors in Germany. It was a less simple matter with Lindsay: he was a considerable figure in diplomacy, and his views on Anglo-American relations could not be ignored. He was summoned to spend the weekend of 8 October at

Balmoral to discuss the treatment the Windsors should receive in Washington.

Lindsay has left an interesting account of his visit to Balmoral. He found the King and Queen, Hardinge and Lascelles almost hysterical on the subject of the Duke. He put forward his views, explaining that Americans would naturally expect the Duke and Duchess to stay at the British Embassy. 'In all the ballyhoo they would notice his going to a hotel – they would infer official coldness towards him – a semi-snub – disapproval of the visit – disapproval of his alleged interest in labour – and all this resulting in a bad reaction in America, which would spread to England – just what we want to avoid.' His royal critics replied that 'the Duke was behaving abominably – it was his duty not to embarrass the King – he had promised not to – and he was dropping bombshell after bombshell, and this was the worst of all. What was coming next? He was trying to stage a come-back, and his friends and advisers were semi-Nazis.[3] He was not straight – he hadn't let the King have an inkling of his plans. . . .' The Foreign Secretary, Anthony Eden, who joined the party at Balmoral, tended to agree with Lindsay; but it was finally decided to defer to the King's wishes and ignore the Windsors in America, except to the extent of giving them a small Embassy dinner. Lindsay found himself won over by the Queen, who 'spoke in terms of acute pain and distress. . . . All her feelings are lacerated by what she and the King were being made to go through. And for all her charity she had not a word to say for "that woman". . . .'

Lindsay remarked that the King did 'not yet feel safe on his throne' and was like 'the medieval monarch who has a hated rival claimant living in exile. The analogy must not be pressed too far because I don't think George wanted the throne any more than Edward. . . . But in some ways the situation operates on the King just as it must have done on his medieval ancestors – uneasiness as to what is coming next – sensitiveness – suspicion. . . .' Opinion at Court was 'certainly violently prejudiced' on the subject of the Windsors, and all seemed to assume that the Duke was a pawn in the hands of a scheming and ambitious wife. Lindsay wondered how far this was really so.

[3] It is difficult to see to whom this might refer, except perhaps Bedaux. The men upon whom the Duke normally relied for advice were Monckton, Allen, Churchill, Beaverbrook and Peacock.

The Windsors returned to Paris from Germany on 24 October, with two weeks to prepare for their American tour. Unlike the German government, the United States Administration would not of course be paying for this trip (which would be financed in fact by Bedaux); but otherwise they seemed willing to treat the Windsors virtually as official guests. The President invited them to the White House, and insisted that they be presented there by the British Ambassador, though Lindsay had been forbidden to do this by his instructions; and Mrs Roosevelt, who was herself interested in the welfare of workers, offered to take them personally to see the housing projects in which she was involved. Government departments offered to attach officials to their party and to give them every facility. Private industry was eager to welcome the Windsors: indeed, there was much competition as to which plants would receive the privilege of a ducal visit. A private Pullman train was hired to take the Windsors and their entire party across the continent from East to West, and General Motors put at their disposal a fleet of ninety of the latest Buicks which would be ready to meet them at their various destinations. The starting-point would be Washington, where the Duke would meet the President, lay a wreath at Arlington Cemetery (since they would be arriving on 11 November), and broadcast to the nation – this broadcast launching his new internationalist role.

The visit to Germany had not aroused much interest in England. Such critical comment which it aroused tended to centre on the Duke putting himself in the public eye so soon after giving up the throne. Churchill wrote to him that the tour did 'not seem to have the effect' of offending anti-Nazi public opinion and that he was 'glad it all passed off with such distinction and success'. The Duke replied that he had gone to Germany 'without any political considerations and merely as an independent observer studying industrial and housing conditions', and that one could not ignore what was happening in Germany, 'even though it may not have one's entire approval'. In America, criticism was deeper and more widespread. The *New York Times* wrote: 'He has lent himself, unconsciously but easily, to National Socialist propaganda. There can be no doubt that his tour has strengthened the regime's hold on the working classes.' By coincidence, two communist labour leaders, Adolf Remble and Robert Stamm, were executed in Germany a week after the Windsors' return; these men were heroes among the American labour movement, where criticism was spreading of the Windsors' decision to come to the United States.

On 1 November 1937, Bedaux arrived in New York to finalize the arrangements for the tour. He badly mishandled the reporters who had congregated to meet him at the quayside, thus alienating an already lukewarm press. Public opinion was building up against his activities in general and the idea of a Windsor tour under his guidance in particular. On 3 November, while he was in Washington conferring with the British Embassy and the State Department, a resolution hostile to the tour was issued by the Baltimore Federation of Labor, making a scathing reference to the fact that the proposed visit would be an advertisement for Bedaux's system,[4] and that it had been preceded by another made 'to Nazi Germany under the personal guidance of Dr Ley, the man who ordered and ruthlessly directed the destruction of all German free trade unions'. It added somewhat superfluously that while resident in Baltimore during her childhood the Duchess had failed to show 'the slightest concern or sympathy for the problems of labor', and warned against 'the potential threat to free labor and free government itself of slumming parties professing to help and study labor and all those who either as emissaries of a dictatorship or as uninformed sentimentalists support a stretch-out system'.

This manifesto proved to be the signal for an avalanche of criticism, and Bedaux returned to New York on the 4 November to be met by a crowd of hostile journalists and angry business colleagues. That night he admitted defeat, and rang the Duke's secretary at the Meurice with the message: 'They must not come.' The following day – 5 November – he sent the Duke a telegram the text of which he issued to the press. 'I am compelled in honesty and friendship to advise you that because of mistaken attacks on me here I am convinced that your proposed study tour would be difficult under my guidance. . . . I respectfully suggest and implore that you relieve me completely of all duties in connection with your American tour.'

Back in Paris, the Windsors were amazed at these developments. They hardly knew what to do. *Bremen* was due to sail from Cherbourg the following day, and their luggage had already been sent to join it. William Bullitt, the United States Ambassador to Paris with whom

---

[4] Ironically, Bedaux had always had satisfactory relations with the American labour movement up to this point, and the American Federation of Labor actually used his system in its offices.

they were on terms of personal friendship, advised them to go ahead regardless of Bedaux. The Duke telephoned Lindsay in Washington, who guarded himself from giving any direct advice on whether to proceed, but confirmed that the advance publicity had taken a disastrous turn and suggested that the Duke's own good sense would guide him to the correct decision. Finally, at ten o'clock that evening, the Duke issued a press statement to say that he had decided to postpone his visit. He had reached the decision 'with great reluctance and after much deliberation', but felt that he was left with no alternative owing to 'grave misconceptions which have arisen ... regarding the motives and purposes of his industrial tour'. He wished to emphasize 'that there is no shadow of justification for any suggestion he is allied with any industrial system or that he is for or against any particular political or racial doctrine'.

'We were so tired after the effort of making up our minds what to do,' wrote the Duchess to her Aunt Bessie. 'We feel we made a wise decision. I am sure Charles did not realise how unpopular he was and I doubt if he is that unpopular, but as labor seems to be fighting so much in the U.S., any excuse sets them off. As for the Nazi idea, it is a pity one can't travel without becoming of the country one is in.' To Fern Bedaux she wrote:

> You can imagine how sad and upset we both are that our lovely innocent trip should have met with so disastrous an end. I only hope that the result will be a clarifying of the [Bedaux] system to the world. It is all very difficult for me to understand, not having been in America for so long. ... In the midst of this American complication we have an English one of nearly equal size[5] – so 7 a.m. to 3 a.m. are the Duke's working hours. . . . One feels rather discouraged trying to do some good in the world when that great organisation of British propaganda never ceases working against the Duke and myself.

The Duke wrote to Bedaux on 9 November, expressing his regret at having had to postpone the tour,

---

[5] Concerning the financial negotiations between the Duke and his brother.

. . . which I know would have been a valuable experience to me. It took me twelve hours to decide the best course to take, and with the whole of the Atlantic separating me from the scene of action, it was doubly difficult to understand the developments on the other side. However, I am confident that I was able to tap the best sources of advice, and that my decision was the only one possible.

If you have been embarrassed in any way I am sorry that I should have been the cause, but, as you know, I had only one aim and object from the outset, which was shared by yourself, that of learning something of the housing and industrial conditions obtaining in America today.

Please let me know what expenses have been incurred that are my liability.

Following his desperate plea to the Duke to forget about coming to America, Bedaux seems to have suffered something in the nature of a nervous breakdown. He relinquished control of his American business empire and fled first to Canada, then to Scotland, finally to Amsterdam, from where he replied to the Duke on 3 December in a tone of paranoia. 'The reasons which led me to say "They must not come" have never appeared in the newspapers. To know them places one in danger and to transmit the knowledge would constitute a greater danger still. . . . Because of my knowledge of these reasons two days after your decision not to come Fern and I were forced to flee. We are still exposed to a systematic persecution and we know we must expect much more.' Bedaux estimated the cost of cancelling tour at the enormous sum of £200,000, 'but not one penny of it is your liability. . . . Fern and I went into this thing at Wasserleonburg with our eyes open and knowing the risks involved. We did it because of the affection we felt for your wife and yourself and because we believed in your cause.'

'While I do not question your reasons for not telling me the whole story now,' the Duke replied on 6 December, 'your obscure references to persecution by mysterious forces naturally puzzle me. I can therefore only repeat my regret that the outcome of your efforts should have proved so unfortunate for us both.'

The Windsors' friend Lord Brownlow, having visited them shortly afterwards, had the impression that 'the failure of the American visit was a disaster in every way'. But Sir Ronald Lindsay, reading through Bedaux's exacting schedule, thought they had had a happy escape. 'Just as the Bedaux system aims at extracting the last ounce of utility out of a working man's efforts,' he wrote to Hardinge on 7 November, 'so the Bedaux tour would have taken up the last ounce of strength of a very strong man, and the Duke is to be congratulated not only on his wisdom in abandoning the tour but on his good luck in escaping it.' The great problem with the ex-King, in Lindsay's view, arose from the question of whether he was now an official person or a private person. 'He is in fact neither one thing nor the other, and tragic as it may be I could wish, for the sake of the future, that he may learn a lesson from the events of this week.'

The collapse of the American tour was followed by a typical incident. Since he would be remaining in Paris, the Duke declared his intention of attending the armistice service on 11 November at St George's Church in Paris, and of observing there with members of the local branch of the British Legion the traditional two minutes' silence. Seats in the front row of the church were duly reserved for himself and his party. On the day before the service, however, a party of journalists visited the Vicar, Canon Dart, to obtain details of the service, and were treated to an extraordinary outburst. 'I would rather the Duke of Windsor did not attend the service. . . . I cannot keep out anyone but I say emphatically that I will not meet him, speak to him or touch his hand. If I did so I would feel that I was betraying all my political and ecclesiastical ideals. . . . I feel that there has pushed in suddenly from outside a man who is entirely hostile. . . . I consider indeed that the Duke of Windsor has committed a sin more grave than any other person who is likely to be in my church tomorrow.'

On learning of these remarks from the *Daily Mail* correspondent, the Duke announced that he would not now be attending the service. The incident caused outrage among his former subjects generally and the British Legion in particular. Dart was deluged with hate mail, and the Duke with letters of sympathy. As a silent protest, the Legion saw to it that the front seats remained empty during the ceremony.

No sooner was one problem out of the way than the Duke had to face another. The cancellation of the American trip coincided with the outbreak of the violent quarrel with the Court over his promised allowance, which (as described in detail in Chapter 2) was now being withheld until he had given an undertaking never to return to England except with the King's consent. 'It seems to me', Allen wrote to him on 24 November, 'that you must now make a determined stand, or for ever, to speak plainly, become a remittance man. I scarcely think that the King and his advisers can realise the insulting and humiliating nature of their proposals.' This bitter argument was to continue into the New Year, and vexed the Duke not only on grounds of pride and honour but also because the holding up of his allowance made it difficult for him and the Duchess to take the desired step of moving out of the Hôtel Meurice and setting up their own house in France.[6]

On 18 December the Duchess wrote to wish her aunt a happy Christmas and give the latest news. 'We are having a long legal battle with King George and the British Government on the money question with Allen and the Duke lined up against that famous Empire, so you see where our thoughts are deeply concentrated.' Lou Viei, the villa at Cannes which had been her refuge at the time of the Abdication, had been generously put at their disposal by its owners, the Rogers, who were in America, and they would be spending Christmas there. They also had a vague plan to take a holiday in Cuba over the winter, but this would involve passing briefly through New York, and 'it may be too soon to come to the U.S. after all the rumpus. . . . But really, people cannot have their private lives interfered with, and just because the world has undertaken to run ours we cannot give in to it. . . .'

On 28 December the Duke wrote a Christmas letter to Aunt Bessie from Lou Viei, which he and the Duchess found

> . . . a welcome change after three months at the Meurice. . . . We passed a very happy and peaceful Christmas, the first we have ever

---

[6] Being an excellent advertisement for the Meurice, the Windsors were able to live there at very favourable rates. In October 1937 the Duchess wrote to her aunt that they paid $30 (about £6) per day for a suite of rooms for themselves and their equerry, a back bedroom which they used as their office, and board and lodging for their entire domestic staff. This sounds amazing, but one must remember the low exchange value of the French franc in the 1930s.

spent together,[7] and have only been out once to dinner as it's much nicer here. . . .

We were very disappointed over having to abandon our tour of America, but I know that you agree that we were wise to postpone coming over under the circumstances. Of course, had we known what we do now, we would never have attempted a tour at all (especially with the Bedaux), and we would have arranged that very interesting visit to Germany for later on. But our greatest regret was the delay in seeing you again.

We may go to Cuba end of January and if we can make the trip we might stop off a week or two in America on the way back. It depends a lot on some legal transactions because as usual my family and the British Government are playing true to form! And another thing that might keep us on this side is our preoccupation in finding a suitable house to rent for a while as we cannot continue to live in hotels. Naturally the big problem is where to 'hang our hat' temporarily and despite temptations of this locality or even Austria we have decided that we must be near Paris for the next year or two to keep in touch with people of the world and our friends. Paris is a world center [*sic*] and everyone passes by during the year and although the political situation in this country is uncomfortably volcanic it seems a reasonably safe chance that it won't blow up to the extent of a revolution. So I expect you will find us ensconced in some French château when you next visit us here. . . .

It was during their stay at Lou Viei that the Duke wrote the letter to Neville Chamberlain quoted in Chapter 2, protesting vehemently against the attempt to make his pension dependent on his renouncing his right to return to his native land. 'I regard such a proposal as unfair and intolerable, as it would be tantamount to accepting payment for remaining in exile. . . . I cannot refrain from saying . . . that the treatment which has been meted out to my wife and myself since last December has caused us acute pain. . . .' As we have seen, this spirited protest changed the tune of the Government, which may have been covering up for a Palace intrigue; and the matter of the Duke's allowance was settled in January to his tolerable satisfaction, though he nevertheless received far fewer advantages than he had been entitled to under the original agreement with his brother signed at the time of the Abdication.

[7] The previous year they were in the middle of their long pre-marital separation, and prior to that the Duke had always spent Christmas with his family at Sandringham.

As we have seen in Chapter 3, the turn of the year also saw a fresh crisis over the Duchess's status. The news that the Court were preparing to give an unfavourable ruling on the question of her official precedence stung the Duke to anger; Jowitt came out to see him in Paris, and he was ready to issue the public statement he had refrained from publishing the previous spring, challenging the legal validity of the Letters Patent of May 1937 and offering to give up his own royal title. But after Allen had delivered a dire warning to 10 Downing Street the Court refrained from delivering the ruling, and so this crisis also passed (with the side-effect that no one was any the wiser about the Duchess's precedence). Both the issue of the money and the issue of the Duchess had threatened to result in a public scandal that late autumn and winter; and such a scandal appears to have been averted only because the Government, having been left in no doubt by Allen of the intensity of the Duke's feelings, got the Palace to change their tune. Although matters were settled for the time being, the events which had occurred had deeply injured the Duke's feelings and further embittered his relations with his family.

The settlement of the money question at last enabled the Windsors to leave the Hôtel Meurice and move into a rented property in France. On 26 January 1938 the Duchess wrote to her aunt about her house-hunting efforts, concluding her letter with some interesting reflections on their attitude towards the publicity they were receiving.

> We have decided not to go to Havana this year as we feel we really *must* have a home before we travel any more. This life of trunks and hotels is very unsatisfactory. I have looked at a number of places in different directions outside of Paris, furnished and unfurnished. The former are hopeless and the unfurnished ones either palaces or too small, the wrong direction or too far from golf, etc., etc., so just to get out of this hotel we have taken a furnished house at Versailles with a small garden and tennis court, belonging to Mrs Paul Dupuy. It is comfortable, no charm but dignity, and we have taken it from February 7 to June 7 – appalling rent as everyone is out to do the Windsors. . . . We have tried to work out a 2 year plan which doesn't involve putting too much money into a place we may not

like – so the Versailles house will give us an idea of how we like living outside of Paris. . .

I am sorry not to be able to see you next month but I think it wiser from every point of view. The U.S. doesn't seem to be able to stop making up fantastic rumours about me. I can't think of any two people except the Lindberghs that have had such press persecution. Think of all the people who think I'm everything I'm not. However one can't let it get one down and that Montague humour has to work overtime. The Duke remains unaffected [by publicity] but furious with his family – though if they read and believe some of the things written I suppose they have a right to disapprove of the marriage. Anyway time will be useful in adjusting it all. . . .

The reference to a '2 year plan' gives an idea of how long the Windsors expected to be remaining on the Continent. On 21 March the Duchess wrote again to describe her housekeeping problems at the Château de la Maye – the grandiloquent name of the Versailles villa they had taken.

I am awfully sorry not to have written, but this house has been very trying. We have had a terrible time with servants – at one moment we had a communist and also a thief. Then there has been the arrival of things from England picked from an inventory and too many came etc. and we have been trying new secretaries at the same time also. The house is too small and everyone [among the staff] hates everyone else. We have continued trouble with the Duke's family who continue to treat him in a most humiliating way – and naturally not being acknowledged by them affects our position here among the snobs. Gradually there won't be many places to consider living in if the continent continues to change hands overnight.[8] . . . We don't go out much. It is hard to make new friends – the U.S. colony is a sad one and the French hard to know. . . .

When she next wrote, on 9 May, the Duchess appeared to have solved her servant problems, and to be entertaining quite happily a number

[8] A reference to the annexation of Austria by Nazi Germany at the beginning of March. Until then, the Windsors had regarded Austria, where they had been made so welcome during their honeymoon, as the natural alternative to France as a suitable place of temporary exile.

of friends from England who came out to stay or dine with them. She also announced that they had taken a two-year lease of La Cröe, a huge shorefront villa at Cap d'Antibes in the South of France belonging to the English newspaper tycoon Sir Pomeroy Burton,[9] where they would be installing themselves the following month.

The three months that the Windsors spent at Versailles witnessed a new crisis in the Duke's relations with the Court and the powers that be. No sooner had they moved there in February 1938 than they were astonished to learn from the newspapers that the King and Queen were to make a state visit to Paris in June. The Duke had been given no official information of this visit, but was naturally anxious to know how it would affect him and whether he and the Duchess would be received by the sovereigns. On 15 February he had Allen, who was with him in Versailles to tie up the loose ends of the financial negotiations, write to Walter Monckton asking if the latter might go to see the King to discuss this delicate matter. As Allen explained:

> The Duke is naturally anxious that Their Majesties' stay in Paris shall be a great success; and while he would, of course, be willing to fall in with any plans which may be made for the visit, he is, at the same time, very hopeful that the King and Queen may take the opportunity which this visit will afford of paying a call on the Duke and Duchess, and of arranging for them to be invited to one of the official receptions. He feels that such an invitation would serve the general interest since it would become known to everyone that the estrangement which has existed in the past is now ended.
> Further, the Duke feels that if Their Majesties come to France a gesture of this nature is essential, otherwise it is difficult to see how the Duke and Duchess can continue to live there in the atmosphere which would thereby be created.

Complicated negotiations then took place between the Duke and the King with Monckton as intermediary, the results of which may be

---

[9] La Cröe had previously been offered to the Duke as a venue for his wedding in 1937, but on the advice of the King he had declined the offer in favour of marriage in Candé.

seen in a letter which the Duke wrote to his brother from Versailles on 30 April 1938.

Dear Bertie,

I have received a letter from Walter Monckton telling me that you are grateful to me for having decided to be away from Paris during your forthcoming State visit to France, and that you fully appreciated the fact that I am doing this in order to avoid any possible embarrassment to you on that occasion. He further says that you and Elizabeth certainly hope that you will be able to arrange to see Wallis and myself later on, but that you feel that this State visit does not afford a suitable opportunity for such a meeting. He also reports that you told him that you had, from the first, personally given instructions to ensure that, wherever we went, we were to be treated with proper attention and respect.

I must confess that I have read Monckton's letter with mixed feelings, although both Wallis and I have at the same time done our best to understand the reasons which have prompted the conclusion you have arrived at.

I do feel most strongly however that, before we go South at the end of May in order to leave the field clear for you in Paris, something should be done to place this gesture on our part in proper perspective. I believe that Monckton discussed this matter with you and that he made the proposal that the right step was for your Ambassador in Paris to give a suitable function for us at the British Embassy some evening before our departure. As there is no reference to this in Monckton's letter, I have decided to write to you myself.

We would be less than human if we did not feel deeply all that has been done to us in the past sixteen months, and we naturally hoped for an end to such treatment. Surely the time has come for some form of official gesture towards us on the continent, where we are at present residing out of deference to you alone, to show that you, as King, require us (to quote from Monckton's letter) to be 'treated with proper attention and respect', so that there may be a termination of the indignities to which we are constantly open, and which are as much a reflection on the Royal Family as a whole as upon us personally.

Some proper recognition of our position as your brother and sister-in-law would seem to be in accord with your stated instructions. We have as yet, I regret to say, detected no evidence that your instructions are being carried out, and we do frankly feel that a formal reception given for us by your diplomatic representative in Paris is distinctly overdue, to say the least.

Had it ever been considered that such a proposal could be in any way injurious to your status, it would not have been suggested. On the contrary, I am convinced that, properly handled as it would be, the atmosphere of your State visit might well be enhanced.

Yours,

DAVID

One of the reasons for the Duke's anxiety to be received at the Embassy was that he and the Duchess were finding themselves shunned by French society in advance of the royal visit; as the Duchess wrote to her aunt on 21 March: 'They are scared of meeting us in case it would put them in the wrong with the British Embassy and they would then not be asked to the parties for the coming visit of the King and Queen. What snobs the world produces and what treatment can be handed out once power has gone. . . .' In the course of May, however, the Windsors were duly received by the Ambassador as ordinary dinner guests; and at the beginning of June[10] they left prematurely for Antibes. 'The King thinks it would make him too nervous to see the Duke, charming little cad that he has shown himself,' wrote the Duchess on 9 May. 'So once again the Duke makes life easier. . . .'

❈

For the next twelve months the Windsors led an extremely quiet life, doing their utmost to keep out of the public eye. Their progress may be summarized as follows. They spent June 1938 moving into La Cröe, which was to be their principal home until the outbreak of war. An enormous and ugly house, the Duchess succeeded in making it both attractive and comfortable, and they were able to give it an intimate touch by filling it with the Duke's memorabilia. In July they took a yacht for a cruise along the Italian Mediterranean coast; and the rest of that summer they spent at La Cröe, completing the

---

[10] In fact it proved unnecessary for the Windsors to have left Paris so early; the royal visit was postponed owing to the death of the mother of the Queen, and only took place towards the end of July.

renovations and entertaining English and American friends. In the autumn they returned to Paris, staying at the Meurice while they searched for another city base; at the end of October they took a lease of 24 Boulevard Suchet, a medium-sized town house in the sixteenth district with a fine eighteenth-century façade. The business of decorating this property, and finding the furniture to fill it, kept them busy until Christmas, when they returned for several weeks to La Cröe. On their return to Paris at the end of January 1939, they moved out of the Meurice into the Boulevard Suchet. They had planned an extended Easter holiday in Morocco; but owing to Mussolini's invasion of Albania and the consequently tense situation in the Mediterranean they were advised to cancel this trip, and so spent the month of April at La Cröe.

An interesting picture of their lives at this time is given by a published memoir of Miss Hood, who took up the duties of the Duke's secretary in the early autumn of 1938. She shows them leading an intensely private, intensely domestic existence, anxious in their desire to avoid publicity. The decoration and management of their two houses constituted their principal occupation. They went out little, and tended to entertain only a few old friends. There could be no doubt of the Duke's happiness in his marriage. 'His wife was constantly in his thoughts. If he went out alone he looked for her the moment he returned home. . . . He never made any attempt to conceal his feelings. More than once I saw him take her in his arms and kiss her tenderly. . . . He bought her exquisite jewellery and other beautiful gifts. Nothing was too good for her. He sought in every way to make her happy. He himself was happy and light-hearted in her presence.'

The Duchess's letters to Aunt Bessie in the summer and autumn of 1938 give other details of their progress during those months. On 16 July she wrote from *Gulzar*, the yacht on which they were cruising:

> We have fled from the trials of decorators and servants [at La Cröe] . . . and sailed last Tuesday night for Portofino and down the Italian coast. Last night we left Viareggio where we have been for two days, having motored from there to Florence and Pisa. I was delighted to see both places for the first time and wish you had been with us in spite of the great heat and terrible crowds every time we moved, which as it interfered with shopping was a good thing! We have come to an island today to rest before taking on Naples. . . .

We return the 28th. . . . In September we are going back to Paris in search of a house for the winter. . . .

Two days later the Duke wrote to his wife's aunt, from Naples.

. . . We are at present having a lovely cruise along the Italian coast which we are enjoying enormously. I have chartered this 200 ton motor yacht from an Armenian for six weeks and we have the Rogers with us. . . . We hope to go on south to Sicily if the weather is good, but the slightest puff of wind damps our ardour as this yacht is so very small. We have been lucky so far, and are having a grand rest from the struggles of getting into La Cröe. I know that Wallis has told you of the difficulties we have experienced as regards the French workmen, decorators, and above all the language, in our attempt to make the house you saw last year something less of a country club in appearance. . . .

That we are gloriously happy I have no need to tell you, and as each day passes I am more firmly convinced that I am the luckiest man in the world. Except for very rare and occasional irritating articles our position publicly is also improving. . . .

The Duchess next wrote from La Cröe on 14 September. Europe was now in the grip of the Czechoslovak crisis.

The house is at last finished and I do want you to see it. I will give you the trip over as an Xmas present if we're not all in the soup by then and our house a bomb shelter. We are not as excited here as in the U.S. and still think there will not be a war. . . . We went to Paris last week-end to look for a *pied-à-terre* – nothing attractive. . . . We will take a flat if necessary. It is really only to be in touch with the world as the Duke is busy with lots of things at the moment that need constant talks with Monckton, Allen etc. Kitty Rothschild wanted us to go to Enzesfeld[11] with her this month but the Government advised against it until things are more arranged – she stayed here for ten days. . . . I feel so out of touch with the

[11] The Nazis had arrested several of the Austrian Rothschilds and were in the process of confiscating their properties.

family [in America]. . . . I have been away so long and have had so many problems and also planning for the future that everything at home seems so dim. . . .

The next letter, again from La Cröe, was sent on 3 October, four days after the Munich Agreement had supposedly saved Europe from war.

I have been thinking of all you have been thinking [*sic*] during these days. We have been perfectly quiet – we simply couldn't believe there could be another war. We were in Paris when it began to look uncomfortable. The French for once were quiet and no-one would have guessed that there was anything in the air. We decided to come back here and pack away lots in the store room in case the Italians liked La Cröe for headquarters. We still have no house in Paris, one possible flat. The latter is difficult as we are so on top of secretaries etc. However there are no nice houses to be let. . . . We expect you for Xmas now that Europe has settled down to slicing up the Czechs. It has been a most unsettled year. . . . This place [Antibes] is deserted, everyone having fled. . . . We hate leaving here as it is the only place where we feel really at home, having our own things. I don't think we will be settled anywhere until the English atmosphere is cleared but the terror of the Duke's return remains – everyone so afraid that it would upset the King's so-called popularity. If that is so well-established as they all say, what is there to worry about? . . .

And on 25 October, writing this time from the Meurice, the Duchess was finally able to announce:

After a long dreary struggle for a furnished house we have now taken an unfurnished one and intend to buy everything from the kitchen to the garret including glass and china, only transporting our silver from the South and not getting any more furniture from England. It will be nice to have some French furniture to add to it all. You can imagine what a state I am now in – and yet house decoration I adore. We are thrilled you are coming for Xmas. . . .

It will have become obvious that, between their marriage and the war, the Windsors always imagined that they would be returning to live in England in the relatively near future. The Duke wrote to Neville Chamberlain in December 1937: 'When I decided to give up the throne last December, I realized that the only dignified and sensible course for me to follow was to leave the country for a period, the length of which was to be determined by a number of considerations. But I never intended . . . to renounce my native land . . . for all time.' And in April 1938 he wrote to the King that he and his wife were residing on the Continent 'out of deference to you alone'. The many knocks they received, and the growing feud with the Court, no doubt made them realize that the moment of return would not be an altogether easy one, and might not take place as soon as they expected, but did not alter their basic intention.

This is clearly shown by the decisions they made regarding their houses. Although property was cheap in France in the 1930s, and the sterling exchange immensely favourable, they never considered buying their own place there at the time. When Harold Nicolson asked the Duchess in July 1938 why they did not buy, she replied sharply that they did not mean to spend the rest of their lives in exile. In January 1938 the Duchess had written to her aunt that they had worked out 'a 2 year plan' for life on the continent – which suggests that they envisaged 1939 as their last year of permanent residence abroad. In June 1938 they took La Cröe for two years, and a few months later they took the house in the Boulevard Suchet for a similar period. All the while, however, the bulk of the Duke's possessions remained in England awaiting his return, housed at Frogmore,[12] a Georgian villa in the grounds of Windsor Castle which since the First World War had served as a great royal storeroom. When they rented La Cröe, they sent for the Duke's silver, a certain amount of furniture, and enough personal memorabilia to make him feel at home; but 'Suchet' they filled entirely with old French furniture which they found in the Paris *antiquaires*, and the great hoard of effects at Frogmore stayed where it was right through to the mid-1950s.

Visitors in the spring and summer of 1938 noticed that the Duke

---

[12] On abdicating, the Duke had asked that his effects be stored at Windsor; but on 15 July 1937 Ulick Alexander had written to him that, although he had tried to keep everything at Windsor 'as long as I could', the King had finally given orders that all should be moved to Frogmore.

was now very homesick. 'When I say that I go back to England tomorrow', wrote Harold Nicolson after seeing him at La Cröe that August, 'his eye twitches in pain.' Another visitor at La Cröe that month was Walter Monckton, and the Duke charged him with a mission to discover from the King and the Government how soon it would be convenient for him to return to England. When Monckton himself returned in September, he went straight to Balmoral, where he discussed the matter with the King, the Queen and the Prime Minister, Neville Chamberlain. Monckton summed up the result of these discussions in a note which has become celebrated:

> The Prime Minister thought that the right course was for the Duke of Windsor to be treated as soon as possible as a younger brother of the King who could take some of the royal functions off his brother's hands. The King himself, though he was not anxious for the Duke to return as early as November 1938 (which was what the Duke wanted), was not fundamentally against the Prime Minister's view. But I think the Queen felt quite plainly that it was undesirable to give the Duke any effective sphere of work. I felt then, as always, that she naturally thought that she must be on her guard because the Duke of Windsor, to whom the other brothers had always looked up, was an attractive, vital creature who might be the rallying point for any who might be critical of the new King who was less superficially endowed with the arts and graces that please.

Some kind of compromise seems to have been worked out between the Prime Minister and the Court, for in November 1938 the Duke and Duchess of Gloucester, returning from a holiday in Kenya, spent a day with the Windsors in Paris. Apart from one or two secret visits which the Duke of Kent may have made across the Channel to see his brother alone, this was the only time the Windsors saw any member of the royal family during their residence in prewar France. As the Duchess of Gloucester states in her memoirs: 'It was Neville Chamberlain's idea, not ours.' Before assigning 'an official role' to the Duke, the Government wanted to assess the public reaction to the meeting between the two brothers and their wives. The Windsors gave the Gloucesters lunch at the Meurice, took them to see the house in the Boulevard Suchet of which they had recently signed the lease, and dined them at a restaurant. The Duchess of Gloucester found them 'more than kind', and was afterwards upset when 'a lot of old ladies wrote furiously disapproving letters' about the meeting. This, however, was enough to discourage the Prime Minister, who had himself briefly called on the ex-King while on an official visit to Paris later the same month. On 22 February 1939 he wrote to the Duke about the undesirability of his return, saying that while there was 'no question of postponement indefinitely' the time was not yet ripe.[13]

The Duke issued a press statement after receiving the Prime Minister's verdict.

> The Duchess and I have been receiving so many enquiries from our friends as to when we intend to return to England, that I feel it would only lead to misunderstanding if we continue to leave such questions unanswered.
>
> First of all I want to say how touched we have been by the many expressions of goodwill that have reached us lately from all parts of the world, and how grateful we are to those who have written, telling us that they are anxious to see us home again. I need hardly assure you that after more than two years, we wholeheartedly desire to see our country.
>
> We had looked forward to making a short private visit to England in the spring, and should have done so had we not been informed that such a visit would not yet be welcome, either to the Government or the Royal Family. In these circumstances we shall be remaining away for the present, and we take this opportunity of expressing our warm appreciation of the hospitality and consideration of the French people, in whose country we are now residing.

Although the Duke had fought vigorously to defend the principle that, as an Englishman, he was free to return to his country whenever he wished, in practice he always sought and followed the advice of the authorities, however unpalatable he found that advice to be. Eventually, Chamberlain indicated that a short visit to England might be arranged in the late autumn of 1939. Clearly the

[13] Only a month earlier a Gallup Poll had found that 61 per cent were actively in favour of the Windsors returning to England, and only 16 per cent actively opposed to this.

circumstances and atmosphere of this visit, the first of the ex-King to his former realm, would determine his entire future relations with his country.

The Duke viewed with deepening concern the deterioration of the international situation and the drift to war. The *Anschluss* in March 1938 made it impossible for him to return to Austria, as he and the Duchess had been planning to do later that year; it is not generally known that he helped a number of Austrian Jews emigrate to England, including his favourite musicians, the pianists Radicz and Landauer, and the Austrian official who had been attached to him at Enzesfeld after the Abdication, Dr Ernst Brunert.[14] Six months later, as indicated by the Duchess's letters, he was preoccupied by the Czechoslovak crisis. He even toyed with the idea of going to Germany again in order to plead with Hitler, but was urgently advised by his friends not to do so in the interests of his reputation. Like the vast majority in Great Britain and France, he hailed Munich as a guarantee of peace.

In the spring of 1939, as we have seen, the international situation forced the Windsors to cancel an overseas holiday. On 14 April the Duke wrote from La Cröe to Aunt Bessie:

We had planned a trip to Morocco for this month and came via La Cröe for a few hours en route to Marseilles to collect a few summer clothes. That was a week ago and thanks this time to Signor Mussolini we have so far spent the Easter holidays on the telephone postponing the Moroccan trip from one boat to the next until we finally decided last night to abandon it altogether. It is a great disappointment as we both wanted a complete change. . . . Actually the tension is eased and there won't be a war as I always predict (touch wood!). . . . But something really has to be done to prevent these monthly incidents of agression [*sic*] and consequent crises, and I personally am convinced that the dictator powers can be made to behave themselves without war which is certain to destroy civilization.

[14] Correspondence and meetings of the author with Dr Brunert, 1983.

The same day as the Duke wrote this letter, the *Catholic Herald* published a dramatic appeal to the world's 300 million Roman Catholics to unite in order to secure peace. 'A major war must put an end to our civilization and initiate a prolonged period of anarchy, poverty and banditry, infinitely worse than anything peoples are suffering today.' The paper called on a figure of world stature (they probably had the Pope in mind) 'to plead in our name to the statesmen of the world, and those in particular whose voices are decisive, to break with the past. . . . Only a last-minute appeal of this nature can save us from war.' The Duke wrote to the editor in support of this idea, and his letter when published provoked a large public response. One of the encouraging replies he received was from his old friend Fred Bate, head of the British and European operations of the National Broadcasting Company of America, who together with his wife, an Italian princess, had been one of the Fort Belvedere set before the Abdication. Bate had always told the Duke that, in the event of his wishing to go on the air, the resources of NBC would be at his disposal; he now proposed that the Duke make a peace broadcast to America.

For eighteen months, since the collapse of his American visit, the Duke had kept his profile low and put aside the dreams of international statesmanship implanted by Bedaux; but given the tensions of the moment, and his awareness of the public longing that someone should speak out, he found this offer irresistible. He and the Duchess had already planned to spend the first weekend in May touring the battlefields at Verdun. Now, under great secrecy, he arranged with Bate to broadcast a short talk from his hotel at Verdun[15] on the evening of Monday, 8 May. What he proposed to say was along the same lines as the appeal in the *Catholic Herald*, and really amounted to no more than an inspiring piece of rhetoric, devoid of political content, calling on the statesmen of the world to settle their differences not by war but by negotiation. It would have aroused no controversy, but for an unfortunate coincidence. The King and Queen had been due to make an official visit to Canada and the United States that spring, but this had been cancelled owing to the international situation. In the first days of May, however, it was decided that the

---

[15] When the moment arrived, the Verdun municipality invited him to deliver the talk from the *mairie* or town hall, but he declined to do so lest it give the episode any kind of official appearance.

visit should go ahead after all, and the royal party sailed at only a couple of days' notice aboard *Empress of Australia* on 5 May. The Duke would therefore be open to the charge that he was seeking to detract attention from the royal visit, that he had chosen a moment to manifest himself when the King would be on the high seas; but as by this time the broadcast had been arranged (though it remained secret) he resolved to go ahead with it.

The Windsors travelled to Verdun on Saturday, 6 May, and that night the news of the imminent event was announced to the press. There followed two days of frantic publicity and preparations. NBC offered to relay the speech to every radio network outside America, while translations were offered to the national radio stations of all European countries. (It was eventually broadcast in French, Dutch and Polish; the German Rundfunk refused to take it, but a German translation was read over Radio Strasbourg.) The press waited to see if it would be carried by the BBC. The Council of the Corporation met on Monday morning to discuss the matter and remained in session for five hours; eventually they decided not to carry it.[16] This caused widespread indignation. The morning newspapers in Great Britain had been critical of the Duke's decision to broadcast, but the evening newspapers were even more critical of the BBC's decision and told their readers how to pick up the NBC transmission on short wave, where it was heard by many of the Duke's former subjects: theatres and restaurants emptied all over London as ten o'clock, the hour of the broadcast, approached. This was the last occasion until his death that the Duke's name was to hold the attention of millions in Britain, and to be the principal item of news in the British press.

The Duke began:

> I am speaking tonight from Verdun. . . . For two-and-a-half years I have deliberately kept out of public affairs and I still propose to do so. I speak for no one but myself, without the previous knowledge of any government. I speak simply as a soldier of the last war, whose most earnest prayer is that such a cruel and destructive madness shall never again overtake mankind. . . . The grave anxieties of the time . . . compel me to raise my voice in

---

[16] Surprisingly, there appears to be no account of this meeting in the written archives of the BBC.

expression of the universal longing to be delivered from the fears that beset us. . . .'[17]

'You have never spoken better,' wrote Bate to the Duke the next day. 'It was a great combination of words, time, place and situation – moving and beyond criticism.' Apart from regrets as to the timing, the broadcast was greeted with enthusiasm in England and hysteria in America, where the text was even included in the Congressional Record. The Duke received thousands of letters of support and congratulation from correspondents all over the world, including such diverse personalities as Marie Stopes, John Foster Dulles and Lord Alfred Douglas. But the episode, historic in that it caught the mood of the moment, was soon forgotten in the developing international crisis.

The late spring and early summer of 1939 were a time of relative contentment for the Windsors. The two houses which they had taken over the previous year had now reached the point of beauty and perfection demanded by the Duchess, and they began to entertain in the elegant style for which they would be famous after the war. They took part in the Paris season, inviting French society to the Boulevard Suchet; and at La Cröe the months of July and August saw a large and jolly house party of friends. They looked forward to visiting England in the autumn; and the international situation, up to the last ten days of August, did not look particularly critical. 'Things look better *re* Poland,' wrote the Duchess to Aunt Bessie on 20 July. 'We still think there won't be a war.'

All changed dramatically on 22 August, with the news of the Nazi–Soviet Pact. The guests at La Cröe vanished overnight, and with them the faithful Austrian manservants whom the Duke had brought back with him in 1937. In what was to be his last act on the international stage, he sent telegrams to Hitler and to King Victor Emmanuel of Italy, begging them, 'as a citizen of the world', not to plunge Europe into war. But, on 1 September, Germany invaded

---

[17] Full text in Appendix III. Astonishingly, the archives of NBC contain no recording of this historic broadcast.

Poland at dawn. The Duke was simultaneously depressed at what he regarded as a catastrophe for mankind, and elated at the confident hope that the bitter quarrels which had raged since the Abdication would now be past, that war would at last reunite him with his family and reconcile them to his marriage, and that he would be able to take up residence in his own country once again.

Chapter Six

A Year of Conflict
1939–40[1]

*T*he outbreak of war proved to be the first of many occasions on which the Duke of Windsor hoped and believed that his exile was about to come to an end, and that he and his wife would finally be welcomed back to England and accepted into the royal fold. As he wrote in 1966:

> The instant war came in September 1939, I offered my services to my country. Notwithstanding the strained relations between me and my brother, it was unthinkable that I should sit on my hands while Britain was mobilizing. He seemed to feel as I did. . . . The King offered to send a plane attached to the King's Flight to take us to London to talk about a war job. His reaction encouraged me to believe that the common sharing that goes with war would prove a solvent of the stubborn things which divided us. . . .

However, the fraternal offer of an aeroplane was withdrawn when the Duke, speaking to the King on the telephone on 1 September, asked if he and the Duchess might be accommodated at one of the royal residences; and the Windsors remained on French soil when Great Britain declared war on Germany on 3 September. It was to be the first of a string of snubs and disappointments. They now had

---

[1] The events of the first year of the war, summarized in this chapter, are described in detail in my previous works *The Duke of Windsor's War* (London, 1982: New York, 1983) and *Operation Willi: The Plot to Kidnap the Duke of Windsor, July 1940* (London, 1984; New York, 1986).

to await Walter Monckton, who was coming out to Antibes as the emissary of the King and Government to inform them of their future.

When Monckton finally arrived at La Cröe on the 7th, he brought the news that the Windsors would definitely not be staying with the royal family and would indeed have to make their own arrangements for travelling to England and accommodation there. Moreover, the Duke would be allowed to return only if he was prepared to accept one of two posts which would be offered to him, both of modest importance; either that of Deputy Regional Commissioner to Sir Wyndham Portal in Wales, or liaison officer with No. 1 British Military Mission to French GHQ under General Howard-Vyse. To this the Duke at once assented.

A few hours later he received a mysterious telephone call from the British Ambassador in Paris asking him to 'start by motor for the Channel coast and stop and telephone the Embassy again', which he correctly understood as meaning that a vessel was being sent from England to pick him up but that the port had not yet been selected. The following day the Windsors set out from La Cröe with their friend 'Fruity' Metcalfe, who was the last to remain of the Windsors' summer house party and had invited them to stay at a country house in Sussex belonging to his wife, Lady Alexandra. It was from Vichy on 10 September that the Duchess wrote the first of her many wartime letters to her Aunt Bessie:

Darling Aunt B,

We never thought it could or would happen. We have to return and left La Cröe with many heartaches on Friday afternoon, spending the night at Avignon – a very changed place. The Riviera was peaceful, but as one goes north one sees signs of war. We came here last night as it is a safe and peaceful spot – one picnics at the hotels as all the male staff have gone – it was the same at La Cröe. We leave tomorrow for the North where we will board an English navy vessel. We then go to the Metcalfes' in the country (Sussex) and the Duke will have a job – he has been offered 2 and that will have to be discussed and decided. If it can be arranged and all is well with our neighbour in the South [i.e. Italy] Lady Norman and myself would like to run our houses as convalescent homes for British officers. I am going to take it up with the army heads as soon as I find out just what the Duke's movements will be. . . . Naturally the Duke wishes to do all he can for the country – quite a different point of view from what they have done for him the last 3 years. I shall miss France where everyone has been more than kind and considerate. . . .

From Vichy they made their way to Paris, and from there – still surrounded by a cloak-and-dagger atmosphere – to Cherbourg, where they were greeted by Lord Louis Mountbatten, commanding HMS *Kelly* which was to take them across the Channel to England, and Randolph Churchill, representing his father Winston who was now First Lord of the Admiralty. This cheered them: the sending of a ship to fetch them had been Churchill's own initiative, and it was evident that they had at least one powerful friend. Churchill had sent a personal letter to the Duke by the hand of Randolph: 'Welcome home! Your Royal Highness knows how much I have looked forward to this day. I know you will forgive me for not coming to meet you, but I cannot leave my post. . . . We are plunged in a long and grievous struggle. But all will come out right if we all work together to the end.'

The news of their imminent return had now been made public in England, and been greeted there with general satisfaction. *The Times* wrote an editorial which reflected the prevailing view:

The announcement that the Duke and Duchess of Windsor are leaving Antibes for England will cause no surprise, still less any kind of contention. It has always been tacitly assumed that war would sweep away the difficulties there may have been in the way of the Duke's earlier return. . . . Now . . . the events and the hour which bring the Duke to rejoin his fellow-countrymen . . . relieve his homecoming of all possible traces of controversy or embarrassment. . . . No-one could dream of the Duke's absence from England at a time in which absence would become intolerable exile, or suppose for a moment that anything would be lacking on the Government's part to speed the fulfilment of his dearest and most urgent wish.

The Windsors sailed from Cherbourg on the night of 12 September, the journey taking six hours on a zig-zag run in a calm sea. The Duke and Mountbatten talked of old times. As they approached

Portsmouth, the Duke said to the Duchess: 'I don't know how this will work out. War should bring families together, even a Royal Family. But I don't know.' Their arrival was dramatic. The dock was in darkness because of the blackout. There was a red carpet and a guard of honour, and the band of the Royal Marines playing 'God Save the King'.

Only two people were on the quayside to meet them, Walter Monckton and Lady Alexandra Metcalfe. No member of the Royal Family was there, nor had they sent a representative or even a message. The landing ceremony had taken place on the sole initiative of Churchill. Lady Alexandra had in fact telephoned the Palace earlier to ask if a car might be sent for them (her own car was taking their luggage); but this had been refused, and no royal instructions had been given even regarding their overnight accommodation, though once again Churchill came to the rescue by getting the Commander-in-Chief of the port to put them up at Admiralty House.

With one exception, the Royal Family were to ignore the presence of the ex-King in England. As Lady Alexandra wrote in her diary, such was their attitude that 'he might not even exist'. His sole contact with them (for the Duchess there was none at all) consisted of a single meeting with the King at Buckingham Palace on Thursday, 14 September, the Duke's second afternoon in England. Even this had been arranged (by Monckton) with great difficulty, and was only made possible by the exclusion of women.

The two brothers were together for an hour. The King later described the meeting as 'very friendly' and 'without recriminations', the Duke as 'cordial enough'. They talked of the two alternative jobs which had been offered to the Duke, who expressed a preference for the civil-defence post in Wales to the staff-liaison post in France. The King assured him there was no urgency in making a decision. They came downstairs together. The King went over to the waiting Monckton and said to him: 'I think it went all right.' The Duke afterwards told Monckton that it had gone all right because he had kept off contentious subjects.

The following day the Duke had a round of meetings with members of the Government. He first went to see Winston Churchill at the Admiralty, where he received a heartening welcome. 'We are all in this together, aren't we?' asked Churchill, possibly having in mind the Verdun broadcast. 'Of course,' the Duke replied, 'that is why I am here.' Churchill's face lit up and he exclaimed: 'And we all want you back.' He then called on the Prime Minister. Chamberlain struck the Duke as a broken man, and appeared to be in a most nervous state. He spoke vaguely of the many people who did not seem to want the Duke back in England. It was when the Duke made his third official call, on the Secretary of State for War, Leslie Hore-Belisha, that the reason for the Prime Minister's embarrassment became evident. The post in Wales for which the Duke had expressed a preference had been withdrawn overnight by the King, without explanation. The Duke would therefore be sent back to France as a member of the Howard-Vyse Mission, giving up his rank of field-marshal for the duration of the war in order to become an acting major-general.

Earlier that day Hore-Belisha had been told by Hardinge, the King's Private Secretary, that the Duke had already been told of these arrangements and agreed to them; this was not true, but now there was little choice but to accept them. As a palliative, Hore-Belisha told the Duke that the Prime Minister was 'making enquiries' as to whether the Duke might spend two weeks touring the English Commands, before proceeding to France. This pleased the Duke, who asked whether the Duchess might accompany him to the Commands.

Next day, Hore-Belisha had two uncomfortable interviews with the King on the subject of the Duke, which he recorded in his diary.

16 September 1939
The King sent for me at 11 a.m. He was in a distressed state. He thought that if the Duchess went to the Commands, she might get a hostile reception, particularly in Scotland. He did not want the Duke to go to the Commands in England. He seemed very disturbed and walked up and down the room. He said the Duke never had any discipline in his life. . . .

2.30 p.m. I went to Buckingham Palace with Ironside.[2] H.M. remarked that all his predecessors had succeeded to the throne after their predecessors had died. 'Mine is not only alive, but very much so.' He thought it better for the Duke to proceed to Paris at once.

[2] Chief of the Imperial General Staff.

This decision had to be broken to the Duke. Hore-Belisha's diary continued:

> 3 p.m. The Duke came to the War Office. He expressed his pleasure in going to the Commands in England and making contact with the soldiers. I pointed out that when a soldier was given an appointment, he invariably took it up without delay. I explained that troops were moving about, the secrecy involved, and that the Duke's presence would attract attention. It would create an excellent impression with the public, I said, if the Duke showed readiness to take up his appointment at once; that Howard-Vyse was waiting impatiently for him in Paris. The Duke appreciated all the arguments and expressed agreement.

In fact they stayed in England for another thirteen days, which was the time it took for the Duke to receive his instructions and sort out such matters as staff and uniforms. Each day they motored up to London to the Metcalfes' town house which they used as their metropolitan base, returning to the country before dusk in order to avoid the blackout. 'All business is transacted from this ridiculous house,' wrote Lady Alexandra in her diary. 'Clerks, secretaries, War Office officials, hairdressers, bootmakers, tailors, with a sprinkling of friends streaming in & out. They have sandwiches and tea from a thermos for refreshment.' The Duke was often cheered in the streets, and received several thousand letters, all but 6 per cent of them favourable. Friends found him looking well. 'He is dressed in khaki with all his decorations and looks grotesquely young,' wrote Harold Nicolson after meeting him and the Duchess at Sibyl Colefax's. 'I have seldom seen the Duke in such cheerful spirits and it was rather touching to witness their delight at being back in England. There was no false note.'

Though he faced his war work cheerfully, the behaviour of his family on this, his first visit to England since the Abdication, had a profound effect on the Duke's state of mind. He had been ostracized, humiliated and snubbed; and he was determined not to expose himself to such treatment when he next returned home. It is important to remember this when considering his attitude nine months later. Nor were his unhappy experiences as a British officer in France over the following eight months calculated to assuage his sense of grievance. As he wrote to King George VI in 1943:

> Granted the first year or two cannot have been too easy for you – I can see that – but ever since I returned to England in September 1939 to offer my services and you continued to persecute [me] and then frustrate my modest efforts to serve you and my country in war, I must frankly admit that I have become very bitter indeed.

Accompanied by Metcalfe in the role of unofficial equerry, the Windsors returned to France on 29 September, putting up at a hotel at Versailles while they decided whether or not to reopen the house in the Boulevard Suchet. The Duke at once reported to his new chief, General Howard-Vyse, at his headquarters at Nogent-sur-Marne, a short distance from the French GHQ at Vincennes.

Several strange ironies surrounded the Duke's war job with No. 1 Military Mission. It had been conceived as a minor sinecure, aimed at getting him out of the way and keeping his profile low. But Howard-Vyse and his men wished to use him for an important purpose. Ostensibly the role of the Mission was to provide the liaison between General Ironside, the Chief of the Imperial General Staff in London, and General Gamelin, the French Commander-in-Chief at Vincennes. But its real task was to spy on the French, who were intensely secretive and suspicious and refused to tell their allies much about their defences and fortifications, and who had not so far allowed any Englishman to inspect the Maginot Line, the basis of their defensive system. In the second week of September, the Mission was wondering how to go about the difficult task of finding out exactly what the French were up to, when they suddenly learnt that the Duke of Windsor was to join them. 'At last we were given a heaven-sent opportunity of visiting the French front,' recalled Brigadier Davy, the Mission's Chief-of-Staff. Royalism was strong in the French army, and the Duke in particular remained popular from 1914 days. It was hoped that he would be allowed to tour French positions which were prohibited to the scrutiny of other British military personnel.

The French suspected nothing. On 19 September their Military Attaché in London, General Lelong, wrote to Gamelin: 'The attachment of the Duke of Windsor to the Howard-Vyse Mission is a purely political matter. They do not quite know what to do with this inconvenient personage, especially in England; but they do not want him to be seen sitting on his hands. . . . General Ironside has told Howard-Vyse to see you about how the Duke might be employed. . . .' Having seen Gamelin, Howard-Vyse reported to London on 21 September that the French military chief had 'no objection to the Duke of Windsor going anywhere in the French zone, which is a great relief to me'.

During the autumn, the Duke made three important tours of major French army zones. As expected, he proved immensely popular. 'HRH was wonderful at lunch, got everything going well and everyone talking and laughing etc.,' wrote Metcalfe of a meeting with French generals. 'He really is 1st class at something like this.' After these tours he compiled secret reports for Ironside on the state of the French defences he had witnessed; and some of his observations were remarkably prescient. He noticed everywhere the general unpreparedness for attack and the poor state of morale. This was what he had to say in October about the Northern Ardennes front near Revin, a spot where Guderian's Panzers were to break through in May 1940:

> The main features are the high and heavily wooded ridges which form the valley of the Meuse. It was difficult to establish what was the general system of defence. . . . The wire entanglements are covered by machine gun fire, but in almost every case there is a very narrow field of fire, and the entanglements could easily be approached up to within a few yards under cover of the trees and very thick undergrowth. There are no anti-tank defences. . . .

In December, this was what he had to say about the Maginot Line:

> In the minds of most of the French officers interviewed on the tour there is one dominant obsession, and that is the excellence, the impregnability of the Maginot Line. . . . The Maginot Line does not seem to be an insuperable barrier. Given the weight of artillery, close support from aircraft, natural or artificial fog, tanks with guns capable of penetrating the armour of the embrasures,

armoured trucks or tractors to carry faggots to fill up the space in the anti-tank rail obstacles, enterprising infantry with flame-throwers, and sappers with explosives, it should be possible to break the crust. . . . After that, there will be nothing but a few demolitions and troops in the open to stop an advance to Paris. . . .

He was also struck by the in-fighting between the French military chiefs, and wrote what has been described by one miliary historian as 'a pungent memorandum in which he expressed the view that the generals were more actively hostile to each other than to the Germans. The French soldiers were, the Duke discovered, dedicated to political feuds. The Roman Catholics look with horror and suspicion upon the Freemasons, for all the world as if the clock had been stopped 50 years previously.' The Duke 'was not alone, but he was among the first to decide that Gamelin was, as he put it, "a weak sister".'

'Having made this appointment for the Duke,' Wing-Commander Vintras, the RAF man with the Mission, later wrote, 'the authorities might at least have had the courtesy, if not the prudence, of listening to what he had to say.' But his prophetic warnings were ignored in London. Indeed, Brigadier Davy came to feel that it had been a mistake to allow him to sign them, since anything bearing his name was likely to have a brief journey to the waste-paper basket. For example, the report questioning the impregnability of the Maginot Line, quoted above, was sent in the War Office by 'J.W.L' to 'D.D.M.O.' with the following minute: 'I do not think you have seen this report by H.R.H. the Duke of Windsor. You will not I think want to read it. . . .'

Another irony was that the Duke, being the only Englishman allowed to have a free run of the French Army, was virtually prohibited from going near the British Army in France. General Alan Brooke noted in his diary that there were instructions 'to guard against his endeavouring to stage any kind of "come back" with the troops out here'. Nevertheless, on 6 October, during a tour of the First French Army Group Sector which included the small British Expeditionary Force, the Duke (with the approval of Howard-Vyse) called at British Headquarters and had tea with the Commander-in-Chief, Lord Gort. 'Everyone there was delighted to see HRH,' wrote Metcalfe, 'and the visit could not have gone better.' Major-General Pownall, Gort's Chief-of-Staff, noted:

He was nice and agreeable and spoke very intelligently. There is, for the moment at any rate, an 'inhibition' against his going round troops, indeed I believe he was not supposed to come to GHQ, but we can't help saying 'yes' if we are told he is coming.

During this visit, the Duke of Windsor also saw his brother, the Duke of Gloucester, who held the high-sounding but empty title of Chief Liaison Officer at Gort's Headquarters and was embarrassed by the encounter.

Eleven days later he returned to the British Sector. The front was in the grip of an invasion scare, and the Duke wished to propose himself for a morale-boosting eve-of-battle tour. He again 'behaved charmingly' at Gort's Headquarters, and at the front struck Alan Brooke as being 'full of go and of interest' – but he blotted his copybook when a guard presented arms and he thoughtlessly took a salute meant for the Commander-in-Chief. For this minor transgression he was astonished to receive a reprimand, and new instructions went out which effectively banned him from the British Sector altogether. As the Duchess wrote in her memoirs, 'we had two wars to deal with – the big and still leisurely war, in which everybody was caught up, and the little cold war with the Palace, in which no quarter was given'. The Duke had 'always had a gift for dealing with troops – the gift of the common touch and understanding. . . . It seemed to me tragic that his unique gift, humbly proffered, was never called upon, out of fear . . . that it might once more shine brightly, too brightly.'

Under the circumstances it hardly came as a surprise to the Duke when he was told to make himself scarce during the King's visit to the front, which took place from 4 to 10 December. 'My brother-in-law arrives in France tomorrow,' wrote the Duchess to her aunt, 'but competition still exists in the English mind – so one must hide so there is no rivalry. All very childish except that the biggest men take it seriously. Anyway the Duke can leave the front and spend those days with me so that the cheers are guaranteed.' The King's visit was followed by the fall from office of Hore-Belisha, the reforming Secretary of State for War. This occurred as the result of an intrigue in which the Court, and in particular Hardinge, played a prominent role, and the involvement of the Palace in military affairs gave the Duke little grounds to hope for an improvement in his position.

During the autumn the Duchess joined the other women of Paris society in engaging frantically in good works for war relief, in which she exhibited her usual organizational skills. 'I have been able to get within the sound of gunfire through joining the French Red Cross automobile section,' she wrote to Sibyl Colefax in December. 'I need not add that the British have not asked me to help them – so time and money have gone to the French.' With her friend Lady Mendl, she also set up and ran a charity known as the Colis de Trianon, sending parcels of food and clothing to needy French troops at the front. In the midst of all this, she found time to reopen the house in the Boulevard Suchet on 'a skeleton staff of people not yet called up or too old to answer to anything but the grave'; and the Duke's dinner table there became a place of relaxation for his French and British colleagues from the Military Mission and Gamelin's GHQ, among whom he was always popular.

⚜

The new year of 1940 found the Duke in a mood of frustration. The Duchess wrote to her aunt that he considered his job 'too inactive, besides a lot of pressure from the Palace which makes it impossible to do well. Even the war can't stop the family hatred of us.' On 21 January he made a short visit to London alone, staying for three nights at Claridges. He had no contact with his family, but saw Churchill. The journey was ostensibly to enable him to make a verbal report to Ironside on what he had seen, which seems to have made no more impact than his written reports with their wise warnings; but he also took the opportunity to complain about the restrictions upon his role.

These representations were not wholly without effect, for when he returned Metcalfe wrote: 'HRH came back from England in great shape, seemingly everything went as he wished.' (Metcalfe was moved to witness the reunion of the Duke and Duchess – *'very* true and deep stuff'.) For the first time since the incident of the salute three months previously, he was allowed to visit British troops – which he did in the course of a tour in early February of the Seventh French Army along the Channel coast. Metcalfe wrote that the Duke was 'very pleased about it', hoping it might be 'the thin end of the wedge. . . . I am glad for him and I also think that something better will come fairly soon for HRH.' He inspected the RAF headquarters in France, and spent an afternoon with a unit which had deep associations for him – the 1st Battalion of the Welsh Guards. But even this episode was cut short since President Lebrun was shortly due in the British Sector, and it was thought undesirable that he and the Duke should meet.

Soon afterwards, painful events occurred which made it clear to the Duke that nothing had been forgiven. On 17 February (as described in Chapter 4) Ulick Alexander wrote to him 'by the wish of the King' to say that Fort Belvedere – which George VI had promised would be kept as the Duke's home whenever he came back to England – had been requisitioned for the wartime use of the Crown Estates (who were never in fact to use it). When the Duke, suspecting the worst, had Allen write to ask if an inventory might be made which would later enable the property to be restored to its former state for his occupancy, Alexander replied that the Duke no longer had any interest in the Fort because the King had never formally confirmed him in possession of it. The Duke wrote bitterly to Allen that it was 'just another example of my brother's failure to keep his word to me of December 1936, when amongst other guarantees it was clearly understood verbally (unfortunately not in writing) that The Fort should be reserved for me until such time as it was considered mutually suitable that I should take up residence in England again'.

That winter, as we have seen in Chapter 2, there was also some threat to cut off the Duke's Palace allowance, on the grounds that he may have given insufficient notice to the King of his visit to London to see his chief Ironside. 'You should be more than ever on your guard', wrote Allen, 'so that there is no excuse for action of this sort.'

In the second week of March, the Duke took his first leave of the war, returning with the Duchess to La Cröe, which they had not seen since they had left it to go to England six months before. Harold Nicolson, who ran into them in Lyons on their way south, found them looking 'very happy'. Francis O'Meara, the British Consul-General in Lyons, remarked to Nicolson: 'He was so charming to me, as though I were the one person in the world he wanted to talk to. It isn't disloyal at all is it, to like the Duke so much?'

By the end of the month they were back in the capital. 'Paris as you know is beautiful at this time,' wrote the Duchess to her aunt. 'It is hard to believe there are so many people who hate each other.' Their evenings were taken up with 'endless galas for war work and talk of war', but the general mood was demoralizing. 'The papers are so censored that it is useless to read them and the political side I think "lousy" with everyone out for himself more than the war.' As for the Duke, his job was 'ridiculous and, instead of using him where he might help the cause, because of jealousy which even the death of men can't temper he has a childish job. . . . he was their best propagandist when P of W and the tax-payer gave a lot for that education and now when they might get a small return family and Government are scared to use him. . . .'

The Duke was full of worries about both the military and political conduct of the Allies. On 3 May he wrote to his friend Philip Guedalla:

It would seem an obvious platitude to say that in my private view, things are going very badly for us indeed at the moment, and they can't possibly go any better until we have purged ourselves of many of the old lot of politicians and much of our out-of-date system of government.

We are up against a formidable foe, not only formidable in the military sense but politically as well. If we are forced to spend millions every day arming and equipping our forces to match Germany's, surely it is equally necessary to equip ourselves politically in order to match ourselves against the calculating shrewdness and freedom of action of the Nazi chiefs?

The trouble with the present lot who are directing our national effort is that they are in the main too old, and are all in some degree tainted with the series of blunders in foreign policy which are responsible for the present mess. We want new blood not caught up in its own bunk, men with common and not necessarily political sense, who can bring clear minds to bear on the phases of the conflict as and how they develop, and who should have greater freedom of action than is possible with the cumbersome parliamentary and departmental machine which strangles us. Granted, there have been signs of improvement in this respect, but there are still far too many 'weeds round the propellor' [sic].

Above all things, we need men who, while applying themselves to the prosecution of war, have an eye open as to the future; for whatever the outcome of this catastrophy [sic] of war, our problems will be infinitely more diverse, complex and serious than those we face today.

If it were as easy to discover the giant or giants (and not too many) as it is to criticise, then I would gladly forgo the pleasure just now. . . .

Three days later, on 6 May, the Duchess wrote to Aunt Bessie:

> . . . We had a nice dinner last week for the British Ambassador and his wife. They are very nice, and certainly brave to come here. . . . We may have to go to London shortly and I think I will go this time just in case I have forgotten their bad manners. As the French are so well-mannered I might forget! . . . My ambulance section is doing well and it is interesting to make trips with them and better in this lovely spring weather. . . . The people are splendid – but there are very few *blessés* happily. From Norway we do not know the casualties as yet, but it is All Quiet on the Western Front.

On 10 May 1940 the Germans at last launched their invasion of France and the Low Countries, and on the same day Churchill became Prime Minister of Great Britain. 'The news that you have accepted to form a Government at this supreme hour of trial for our nation', the Duke wrote to him, 'is dramatic indeed.' For a few days he was able to perform useful liaison work between his headquarters and the front. He was thus fully aware of the disaster which manifested itself on the 15th, by which date Guderian's three Panzer divisions, having crossed the Ardennes and the Meuse against minimal opposition, had overcome the anti-tank defences about which the Duke had expressed such doubts the previous autumn, and were smashing through the French lines. The following day – Thursday, 16 May – was one of panic in Paris, it being incorrectly imagined that the Germans would now be making directly for the capital. The wives of all British diplomats and officials were hurriedly evacuated, and the Duke insisted on driving the Duchess, in spite of her protests, through refugee-choked roads to Biarritz.

Back in Paris, which seemed to be out of immediate danger, the Duke continued to attend his headquarters daily, but there was little for him to do. As the Duchess wrote to her aunt, 'his job ceased to exist the day the war really got started as it was to visit the French troops and they are hardly receiving at the moment'. He obtained leave to go to the South of France, with a view to packing up his possessions at La Cröe ('I don't intend to let my family silver fall into Mussolini's possession') and performing some liaison function with the French Army of the Alps, at a moment when Italian invasion was hourly expected. Picking up the Duchess at Biarritz, he arrived at Antibes on the 29th. He had originally intended to return to his headquarters, but on 4 June he wrote to his aide, Major Gray Phillips, who had been left in charge of the house in the Boulevard Suchet, describing his position.

The Duchess and I are very glad to be here and, while awaiting the Duce to declare his hand, have been able to make some dispositions to meet any eventualities. Those days of inactivity in Paris were intolerable, and exposed more definitely than ever the fact that the futile role I played at the Mission died a natural death with the German offensive. It is not in my make-up to sit in Paris without a job when I should be with the Duchess who, in view of the uncertainty of Italy's attitude towards the war, I cannot and will not leave here quite alone.

I have heard from Fruity [Metcalfe] that he is returning to England which is by far the best thing he could do, only I do think that he should first of all have submitted his intention for my approval and not left without my permission. However, it is a typical Fruity gesture and one would not expect him to behave otherwise.[3]

'So far so good' is the news from this coast, which is in suspense and the military so active that a request I made in person five days ago at the French Corps HQ to visit their defences in the mountains has so far met with no response. The B.E.F. have made an amazing getaway; that so large a proportion have been snatched away right under the nose of the enemy is nothing short of a miracle.

It must be very lonely and boring in Paris and I hate asking you to remain there for the present. But it is important that there is someone . . . with whom we can keep in touch. Of course, in the event of your having to mount your saddled horse, then you must ride here with all speed.

---

[3] Metcalfe appears to have quarrelled with the Duke in Paris and parted from him there. Afterwards, each of them seems to have regarded himself as abandoned by the other.

On the 9th, the French Government and Army (along with Major Phillips) abandoned the capital; and on the 10th the Duchess wrote to her aunt from La Cröe:

> It really is becoming a most awful mess. We haven't decided what we will do yet exactly but will stay here for a few days anyway. You can imagine how difficult it is to make a real plan. I had just taken 2 Italian servants. . . . The Duke is with the army here for the moment but can do more or less as he likes. . . . France is having a tough time. I can't believe they will go for the Island – and I believe you will be in it before long. It is 'the old order changeth giving place to new' I am afraid. . . . The battle is supposed to start tonight here. The Duke thinks the defences in the Alps excellent. Everyone is calm and the gardeners (all Italians) planting flowers for the summer. The sky is blue, the sea smooth – but the mind ruffled. . . .

The Italians were heroically repulsed along the coast, but the Germans were now racing down the Rhône Valley. At La Cröe, the Duke dithered. He had heard nothing from the British authorities, and was reluctant to move until he had some word from them about his future. It was not until the 16th that he asked the advice of the British Consul-General at Nice, Major Hugh Dodds, who urged 'that he should leave France without delay, as with the rapid advance of German troops he might find himself cut off. I had visions of H.R.H. being held as a hostage by the enemy.' On 19 June, accompanied by Dodds and by a small party of friends, the Windsors finally set out from Antibes in a motor convoy bound for the Spanish frontier. In her memoirs, the Duchess recalled their departure from La Cröe, where during the fifteen months before the war she had worked so hard to create a pleasant life for the Duke:

> The staff were grouped round the entrance to say goodbye. As I was about to enter the car, the gardener stepped forward to press into my arms a huge bunch of tuberoses. 'Your birthday present, darling,' whispered David.[4] I buried my face in the sweet-smelling

---

[4] The Duchess was forty-four.

mass, grateful for being able to take away with me at least this lovely reminder of La Crōe. Our staff wept as we left; and so did I.

There was no guarantee that they would succeed in getting to Spain, for they had no papers, and even if they managed to cross the frontier there was a risk that the Duke would be arrested by the Spanish authorities as a serving Allied officer on neutral soil. And the route to the frontier was blocked by barricades manned by veterans. But the Duke managed to get through by announcing: *'Je suis le Prince de Galles. Laissez-moi passer, s'il vous plaît';* and after a long wait at Perpignan and futile meetings with consuls he finally managed to get visas for himself and his party by appealing on the telephone to the Spanish Ambassador to France. By midnight on the 20th they had reached Barcelona, from where the Duke telegraphed Churchill: 'Having received no instructions have arrived in Spain to avoid capture. Proceeding to Madrid. Edward.'
Edward.'

The Windsors arrived in Madrid on 23 June, the Duke's forty-sixth birthday, and went to stay at the Ritz. It was a tense city which bore the scars of the Civil War which had ended only twelve months before; but the recently appointed British Ambassador, the veteran Conservative politician Sir Samuel Hoare, was something of an old friend of the Duke. Hoare had at first received instructions to send the Windsors straight on to Lisbon, but these instructions had been changed at the last minute because Prince George, the Duke of Kent, was about to arrive in Portugal to lead the British delegation to the eight hundredth anniversary celebrations of Portuguese independence, and it was thought undesirable that the two brothers should coincide. The Windsors therefore spent nine days in the Spanish capital under the Ambassador's aegis.

The War Cabinet had now discussed the Windsors' position, and the Duke found in Madrid a telegram from Churchill saying that they wanted him 'to come home as soon as possible' and that the Ambassador would explain the arrangements. The Duke received this news with mixed feelings. He remembered painfully how he and his wife had been ignored and ostracized on their return in September 1939, and wanted to know exactly what he would now be coming home to. Would there be work for him to do? Hoare was able to tell him nothing except that Saighton Grange, a house near Chester (and thus two hundred miles from London) belonging to the Duke of Westminster, might be made available to him as a residence.

The following day, Hoare telegraphed Churchill that the Duke was 'ready to leave Madrid provided his stay in Lisbon does not overlap with the Duke of Kent's'. But before leaving he was 'most anxious' to know if he was to have a job in England. 'He does not want to appear to be returning as a refugee with nothing to do. I hope you can help him with a friendly answer as soon as possible. I have told him that if he fails to return to England within a few days, all sorts of mischievous rumours will circulate about him.'

As the Duke settled down in Madrid to await his brother's departure from the Peninsula, Hoare faced two worrying problems. First, Axis propaganda was rife in Spain and had set out to exploit the Duke's presence. 'All sorts of rumours were being spread about his visit,' wrote Hoare to the Foreign Secretary, Lord Halifax on 26 June, 'that he had come to make a British peace negotiation, that he had come to make trouble against the British etc., etc. I felt that the only possible course was to take him as much as possible under my wing and to make it as clear as I could to the whole world that he was in friendly relations to all of us and merely stopping in Madrid on his way to England.' The other problem was more serious. Hoare felt that, unless the Duke received some encouraging news about his future, he might in the end decline to return. He wrote to Churchill on the 27th:

> . . . May I say a word about our friend, the Duke of Windsor. . . . Whenever I see him – and this is very often – he returns to the charge about being given a job in England. I know as well as you do the difficulties of the position. Nonetheless I feel that you will never have peace and perhaps I shall never get him away from here unless you can find something for him. Could you not give him a naval command of some kind? He still loves the sea better than anything else and anything actually in Great Britain might be troublesome to the Palace and you. I do feel strongly that this is the moment to get them both back to England and clear up the situation. If the chance is lost, there will be a prince over the water who will be a nuisance and possibly an embarrassment. . . .

In London, Churchill, however much he might have liked to do so, was unable to arrange anything for the Duke. The very decision to ask the Windsors to return to England had been taken by the War Cabinet in the face of opposition and alarm from the Palace. Churchill's position only six weeks after he had assumed the premiership was such that he had to defer to the King's wishes; and Hardinge wrote that he did not see how it was possible for the Duke 'as an ex-King to perform any useful service in this country'. Churchill was therefore only able to reply to the Duke that it would be 'better for Your Royal Highness to come to England as arranged, when everything can be considered'.

This suggestion, however, did not satisfy the Duke, who had now decided that, as a matter of honour, he could only go back to his own country if some small gesture of recognition was made towards his wife. As he wrote a quarter of a century later: 'His [Churchill's] personal advice to me was not to quibble about terms but to come home and wait patiently while he worked things out. But I could not in honour take this line. The year before, while we had been in England, the Duchess's presence at my side had never been acknowledged, even perfunctorily. Before going back I wanted an assurance that simple courtesies would be forthcoming.' He did not choose this moment to insist that the Duchess be accorded royal status, merely that she be received with him by the King and Queen to dispel the public impression that she was in disgrace. What he sought was no more than a gesture for the sake of public appearances. 'In the light of past experience', he wrote to Churchill on 27 June, 'my wife and myself must not risk finding ourselves once more regarded by the British public as in a different status to other members of my family.' To this request, however, the Court refused to yield. In a fierce telegraphic exchange lasting two days, Churchill continued to urge the Duke to return without conditions. This the Duke still hesitated to do, though he declared his willingness, should his terms not be accepted, to serve his country anywhere in the Empire.

Hoare, who was appalled to see the family quarrel rage at such a critical moment, did his best to settle the affair. On the 29th he wrote to Churchill that he had got the Duke to whittle down his demands to very little. He had now dropped his request for a job in England. As for the other matter, it 'boiled down to both of them being received only once for quite a short meeting by the King and Queen, and notice of this fact appearing in the Court Circular'. All that was at issue, Hoare stressed, was a 'once only' meeting of 'a quarter of an hour', and Hoare earnestly hoped the King could agree to this.

Having had no final reply to their queries, the Windsors left Madrid for Portugal on 2 July, the day the Duke of Kent departed from Lisbon. Hoare was relieved to see them depart. He wrote to Halifax, the Foreign Secretary, that they had 'behaved admirably during their stay here. They have made themselves extremely popular with the many Spaniards whom they have met and apart from the family row in which once again I have been unwillingly involved, they have been both easy and affable.' But, to Churchill, Hoare wrote:

> I did my best with them while they were here and I greatly hoped that you would come to some accommodation over the offer. I am certain that this is the moment to end the trouble and if it is not ended now, the rift between them and the rest of the family will become deeper and more dangerous. The trouble is that he has no one who knows anything about England to advise him. As it was, I argued with him and with her for hours on end that this was not the moment for bargaining over details. They replied that they agreed provided both sides in the controversy behaved in the same way. . . .

Arriving in Portugal on 3 July, the Windsors went to stay at the house that had been prepared for them, a seafront villa at Cascais, near Lisbon, belonging to a Portuguese banker, where they were greeted by the British Ambassador to Portugal, Sir Walford Selby, and informed that two flying boats of RAF Coastal Command were waiting in the Tagus to take them back to England. Hoare's last message to the Foreign Office had stated that he did not think that they would return 'without further assurances', and it may well have been that the Duke still intended to stick to his conditions, minimal though they now were, for going home. But Selby handed him a telegram from Churchill which amounted to a command: 'Your Royal Highness has taken military rank and refusal to obey direct orders of competent military authority would create a serious situation. I hope it will not be necessary for such orders to be sent. I most strongly urge immediate compliance with wishes of the Government.' In the face of this ultimatum, the Duke capitulated, and agreed to return without delay and without conditions. A telegram was sent to London, advising that the Windsors would be flying from Lisbon to Poole Harbour the following night. This telegram, however, crossed with yet another from Churchill to the Duke, which he received when he called at the British Embassy in Lisbon on the morning of the 4th. This read:

> I am authorized by the King and Cabinet to offer you the appointment of Governor and Commander-in-Chief of the Bahamas. If you accept, it may be possible to take you and the Duchess direct from Lisbon dependent on the military situation. Please let me know without delay whether this proposal is satisfactory to Your Royal Highness. Personally I feel sure it is the best open in the grievous situation in which we all stand. At any rate I have done my best.

The appointment was extraordinary and unprecedented, being the only time in modern history that a member of the Royal Family had been given a colonial governorship or indeed any position involving political responsibility. Its origins are still not wholly clear. According to Lord Lloyd, the Secretary of State for the Colonies, it was 'the King's own idea, to keep him at all costs out of England'. But, in a conversation with Beaverbrook, Churchill took the credit for it. The Prime Minister asked, 'Max, do you think he'll take it?' to which Beaverbrook replied, 'He'll find it a great relief,' whereupon Churchill commented: 'Not half as much as his brother will.' Such an appointment, however, was urgently necessary in order to get him out of Europe, since, as Churchill wrote to Roosevelt,

> ... though his loyalties are unimpeachable there is always a backwash of Nazi intrigue that seeks to make trouble about him now that the greater part of the continent is in enemy hands. There are personal and family difficulties about his return to this country. In all the circumstances it was felt that an appointment abroad might appeal to him, and the Prime Minister has with His Majesty's cordial approval offered him the Governorship of the Bahamas.

The Duke lost little time in accepting the offer. He told the Duchess: 'Governor of the Colony of the Bahamas. One of the few parts of the Empire I missed on my travels. Well, Winston said he was sorry, but it was the best he could do, and I shall keep my side of the bargain.' (This was a reference to his earlier assurance to Churchill that, if family circumstances made it impossible for him to return, he was ready to serve anywhere in the Empire.) A few hours after receiving Churchill's telegram, he replied to it: 'I will accept appointment of Governor of the Bahamas as I am sure you have done your best for me in a difficult situation.'

'I am very glad Your Royal Highness has accepted the appointment', wrote Churchill, 'where I am sure useful service can be rendered to the Empire at the present time. . . . Sincere good wishes.' The King also wrote to his brother expressing his pleasure and relief, adding how glad he was that the Duke had realized how impossibly difficult it would have been for him to return to England. It was evident that the Court had played no part in the Government's action of the previous month inviting the Windsors to return, and had been only too happy that the Duke had made conditions for his homecoming that might be refused.

The governorship was made public on 9 July, and the Windsors stayed on in Portugal for the rest of the month busily making preparations for it. At first they seem to have been relatively happy that their immediate future should at last have been settled. The Duke wrote on 12 July to Lloyd, whom he had first known in the twenties as Governor of Bombay, that he was glad that 'by good fortune, my immediate political chief should happen to be an old friend'. Although the role of colonial governor was a novel one for him, the fact that 'Winston considers it [one] . . . in which I can serve the Empire' made him take up his duties 'with enthusiasm'. On the other hand, the post was hardly flattering to the ex-King, being extremely minor: the Bahamas were among the most insignificant of the thirty-five territories under the control of the Colonial Office. The Duchess wrote to her aunt from Cascais on 15 July:

> The St Helena of 1940 is a nice spot. At least the British have got the Duke as far [away] as possible. We refused to return to England except under our own terms, as the Duke is quite useless to the country if he was to receive the same treatment as when he

returned to offer his services wholeheartedly in Sept only to receive one humiliation after another. Once bitten twice shy, and they would guarantee him no different treatment – so he asked for something out of England and he got it! . . . Can you fancy a family continuing a feud when the very Empire is threatened and not putting every available man in a spot where he would be most useful? Could anything be so small and hideous? What will happen to a country which allows such behaviour?

Surprising as it may seem, in view of Churchill's eagerness to get them out of Europe, the Windsors were left to make all their own travel arrangements for getting out to the Bahamas. They hoped to travel by way of New York (which was the normal route) in the American packet-steamer *Excalibur*, due to sail from Lisbon on 1 August, but a mass of refugees were trying to leave Portugal and this ship and all others were fully booked. There was also the question of whether an American ship could carry them under the United States neutrality laws. 'I feel this obstacle would be overcome', wrote the Duke to Churchill on 12 July, 'if our voyage to America be arranged officially between His Majesty's Government and the United States Government.' Both the British and American governments, however, were unhappy about the idea of the Windsors passing through the United States. They would be the subject of massive press interest there, and it was feared in London that the Duke might drop some indiscretion concerning the war, and in Washington that his arrival might be exploited by the Isolationists, who were hoping to unseat Roosevelt at the presidential election in November. It therefore happened that, although the two governments did indeed officially arrange the ducal party's passage, it was not the journey the Duke had been expecting. On 18 July the Prime Minister telegraphed to say that *Excalibur* would now be diverted to Bermuda, where another ship would take them directly to the Bahamas.

This news infuriated the Duke, who had been looking forward to a short visit to America, and who was undoubtedly living in a state of great frustration and tension, having been isolated with the Duchess for two weeks in a remote seaside villa under conditions of strict security which amounted to house imprisonment. He also had another cause of grievance: the Government had refused to allow Piper Fletcher of the Scots Guards, who had been his batman since the beginning of the war, to join him in the Bahamas, on the grounds that he was required for active service. That the Duke should have pressed this matter seems petty: but he considered that, having made the grand gesture of accepting an appointment which was at the same time insignificant and unprecedented, he was entitled to the use of a tried and trusted servant who could attend properly to his personal needs in such a post. At all events, a brief but unpleasant telegraphic row broke out between the Government in London and the Duke in Lisbon, who wrote to Churchill on 18 July: 'Have been messed about long enough and detect in Colonial Office attitude very same hands at work as in my last job. Strongly urge you to support arrangements I have made as otherwise will have to reconsider my position.'

This seems to have represented no more than a momentary outburst of spleen; in his next telegram, sent only a few hours later, the Duke felt 'diffident' in advancing his claims and merely wrote: 'Feel sure you do not know red tape we are up against as regards new appointment.' A deal was arranged, whereby the Duke would be allowed to keep Fletcher but not to visit America. On 25 July the Duke accepted this, asking for one further assurance – that the American prohibition was only to apply 'until after the events of November', and that it was 'not to be the policy of Her Majesty's Government that I should not set foot on American soil during my term of office in the Bahamas'. Churchill replied evasively but politely that 'we should naturally wish to fall in with Your Royal Highness's wishes. It is difficult to see far ahead these days, but . . . we should naturally do our best to suit Your Royal Highness's convenience.'

Although all now seemed ready for the Windsors' departure, the brush with officialdom had briefly instilled in the Duke, given the isolated circumstances in which he was living, a dangerous mood of melancholy and resentment. He described his state of mind in a frank letter to Allen of 20 July:

> We are encountering every conceivable form of governmental obstruction and red tape in the making of our arrangements for the voyage and the taking up of this wretched appointment. Any keeness [*sic*] that I had at first been able to evoke has been completely knocked out of me, and I view the prospect of an indefinite period of exile on those islands with profound gloom and

despondency. However, as I refuse to accept an appointment in England under the conditions which prevail, I suppose there is no alternative but to go, although I am at times sorely tempted to chuck the whole project and retire entirely from the contest. . . .

⚜

During July 1940, while the Duke was waiting in Lisbon for the ship that was to take him and the Duchess to the Bahamas, the Germans hatched a plot of amazing complexity to bring him under their control in the Peninsula.[5] The author of this plot was Ribbentrop, the German Foreign Minister, and what exactly he meant to do with the Duke once he had got hold of him is not entirely clear. No doubt the long-term idea was to try to set him up as the ruler of a pro-German Britain; in the short term, the idea seems to have been to weaken Great Britain's will to continue the fight by exploiting the ex-King as part-collaborator, part-mediator, part-hostage. Ribbentrop, however, was far from sure that the Duke would go along with his plans, and his instructions to his agents stressed that he was not to suspect German interest in him until he had been safely lured into German hands by trickery. The Duke consequently knew nothing of the web of conspiracy that was then being woven around him, and was astonished when he learnt of it thirteen years later; yet he had unwittingly encouraged the plot at the time by indiscreet talk with neutral friends, which eventually got back to the Germans, in which he expressed his dissatisfaction both with his personal situation and the continuation of the war. On the other hand, it is a bizarre fact that the plot may possibly have saved England, for it contributed indirectly to two results which proved vital to British survival at that critical moment – the continuance of Spanish neutrality, and Hitler's fatal decision to delay his attack across the Channel from mid-July to mid-August. It can be no mere coincidence that 1 August – the day that the German plot failed and the Windsors departed safely for the Bahamas – was also the day that Hitler, after weeks of otherwise inexplicable hesitation, finally issued his Directive No. 17, launching the air war against England.

On 11 July – a week after the Duke's arrival in Portugal, and two days after the public announcement of his Bahamas governorship –

[5] I have tried to unravel these complexities in *Operation Willi*; the account here is necessarily very abbreviated.

Ribbentrop sent an extraordinary telegram to Stohrer, his Ambassador in Madrid, to say that he urgently wanted the Duke brought back from Portugal to Spain,[6] but that it was 'decisive for the success of such a plan that our interest should in no way become known'. Some pretext had therefore to be found to lure the Windsors across the frontier without their realizing that they would not be going back. Perhaps some of their Spanish friends could invite them for a visit; if that failed, perhaps the Spanish authorities might be persuaded to warn the Duke that there was a British plot to assassinate him, and that he should flee to Spain for his own safety. 'After their return to Spain', continued the German Foreign Minister, 'the Duke and Duchess must be persuaded or compelled to remain on Spanish soil.' If the Duke proved uncooperative, the Spanish would have to imprison him as 'a deserting military refugee'. At any rate, once the Duke was safely in Spain under German control and unable to leave, he would be told

> . . . that Germany wants peace with the English people, that the Churchill clique stands in the way of that peace, and that it would be a good thing if the Duke were to hold himself in readiness for further developments. Germany is determined to force England to peace by every means of power, and upon this happening would be prepared to pave the way for the granting of any wish expressed by the Duke, especially with a view to the assumption of the English throne by the Duke and Duchess. Should the Duke have other plans, but still be prepared to cooperate in the restoration of good relations between England and Germany, we would likewise be prepared to assure him and his wife an existence which would enable him, either as a private citizen or in some other position, to lead a life suitable for a king.

On receipt of this telegram, Stohrer (who was in fact a secret oppositionist to Hitler) consulted Ramon Serrano Suñer, Franco's powerful brother-in-law who was Spanish Interior Minister. The two men were close friends, and although sceptical about the plot they decided to play it for all it was worth in the hope that it would

---

[6] The Portuguese secret police were protecting the Duke during his stay in that country, while the Spanish authorities were strongly pro-German. It was only in Spain, therefore, that the Duke could be brought under German power.

induce Ribbentrop to shelve another scheme to which they were both opposed – that of dragging Spain, exhausted after her Civil War, into a military alliance with Germany. With a view to getting the Windsors to return to Spain as the German Foreign Minister wished, they arranged for a Spanish Government emissary to be sent out to the Duke in Portugal. The man chosen for this mission was Miguel Primo de Rivera, a somewhat lightweight character from a famous Spanish family who held the post of Civil Governor of Madrid and happened to be the oldest Spanish friend of the Duke of Windsor.

Primo de Rivera visited the Windsors at Cascais, and begged them to slip over to Spain in order that they might receive from the Spanish government an urgent message concerning their personal safety. By an unhappy coincidence, this suggestion came at exactly the moment that the Duke was in the midst of his quarrel with the British government over the preparations for his Bahamas governorship, when he was writing to Churchill that he had been 'messed around long enough', and to Allen that he was suffering from 'profound gloom and despondency' and 'sorely tempted . . . to retire from the contest'. He therefore seems to have taken Primo de Rivera's plea more seriously than he might otherwise have done. After the emissary's return, Stohrer telegraphed to Ribbentrop that

> The Duke expressed himself most freely. He felt almost a prisoner and surrounded by spies etc. Politically the Duke has moved further and further away from the King and the present English Government. The Duke and Duchess do not fear the King, who is utterly stupid, as much as the clever Queen, who is constantly intriguing against the Duke and particularly the Duchess.

The Duke and Duchess had been 'extraordinarily interested' in the information about their security possessed by the Spanish Government; and although the emissary had been unable to tell them anything definite about it they had said that they 'very much desired to return to Spain'. Their fears that they might be interned in Spain had been dispelled by the emissary, who assured them that the Spanish authorities would allow them to reside freely in the south of the country. This report is a biased and suspect document, drafted with a view to telling its recipient what he wanted to hear; yet Stohrer had to admit to Ribbentrop that, when Primo de Rivera, 'knowing nothing of any German interest in the matter', asked 'on his own account' whether the Duke 'might yet be destined to play a large part in English politics and even to ascend the English throne, both the Duke and Duchess seemed astonished. Both seemed completely enmeshed in conventional ways of thinking, for they replied that under the English constitution this would not be possible after the Abdication.'

Receiving this news, Ribbentrop decided to press ahead with his plan, all the more so since that same day (23 July) the British government, in the form of a broadcast by the Foreign Secretary, Lord Halifax, had categorically rejected Hitler's demand for a negotiated peace. It was decided to send a second Spanish government emissary out to the Windsors to organize their flight to Spain, and at the same time to dispatch a German secret agent to the Peninsula to ensure that this flight succeeded and that they found their way into the hands of German commandos who, as they could hardly have suspected, would be waiting for them across the frontier. The Spaniard (who was to meet the Duke) was a civil servant and Abwehr agent called Angel Alcázar de Velasco, and the German (who would be operating secretly behind the scenes) a senior SD officer called Walter Schellenberg. When these two arrived in Portugal on 26 July, however, they soon discovered that the Duke had abandoned the idea of going to Spain, if indeed he had ever really had it. That it had never been a serious intention is suggested by the fact that the whole time he had carried on with his preparations for the Bahamas. By now his quarrel with the British Government, in the form of a broadcast by the Foreign Secretary, Lord Halifax, had categorically rejected Hitler's demand for a him of the dangers which surrounded him and stress the need for prompt departure. In his report, Alcázar de Velsaco stated that the Duke definitely wished to proceed to the Bahamas, and believed that 'no prospect of peace existed at the moment', though he had 'nevertheless given consideration to the possibility that the role of an intermediary might fall to him' at some future date.

This last remark, though it may not have meant anything very much, further encouraged Ribbentrop, and desperate efforts were made to prevent the Windsors sailing from Lisbon, which they were due to do in two days' time. Schellenberg staged a series of frightening incidents designed to increase their already considerable sense of insecurity; and the idea of abducting the Duke was considered by the Germans, though finally thought 'inadvisable . . . in view of the political designs we have with regard to him'. Various neutral friends – the Spanish Ambassador to Lisbon, Primo de Rivera again, and the Duke's Portuguese host – urged him up to the last moment not to leave Europe for the sake of the British Empire and himself; but Monckton was on hand to nullify their exhortations, and the most the Duke ever did was to suggest in a roundabout way that, although it was his duty to go out to the Bahamas, he might in the event of disaster befalling his country consider returning to try to mitigate her misfortunes. This further hopeful but insubstantial hint may have saved him from capture; and he and the Duchess departed safely on 1 August 1940 aboard *Excalibur*, the ship by which they had always intended to travel, arriving in the Bahamas on 17 August.

Chapter Seven

The Bahamas
1940–43

*T*he Bahama Islands (from the Spanish *bajamar*, the shallow seas) consist of a coral archipelago some 400 miles long, lying north of Cuba and south-east of Florida. They are blessed with a pleasant winter climate and fine sandy beaches, but very little else; in particular, unlike the lush volcanic islands of the Caribbean group, they are infertile, the harsh, porous limestone sustaining little agriculture. The Spanish were the first Europeans to arrive there – Columbus' first American landfall was on the island of San Salvador on 12 October 1492 – but they had no use for so arid a place and abandoned it after carrying off the native Arawaks as slaves. The Bahamas were then virtually forgotten until the late seventeenth century, when they became the principal base of the English pirates who waylaid the Spanish treasure ships bound for the rich colonies of Cuba and Hispaniola. It was not until 1717 that the British Crown reluctantly moved in to bring these vagabonds (who supported the Jacobite pretender) under control. Although the pirates accepted the rule of the Crown Governor, they did so reluctantly and sullenly; and the whole history of the Colony from beginning to end was one of struggle between the Governor's administration and the tough local white settlers, who resented being ruled from London at all.

By the time the Duke of Windsor arrived as Governor on 17 August 1940, the Bahamas remained one of the most backward and difficult to govern of all territories in the British Colonial Empire. Its population was a mere 70,000 of which about 60,000 were negroes or men of mixed race (descended from slaves imported in the late eighteenth century) and 30,000 lived on the principal island of New

Providence, which was eighty square miles in extent and included the capital of Nassau. The economy depended entirely on the reputation of New Providence as a smart winter resort for rich visitors from the American mainland – but this reputation was extremely recent, being largely the personal work of the last Governor but one, the jolly and aristocratic Sir Bede Clifford (1932–37). Before that, the main economic activity had been bootlegging during the years of American Prohibition.

For all practical purposes, the colony had been run for more than a century by an avaricious mafia of white Nassau merchants known as 'the Bay Street Boys' (Bay Street being the main thoroughfare of the capital running parallel to the shore). These men, brutal and independent, were the true heirs of the original pirate settlers. Using gangster methods in elections, they completely controlled the local legislature, the House of Assembly, which in turn controlled the colony's purse strings. As the Bay Street bosses made most of their money importing food and drink (and the House raised its revenue from levying duties on these imports), it was in their interest to keep the agriculture of the islands as primitive as possible. They were also a racial élite whose power depended on the blacks being kept firmly in their place, and they rigidly enforced the colour bar (which was stronger in the Bahamas than in any other British colony), opposing all measures designed to promote the social betterment of the majority. The Colonial Office, with its reformist intentions, was always regarded by them as the enemy. According to Sir Alan Burns, who served in the Bahamas in the 1920s with the rank of colonial secretary, the Governor had little real authority,

> . . . only the power of veto and such executive powers as he can exercise without money, or with such sums of money as he may be entrusted by a reluctant and suspicious legislature. . . . It was in the Bahamas that I realised, more than in any other Colony in which I served, the local hostility to the imported official. . . . The House of Assembly refuses to increase the salaries of officials, hoping that if they are kept low enough no one will want to accept the appointments. . . . This policy places the civil service at the mercy of the legislature. . . . The Secretary of State has the greatest difficulty in filling these posts in the Bahamas. . . . If in the circumstances one half of the officials prove to be successful in their posts, the Colony is more lucky than it deserves. . . .

The Duke's predecessor as Governor, Sir Charles Dundas, had
tried in vain to do something about this lamentable situation. He
sought to stimulate agriculture in the Out Islands (islands other
than New Providence, all primitive and impoverished) by granting
large farming estates to enterprising pioneers from Europe and
America: these efforts were consistently sabotaged by local interests.
He attempted to break the power of Bay Street by introducing
legislation for an income tax and secret voting in elections. Both of
these measures were thrown out by the House of Assembly, and such
was its hatred of the Governor that, when war was declared in
September 1939, it refused to pass the Trading with the Enemy Act
and other vital legislation, which had to be brought into force by
Order in Council. A serious constitutional crisis was only averted by
Dundas's sudden removal in July 1940 to make way for the Duke.

Bay Street greeted the news of the Duke's appointment with
incredulity and delight. Their pockets were now filled by the profits
of American tourism, and nothing would do more to stimulate this
than the presence of the glamorous ex-King and his American wife at
Government House. But they were not prepared to tolerate from
him, any more than from his predecessor, any programme of
economic or social reform. As Sir Harry Oakes, the legendary Canadian gold millionaire who was the Bahamas' richest resident,
remarked:

> He will learn . . . that the best way to govern the Bahamas is not to
> govern the Bahamas at all. If he sticks to golf he will be a good
> Governor and they'll put up statues to him. But if he tries to carry
> out reforms or make any serious decisions or help the niggers he
> will just stir up trouble and make himself unpopular.

Being four thousand miles from Europe, and the British colony
nearest to the still-neutral United States, the Bahamas seemed very
distant from the war in the summer of 1940. There was no conscrip-
tion, the U-boat menace in the Atlantic was not yet serious, and
censorship and security measures remained perfunctory. The previous winter Nassau had enjoyed a successful tourist season, and the
coming season, thanks to the Windsors, would be even more successful. It was entirely open to the Duke to 'stick to golf' and regard

himself as a mere figurehead; but this was not the course he chose. As soon as he grasped the political situation, he resolved that something must be done.

On arrival in Nassau, the Duke telegraphed to Lord Lloyd, his new chief in London: 'Many thanks for your message of welcome and good wishes on my arrival in the Bahamas. The Duchess and I have been most cordially welcomed here, and we look forward to helping Bahamians in their various problems and industries.' The Windsors' first reactions, however, were those of discomfort and depression. They came in mid-August, when the heat and humidity are suffocating; and they discovered that their residence, Government House on Prospect Ridge, was in a near-derelict state. It was customary for the Governor of the Bahamas to spend the summer on the mainland, and the Duke asked if he might retire for a few weeks to his ranch in Canada. This request Lloyd refused, wishing to keep the Duke out of America at least until after the presidential elections in November. After a few days the Windsors moved out of Government House, and for the rest of the year they lived in private houses rented from British residents of the Colony. Meanwhile Government House was rebuilt with the aid of £5,000 reluctantly voted by the House of Assembly; the interior redecoration the Windsors paid for themselves.

Coming straight from war-torn Europe, they also experienced a violent culture shock at the backwardness, placidity and parochialism of Nassau. The Duchess's letters to her Aunt Bessie that late summer and autumn give an idea of their private impressions:

31 August 1940: As you have been to Nassau I don't have to describe it to you. In fact you described it to me and you were right! . . . I can't get used to being so far from the war. Although one has to go where one is told in wartime I really would have preferred air raids in England . . . to feeling so absolutely far away. . . . After having had a taste of it for six months one gets wrapped up in the war. To come to a place which gives no idea of war makes me quite restless. I even miss air raid sirens – the nearest thing here is the twelve o'clock whistle. . . .

The Bahamas

16 September 1940: The heat is *awful.* I long for some air that isn't caused by electric fans. . . . I hate this place more each day. . . .

7 October 1940: Where did you stay when you came to this dump and why did you come here?

25 October 1940: One might as well be in London with all the bombs and excitement and not buried alive here. . . .

21 November 1940: We both hate it and the locals are petty-minded, the visitors common and uninteresting. . . .

Under the circumstances it was natural, in their heart of hearts, that the Windsors should come to see their appointment to the Bahamas as a banishment to a backwater as a result of family vindictiveness. Two months after taking up his post, the Duke relieved his anguish by drafting (but not sending) a long letter of protest to Winston Churchill. It begins with a sober recital of the many personal and practical difficulties he was experiencing in his post, but ends on a passionate and bitter note.

In time of war, and more especially just now that Great Britain is subjected to intensive bombing attacks and threatened with invasion, and when the fortitude and behaviour of her populace in the face of these onslaughts are the admiration of the whole world, I would generally regard it as a man's duty to accept without complaint whatever the appointment he was given. There are however even in moments of national danger always exceptional cases where a man would be doing a disservice to his country's cause were he not honest enough to bring to the notice of the Government the fact that he is 'a square peg in a round hole' or sufficiently frank in giving his reasons for such a state of affairs.

It is because I find myself in just such a predicament that I am addressing myself to you as the present head of the Government of my country in order to place certain facts before you as to why I must sooner or later tender my resignation as Governor of the Bahamas.

In the first place this appointment was offered and accepted in extraordinary circumstances. I used to have your support until you reached the supreme power of P.M. since when you seem to have subscribed to the Court's hostile attitude towards me. Due to negligence of both our military and diplomatic authorities in France I got lost in the shuffle of war and, left to my own devices to avoid capture by the enemy, I duly informed you when I had reached a neutral country. You thereupon summoned me back to England, and when I felt bound in my own interests to make my compliance with this summons contingent upon a simple and fair request which my brother evidently turned down, you threatened me with what amounted to arrest, thus descending to dictator methods in your treatment of your old friend and former King.

I will never forget that telegram which you sent me via Madrid and which I received in Lisbon, nor can I describe my surprise upon my going to the Embassy the next morning to find another telegram offering me the Governorship of the Bahamas. I am inclined to think that the offer of this job was an impulsive gesture and that you did not stop to bring your experienced mind to bear on the consequences. That the appointment is a mistake from every angle is patently clear to me after two months in Nassau.

As a member of the Royal Family, I have been raised under the protective wing of successive British Governments. Now I find myself in a post in which the tables are reversed for, as one of my officials explained to me the other day, he had been brought up by the Colonial Office to regard the position of Governor as protection for the Secretary of State in all matters of policy affecting the colony to which he was appointed administrator.

That in itself at once constitutes a problem for me, for having been taught all my life to avoid controversial matters, I am now expected to hand out the instructions of the S. of S. as if they were my own orders and to take all local blame for them. Needless to say, the American newspapers have made full use of this embarrassing position, for whereas an order issued by the Governor of the Bahamas was not even news, one by the Duke of Windsor is a headline.

But the most disagreeable feature of all in this place is the fact that I am being exploited in all manner of ways.

Take the colour problem, for example, which is an outstanding one in the British West Indies and the subject of an exhaustive report by the Moyne Committee in 1939. It is particularly acute in the Bahamas due to these islands' close proximity to America and the fact that local politics are controlled by the reactionary lawyers and merchants, for while they will not let up an inch, the Governor must be conciliatory without queering the pitch for the native European element. This is by no means easy to achieve and ever since my appointment was made known in July the two rival coloured newspapers have each used me as a stick to beat the other, the one proclaiming that my coming here heralded a new era of miracles for the negro population, while the other pursues a policy of criticism regarding my smallest administrative action or any slight change that I have considered it in the Colony's interest to make. This feud, which is meat to the American press, has assumed proportions which have needed drastic indirect attention, and although I think I have it in control for the moment, I could never guarantee it as fool proof.

Then another thing which makes me vulnerable for exploitation purposes is that the revenue of the Bahamas as you know depends entirely on three or four months' tourist traffic from America in the winter. It is unfortunate but it cannot be helped. For one good reason or another various attempts at raising, canning and exporting such climatically suitable agricultural produce as pineapples, tomatoes, sisal and sponges have all failed, and for better or worse the Bahamians have literally to rely on the tourist for a livelihood. For worse as it has turned out, for it has had the effect of inculcating a spirit of indolence among the coloured people who now prefer to exist for eight months on what they have been able to make out of the visitors in Nassau than to work reasonably hard all year round in the Out Islands and as likely as not earn less.

What with the Exchange and Import control operating adversely in countries not in the sterling block it is of course going to prove increasingly difficult to maintain this source of revenue up to the normal level in wartime, and local interests have already quite naturally begun to use both the Duchess and myself to boost the American tourist trade for the coming season. I will not go so far as to say that they have as yet done so in an undignified manner, and of course as Governor I have a certain amount of control. But it does not require much imagination to see how we are the draw in this down-at-heel place, and enquiries have already come from American tourist agencies as to how they can advertise to their clients the assurance that they will get a good look at us if they go to Nassau on a cruise from New York.

Here again is a definite snag, for if we do not allow ourselves to be used to a certain extent to encourage American tourists to visit the Bahamas we shall be doing the Colony a bad turn; on the other hand, it goes against the grain to play the part of 'greeter' amidst all the horrors and misery that this war inflicts and which we have seen with our own eyes, a role that has never been in our make up and a form of publicity which, while helping these islands, would obviously react very badly on ourselves at this time.

The truth of the matter is that this place is far too small to carry anyone who has been the subject of so vast an amount of publicity, good and bad, that I have. While the situation created by my being sent here is merely very unpleasant so far as I am concerned, it is in my opinion reacting to the detriment of the Colony's interests as a whole, and they will never, poor people, be able to take the fierce glare of the spotlights that have quite accidentally been suddenly switched on to them.

Last but by no means least, I am up against the famous Court ruling published in the Gazette the last days of May 1937, a few days before our wedding, whereby the King (or shall we say the Queen?) decreed that the Duchess shall not hold Royal Rank. I will admit to being apprehensive of the possible effect of this difference in our official status on our position in a small community like this British Colony; but somehow I felt that, in view of the gravity of the war situation, this chronic insult to my wife might well be overcome if not entirely lost in the vast changes that are taking place before our eyes.

But NO! The Colonial Office had to circulate instructions, with the approval of the Lord Chamberlain, before we had even sailed from Europe, on the official etiquette to be observed regarding the Duchess and emphasising the difference of her rank to mine. I saw one secret telegram from the S. of S. (of 24th July) in a file on my arrival here, and it is of course available to you in Whitehall. However to save trouble here is the text.

> Secret and personal. My telegram 134 secret. You are no doubt aware that a lady when presented to H.R.H. the Duke of Windsor should make a half-curtsey. The Duchess of Windsor is not entitled to this. The Duke should be addressed as 'Your Royal Highness' and the Duchess as 'Your Grace'. Ends.

Although it is irrelevant, I cannot but hold it to a certain extent against those whom I regarded as my friends not to have warned me at the time of the Abdication of the way in which Great Britain can treat their public servants once they have been discarded; I might then have been able to safeguard myself from the mean and petty humiliations with which a now semi-Royal Family with the cooperation of the Government has indulged itself over the past four years. But you must not for one instant infer from this that the Duchess has the least desire ever to be considered a member of my family after the way they have behaved to both of us. I only include it in this letter as a final illustration of the unsuitability of my holding this appointment, and I am quite sure that had your wife been the target of the vindictive jealousy of a few royal women you would have the same repugnance to service under the Crown that I have – war or no war.

This eloquent and despairing letter enables us to peer into the Duke's mind at the outset of his governorship; but it was drafted merely to let off steam.[1] He never sent it; and such anguished feelings were kept entirely to himself. Outwardly, indeed, both the Windsors devoted themselves cheerfully and uncomplainingly to their official duties. The Duchess immersed herself in the local Red Cross and war charities, while the Duke learned the administrative ropes of governorship.

Almost at once, he made it clear that he meant to be a reformer and was prepared to take on the local establishment. 'As regards these islands,' he wrote to his friend Philip Guedalla on 15 October, 'we have already discovered a host of problems which require immediate attention. Unfortunately the House of Assembly, which votes the money, is in the hands of the unscrupulous merchants of Bay Street, and they are a very tough nut to crack.' Speaking at an open-air ceremony of welcome only six days after his arrival, and proroguing the House of Assembly a week after that, he spoke approvingly of his predecessor's policy of promoting agriculture in the Out Islands and advancing the social welfare of the majority. He had his first clash with Bay Street that September when, appalled at local unemployment outside the tourist season, he proposed the establishment of a Labour Department and was bluntly told by the local bosses that the necessary funds would never be voted by the House. When he asked Lloyd whether he might raise the money for this vital reform through his emergency wartime powers, his request was tactfully but firmly refused. 'I am of course aware of the attitude the House of Assembly has adopted in the past', wrote the Secretary of State, 'but am confident that as time goes on Your Royal

---

[1] Drafting strongly worded letters to people in authority which he never intended to send became something of a habit of the Duke's during these difficult years as a means of working off his frustrations. In February 1941 he wrote to Beaverbrook: 'I am quite decided that I must not only relinquish this appointment in the Bahamas but cannot accept any other post under the Crown so long as Queen Elizabeth holds her sway.'

Highness's personal influence will steadily wax and by biding your time you will get them to agree.'[2]

On 29 October 1940 – only ten weeks after his arrival – the Duke opened the new session of the Legislature in Nassau with a vigorous speech in which he made clear his reformist intentions. He spoke again with approval of the policy of his detested predecessor to revive local agriculture. And he continued by stating the policy which he evidently meant to make his own:

> I have been giving special thought to a problem which confronts all governments, namely unemployment. . . . It would be foolish to adopt an attitude of complacency in this matter and a policy of hoping for the best. . . . In my opinion it is essential that some form of central organisation be set up to take care of any serious shortage of employment the moment it arises, and with this in mind I hope after careful personal investigation to submit a concrete scheme for you to consider during the forthcoming session. In the meantime I am taking steps to appoint an Advisory Board to consider wages in relation to the cost of living.

This determination to improve the economic lot of the black population created a deep impression. John Dye, the United States Consul in Nassau, wrote in his dispatch to the State Department:

> The speech is one of the most sensible and business-like that has been delivered by a Governor for many years. It . . . indicates that the Duke is already familiar with local conditions and has a determination to improve those conditions. . . . It may be true that he and his Duchess were sent out here to get rid of them, so to speak, but he is taking his job seriously and is showing a keen interest in the welfare of the Bahamas.

---

[2] This advice proved to be over-optimistic. The Duke laid urgent proposals for a Department of Labour before the House in the autumn of 1940, the winter of 1941 and the winter of 1942: on each occasion the House voted them down. As a consequence of the lack of organized labour relations, serious rioting occurred in June 1942 (see pp. 195 ff). A year later the Duke laid his proposal before the House for a fourth time. Again it was thrown out, but this time the Duke did what he had wished to do three years earlier and raised the money through his emergency powers (14 September 1943), the only time they were ever used.

For the Windsors, one of the few advantages of the Bahamas was its proximity to the United States, which they greatly looked forward to visiting. The Duke had not been there since 1927, while the Duchess had seen nothing of her native land since 1933. It was customary for the Governor of the Bahamas to spend much time on the mainland, and to exchange regular friendly visits with the Mayor of Miami, a city only 180 miles distant from Nassau. Moreover, only two weeks after the Windsors' arrival a situation arose whereby the Duke would have official business in future with the American authorities. Under the Anglo-American Agreement of 2 September 1940, the United States offered Great Britain fifty destroyers in return for the right to set up bases in a number of British West Atlantic territories – including the Bahamas.

Upon accepting his appointment, the Duke had been told that he could not visit America before the Presidential elections in November. On the fifth of that month, President Roosevelt was re-elected by a comfortable majority; but still the Colonial Office would not give the Duke permission to leave his territory. 'I think we are fated never to go to America,' wrote the Duchess to her aunt. 'Great Britain hates the idea of us going, because you know the Duke is an independent thinker and they don't want him to open his mouth. Also Lothian [the British Ambassador to Washington] is controlled by Nancy Astor – as you know, an arch-enemy of ours – and L. will advise against coming on account of the press. That will be the excuse. . . .'

No doubt the fear that the Duke might let fall some chance remark which would encourage the American isolationists was part of the reason for the official reluctance to allow a visit: but, as the Duke saw it, the main reason was that the British authorities simply did not want him to enjoy any kind of popular success. He was outraged to discover from contacts with newspaper bosses that the American press was basically favourable to him but acted on unfavourably slanted information supplied by the British Embassy in Washington. On 15 October, the Duke wrote bitterly to Philip Guedalla that

> . . . we have ample evidence of their activities on this side of the Atlantic, and the persecution of the Windsors goes on relentlessly. We know from reliable sources that they more or less control news

regarding ourselves in America, and that they go so far as to encourage any lousy publicity, and that disgraceful and libellous lies are rife even in Washington. I have good reason to believe that the latter emenate [*sic*] from the FO; at any rate, the British Embassy has taken no steps to deny them. . . . However, who knows that this appointment in the Bahamas, in itself the end so far as we are concerned, may, on the other hand, prove to be the first opportunity we have as yet had to frustrate their game and change the unfavourable atmosphere that over four years of intensive pernicious British propaganda has created for us in the United States. . . .

The Windsors were to visit the mainland sooner than they thought. In the late autumn of 1940 the Duchess had some serious dental trouble and was advised by the Nassau dentists, who lacked the facilities to operate on her, to go into hospital in Miami. The Duke asked for a week's leave to accompany her there; to his surprise and relief, the request was agreed to with alacrity. The reasons for this indulgence were extraordinary, however. President Roosevelt was planning a West Indian cruise in USS *Tuscaloosa* to inspect the proposed American base sites under the Destroyers–Bases Agreement; and he had told Lord Lothian that he hoped the Duke would join him on his ship as it passed through Bahamian waters. When Lothian reported this to the Foreign Office, the reaction was almost hysterical. The meeting was one which the British Government 'was not anxious in any way to encourage', and Lothian was to use every means 'to discourage the President from pursuing his idea about meeting the Duke of Windsor, who has been left in ignorance of the suggestion'. When Roosevelt persisted in his idea, the Duke's request for leave seemed too good an opportunity to miss. Roosevelt would be sailing through the Bahamas on 12 and 13 December; the Duke was therefore given permission to absent himself from the Colony from the 9th to the 14th. 'There is now presumably no physical possibility of a meeting,' wrote the Foreign Office to Lothian with satisfaction. Through a mix-up with official telegrams the Duke did in fact discover the deception before his departure – but too late to change his plans, and there was nothing to do but make the best of their first trip to America, mere hospital visit that it was.

The Foreign Office need have had no fears about the effect of the

Duke in the United States. This was how the British Consul-General in Florida, James Marjoribanks, later remembered the visit.

> To be frank, there had been some doubt in official circles about how things would go. Britain was at war; the US was not. Would the American press highlight the Duke on the golf course? I think he, as an ace operator, may have had a round or two during the hurried official schedule. But the pictures I remember from this and other visits were of conversations with factory hands, visits to RAF trainees. He never missed a chance to perform some act of public relations in aid of the British war effort. On one occasion I remember him addressing in Spanish a group of fifty South American businessmen whom he ran into by chance in the company of Mr Orr, Mayor of Miami – whose obvious delight in his guests contributed to the general euphoria. The Duke and Duchess took everything in their stride. A holiday atmosphere prevailed; Britain's stock soared with the advent to Miami of our former monarch. I remember recording in my despatch to the Foreign Office that the visit had been 'a success from every point of view'. This was no exaggeration.

On 12 December, while the Duchess was still in hospital recovering from her operation, the Duke received two extraordinary items of news. The first was of the sudden death of Lord Lothian, the Ambassador to Washington; the second was an unexpected but welcome invitation from Roosevelt, whose ship was now off the Bahamian island of Mayaguana, and who offered to fly the Duke out there on a United States Navy seaplane so that their meeting might take place after all. The Duke gladly accepted this offer, and spent five hours with the President on board *Tuscaloosa*, lunching and talking. It has been alleged that he went out to see the President by way of an intrigue to obtain for himself the now vacant Washington Embassy; but there is no evidence for this. The meeting was entirely at the prompting of Roosevelt himself, who was fascinated to meet the man who had given up his throne for love; they were to meet many times during the war and to become friends. The Duke did not expect or want the Washington post, with its immense political responsibilities. But, having just witnessed with satisfaction the beneficial effect that his presence had in America, he would certainly have liked to help his country there in the sphere of public relations; and he hoped that the new ambassador would be more friendly to him than his predecessor.

In this he was to be disappointed. The man chosen was the Foreign Secretary, Lord Halifax, a traditionalist and fierce High Anglican who had been a leading member of the Baldwin cabinet at the time of the Abdication Crisis. He was a friend of the King, who would have preferred him to Churchill as Prime Minister; and (though he remained a titular member of the War Cabinet) Churchill was no doubt relieved at the opportunity to get him out of the way. Though an astute politician, he was never popular in the United States, unlike the Duke of Windsor, with whom he had little sympathy.

When the Windsors returned to Nassau on 14 December 1940 after their five days in Miami, the refurbished Government House was at last ready for their occupation, and preparations were under way in the colony for the winter tourist season. Inevitably, this was to be the best the Bahamas had ever known. Twenty thousand people came over from the mainland, as opposed to fourteen thousand the winter before, and the amount of dollars spent increased by one-half. This was due to the glamorous presence of the Royal Governor and his American Duchess at Government House. As we have seen, they did not relish their role as the mascots of a tourist paradise. The Duchess had written that she would rather face bombs in England than be 'buried alive' in the Bahamas, the Duke that the 'role of greeter' went 'against the grain' in wartime. They nevertheless did what was expected of them. Although they entertained prominent visitors at their new residence, they refused all social invitations except those to events which were in aid of war charities – and the funds raised on these occasions were impressive.

The financial success of the season only intensified the Duke's desire to make the Bahamas less reliant on tourism and to foster other forms of economic life. At the end of March he and the Duchess made an important tour by sea of the Out Islands to see what could be done to improve their wretched agriculture and give employment to their languishing populations: it was the first time a governor had ever made such a voyage. In order to alleviate the worst hardships, he set up a 'Bahamas Assistance Fund', to which he made over the income from a charitable trust he had founded as Prince of Wales. This was run by the Duchess, who showed extraordinary energy and powers of organization in her charitable work in the Bahamas, where she also took charge of the Red Cross and set up two infant welfare clinics to cope with Nassau's appalling infant mortality problem.

Charity was one thing, reform another. That summer the Duke presented his programme to the House – and one measure after another was resoundingly defeated by the Bay Street caucus. He asked for a programme of public works (which he had already worked out to the last detail) to relieve unemployment: this was thrown out on second reading. He asked for a rise in the standard wage to offset the huge rise since the war's beginning in the cost of food: this was referred to a select committee, who rejected it. Finally he asked for a package of measures to stimulate Out Island agricultural projects, notably a waiver of Customs duties on the importation of farming machinery: this too was refused. The Duke felt angry and frustrated at the endless obstruction to his plans; biding his time, he resolved to take the offensive against the Bay Street Boys and find some means of reducing their power.

True to form, the House also refused to grant adequate funds to safeguard the colony against enemy attack. Nevertheless, the Duke devoted much time to security preparations in 1941. He had been made uncomfortably aware that 'a U-boat suddenly appearing off this island could easily shell the cable and wireless station and carry off the entire occupants of Government House before anyone realised the island was being attacked'; in particular, after Rudolf Hess's flight to England in May he was concerned that he might be kidnapped by the Nazis and held as a hostage against Hess's release. But it was not until the following year that the British government responded to his entreaties and sent a company of crack troops to garrison Nassau.

Following the success of 'tooth week' in Miami, the Windsors were hopeful that they would at last be allowed to make a tour of the mainland in the spring of 1941, once the Nassau season was over. At their meeting in December, Roosevelt had invited the Royal Governor to visit the camps of the Civilian Conservation Corps he had set up in 1934 to alleviate American unemployment, and the Duke much wished to accept this, having in mind his own local projects. Halifax wrote to the Foreign Office on 14 March that, while he did not welcome such a visit, 'any overt attempt on our part to prevent it' might result in bad press publicity for Great Britain in America. It seemed that the trip would go ahead, when the Prime Minister himself took a hand. In a telegram of 18 March – the first communication to have passed between them since the summer of 1940 – he wrote to the Duke that 'after much consideration and enquiry, I have reached the conclusion that Your Royal Highness's proposed visit to the United States would not be in the public interest or your own at the present time'. The reason for this veto became clear at the end of the telegram:

> Exception is taken . . . to Your Royal Highness's recently published interview . . . of which it is said that the language . . . will be interpreted as defeatist and pro-Nazi and approving of the isolationist aim to keep America out of the war. . . . I must say it seems to me that the views attributed to Your Royal Highness have been unfortunately expressed by the journalist. . . . I could wish indeed that Your Royal Highness would seek advice before making public statements of this kind. I should always be ready to help as I used to in the past.

'We can *not* come to the U.S. in April,' wrote the Duchess to her aunt on 31 March. 'W.C. wishes us to wait a while. The Duke is in a rage. I am used to "no" so am calm. We shall now try for August and September. Only when the war stops will we regain our independence from H.M. Government. . . .'

The interview which had aroused Churchill's anger had been given in Nassau in December to the American novelist Fulton Oursler, and published in the magazine *Liberty* on 12 March – six days prior to the dispatch of the admonishing telegram. Read today it sounds very harmless. Though his interlocutor evidently held isolationist sympathies, the Duke did little more than ask polite questions and utter platitudes. This was the passage to which the Prime Minister took exception:

> The Duke heaved a sigh.
> [Duke:] 'Is there much sentiment for your going in [to the war]?'

[Interviewer:] 'Some for it, a great deal against it. . . .'

[Duke:] 'Do you think there is ever such a thing in modern war as victory?'

[Interviewer:] 'I am inclined to doubt it. . . . The Germans might say there will always be a Germany so long as one German remains alive.'

[Duke:] 'And you can't execute the death sentence on 80,000,000 people?'

[Interviewer:] 'That is what I mean. . . .'

[Duke:] 'Do you think he [Hitler] will be overthrown from within . . .?'

[Interviewer:] 'No I do not. I think they have him because they want him. . . .'

[Duke:] 'I agree with that. . . .'

The Duke replied indignantly to the Prime Minister on 19 March. He had received Oursler on the recommendation of President Roosevelt's personal secretary, and most of the views expressed in the articles had been put into his mouth. Anyway, what could London expect when they dumped him in the Bahamas and did not even allow him an official to help him deal with a sensationalist American press to which he was constantly exposed? 'My first six months here have been spent doing my utmost to strengthen Anglo-American relations and I think I have had some success with prominent American business men and others. Now you say it would not be in the public interest or indeed my own to visit America. Personally I do not share this view and . . . if your message infers that I am more of a detriment than an asset to these vital relations then I would prefer to resign.'

Churchill returned to the Duke in this heated telegraphic exchange the following day.

. . . The article in LIBERTY which has not been repudiated by Your Royal Highness gives the impression and can indeed only bear the interpretation of contemplating a negotiated peace with Hitler. That is not the policy of His Majesty's Government; nor is it the policy of the Government and vast majority of the people of the United States, where there is a very fierce and passionate feeling rising. . . . Later on when the atmosphere is less electric, when the issues are more clear-cut and when perhaps Your Royal Highness's public utterances . . . are more in harmony with the dominant tides of British and American feeling, I think that an agreeable visit for you both might be arranged. Meanwhile in this sad time of sacrifice and suffering it is not I think much to ask that deference be shown to the advice and wishes of His Majesty's Government and of Your Royal Highness's friends, among whom I have always tried to play my part.

In a further telegram of 27 March, the Duke protested bitterly to Churchill against these insinuations. He could not understand how his visit to America might be harmful, for he had been 'able to handle the hordes of reporters in Miami last December when our visit was most dignified and no harm was done to British interests that I am aware'. Any repudiation of the unfortunate article would 'only serve to attract attention and publicity. Besides, were I to hold views at complete variance with your policies I would use more direct means of expressing them.' And since the Prime Minister attached such importance to American magazine articles the Duke wished him to know 'that I strongly resent and take great exception to an article in . . . LIFE entitled THE QUEEN, in which the latter is quoted as referring to the Duchess as "that woman". I understand that articles about the Royal Family are censored in Britain before release and this remark is a direct insult to my wife. . . .' As for Churchill's parting thrust:

It is not necessary for you to remind me of the sacrifices and sufferings that are being endured by the people of Great Britain. Had my simple request conveyed to you by Sam Hoare been granted by my brother, I would have been proud to share these sad and critical times with my countrymen. I have both enjoyed and valued your friendship in the past but after the tone of your recent messages to me I find it difficult to believe that you are still the friend you used to be.

Three months passed without further communication. Finally the Duke (who now hoped to visit America in the autumn) pocketed his pride and wrote Churchill a mild, conciliatory, almost pathetic letter. This letter, dated 30 June 1941, is very different from the one of spirited protest the Duke had drafted nine months previously but never sent. It is strenuous in its desire to assure the Prime Minister of its author's loyalty and good behaviour and determination to carry on in the Bahamas, and its tone is one of sadness and resignation.

'I have long hesitated in disturbing you with a letter,' the Duke began, 'knowing that the momentous task you have undertaken leaves you with little time for other thoughts.' He had come to accept that 'my banishment to these islands was as good a wartime expedient for a hopeless and insoluble situation as could be found'. He could hardly be expected to like it, however, for it implied one of two things. 'Either that my services are not rated very high by any British Government or that I have the same Court clique to thank for keeping me out of my country. I hope the latter is the correct conclusion. . . .' Nevertheless, he was 'prepared to carry on here so long as I can conscientiously feel that I am pulling as much of my weight as this restricted appointment allows'. He had hoped, all the same, that Churchill would have made his position easier by getting the King to grant royal rank to the Duchess, 'and so put an end to a situation in which I am sure you would not allow your wife to be placed'.

The Duke referred to their 'lively exchange of telegrams' during March, and assured the Prime Minister of his loyalty and discretion. 'I think you know me well enough to realise that as long as I hold an official position, I play the game of the Government that appointed me. . . .' He then asked for permission to go to America that autumn. He had official business to transact on the Colony's behalf in Washington, and wanted to visit his ranch in Canada.

> I need hardly say how much I would welcome your consent and help regarding this trip. It would indeed be difficult for me to explain to my Executive Council that I was virtually a prisoner here, and could not go to Washington on the business of the Colony. I want to assure you that I have no idea of making any utterances, public or private, that are not in line with your policy. Indeed, I have no desire to make any speeches outside the Bahamas or to discuss politics. . . . That I leave to Lord Halifax. . . . I only wish you would do something to dispel this atmosphere of suspicion that has been created around me, for there is a good deal more I could do to help on this side of the Atlantic. . . .

In his colony, the Duke concluded, 'one naturally feels very out of touch with all that is happening in Great Britain. . . . Amongst the few high spots to which we are treated in Nassau are your radio addresses, which the Duchess and I invariably make the occasion for a small gathering of our friends to listen in. We hope you and Mrs Churchill are standing up to the great strain; the welcomes we see you receiving are most inspiring.'

'We have written to London about a trip to America', the Duchess wrote to her aunt, 'and it remains to be seen if the naughty boy is allowed to leave Nassau.' Receiving the Duke's letter, Churchill relented. On 16 July he wrote the following minute to the Foreign Secretary and the Colonial Secretary:

> I see no reason why the Duke of Windsor should not towards the end of September visit Canada and the United States if he so desires. Such a request would not be denied to any Governor of Nassau. . . . I presume he would go to New York where he would stay at a hotel rather than with Society people and do any shopping which the Duchess may require. Thereafter they would go to the EP Ranch of which I expect they would soon tire and after that return via Washington where the President has promised to give them a luncheon. . . . There is no reason why this tour should not be worked out and everything done for the comfort and honour of the former King-Emperor and his wife. But all must be planned beforehand.

❧

The Windsors' first mainland tour lasted six weeks, from 25 September to 7 November 1941. Apart from the ten days of genuine holiday they spent on the Duke's ranch in Canada, a hilly and isolated spot in the Alberta prairies, they visited Washington, where they lunched with the President; Maryland, where the Duchess saw her own family for the first time in eight years; and New York. Everywhere they were greeted by huge and enthusiastic crowds. In Washington the crowds were far larger than those which had welcomed the King and Queen on their state visit in June 1939, and in Baltimore where the Duchess had spent her childhood she was mobbed by her own people. Owing to the fact that the Duke's uncle Lord Athlone, the Governor-General of Canada, refused to receive the Duchess, their journey to Alberta did not follow the usual rail route through Winnipeg and Ottawa, but crossed the American Mid-West, which was notoriously isolationist and anti-British. Here if anywhere the Windsors might have been expected to receive a lukewarm, perhaps hostile reception: but even in Chicago, the home of isolationism and of the anglophobe *Chicago Tribune*, their welcome was rapturous.

The United States, while giving the Allies 'all aid short of war', had not yet abandoned neutrality; and the Windsors went visibly out of their way everywhere to do something on behalf of the British war effort. The Duke presented wings to Canadian pilots, visited wounded British merchant seamen in Baltimore. In New York they spent some time with all of the many organizations involved in British war relief. Most of their itinerary was carefully controlled by the British Embassy in Washington: but the most successful episode of the whole trip, the Duke's two-day visit alone to Detroit, was unscheduled and took place against the wishes of Halifax. Even the British Press Service in New York, which circulated consistently hostile reports about the Windsors, had to admit that his tour of the factories there 'brought back memories of the Prince of Wales in his most popular days'; and it was after being visited by the Duke that Henry Ford announced that, contrary to his previous policy, he was now prepared to make arms for England.

After his first wartime meeting with the Duke in Washington, Halifax wrote to Churchill:

His [the Duke's] visit seems to have gone off all right, and not attracted too much publicity, and on the whole the press, with the exception of one or two rags, have behaved all right.

I had a long talk to him a few days ago, in which he opened his heart and talked quite freely. He feels pretty bitter about being marooned in the Bahamas, which he says is a foul climate, and where there is nobody except casual American visitors he can see anything of as a friend. I must say it certainly sounds pretty grim.

He said that he had done his best to play the game and avoid making difficulties, but that his family had not responded, and he never wanted to see them again. He meant to stick out the war in the Bahamas, but couldn't stay there for ever, and talked a bit about where he might live afterwards. France didn't look as if it was going to be very good; the . . . United States would be all right, but was very expensive!

He left pretty clearly on my mind the idea that he was not going to force himself on England again against the King's wishes,[3] but he has very little appreciation of the difficulties inherent in his position.

I told him that I thought it would be wise to give time a chance to heal the past, which it hadn't fully done yet, and that he ought to remember the danger of excessive publicity resurrecting old feelings and criticisms. He took all this very well, but of course thinks it wholly unreasonable. He spoke very nicely of you, and said he was completely happy with the most wonderful wife in the world, and certainly looked very well himself – much less nervous and much less on edge.

He is going back to the Bahamas in a week or two and I should guess that he will want to pay periodic visits to the United States, which personally I think it would be rather cruelty to animals to prevent him doing, so long as he will behave with discretion. And I think that when the ice gets well broken, his coming here will not probably attract too much attention. . . .

In fact, the Windsors' visit had been a British propaganda victory in the United States, inclining American sympathies yet further to the Allied cause. A nationwide press survey showed that 96 per cent of the hundreds of thousands of column inches concerning them had been favourable, and that most of the remaining 4 per cent came from a single, isolationist newspaper – the *New York Daily News*. But the British Press Service Report, sent to London for the guidance of the British papers, gave a very different picture: 'The general impression created was that of a rich and carefree couple, travelling with all the pre-war accoutrements of royalty, and with no thought either for the sufferings of their own people or of the fact that the world is at war.' It was evident that the Duke's desire to play a wider role in furthering Anglo-American relations would be frustrated, and that he would be allowed to gain little kudos at home from his successes abroad.

[3] On 3 March 1942, the King wrote to Halifax expressing his relief at this news, adding that he and Churchill both believed that the Duke 'having occupied the throne of this country can never live here as an ordinary citizen'. The Duke, however, did not understand this fact and it was impossible to explain it to him 'in so many words'. (Quoted in Patrick Howarth, *George VI*, Hutchinson, 1987, pp. 142–3.)

Back in Nassau in November 1941, reinvigorated by his trip abroad with all its excitement and acclamation, the Duke opened his long-prepared offensive against the Bay Street Boys, the reactionary local political caucus which controlled the House of Assembly and had frustrated his every attempt at economic and political reform. He sacked the main Bay Street figures from his Executive Council, where they regarded their positions as held by right, and replaced them by men more in tune with his own ideas. The Executive Council ('ExCo') over which the Governor presided was the Colony's main decision-making body, but depended entirely on funds voted by the House, which was now in uproar. In the hope of obtaining a legislature more favourable to him, the Duke eventually dissolved the House and ordered new elections (the Bahamas was the only British colony to have a general election in the middle of the Second World War); but such was Bay Street's stranglehold that the new chamber differed little from the last. After that his policy was to cultivate a party of his own supporters in the House by the exercise of charm, hospitality, and his control of the honours system – an aim in which he gradually succeeded as time went on.

Only a month after his return from America, however, this fierce political struggle which promised to dominate his governorship suddenly seemed to become irrelevant. For in the early hours of Sunday, 7 December 1941 the Japanese bombed Pearl Harbor, and the United States – the Bahamas' great mainland neighbour – ceased to be the world's most powerful neutral and joined the hostilities. This great event aroused all the patriotic instincts of the Duchess. 'I am glad we are going to be *in* the war,' she wrote to her aunt, 'which is better than being on the outside.'

America's entry into the world conflict plunged the Colony into darkest crisis. During the First World War, with the German submarine offensive in the Atlantic, the Bahamas had been isolated and its population reduced almost to destitution; but at least it was able to survive off a marginal local agriculture. Now agriculture had been forgotten and the Colony existed almost entirely off the profits of American tourism. The Duke wrote to George Allen:

> With Japan's unparalleled treachery and the entry of the United States into the war, the Bahamas winter tourist season dies a natural death. This Colony will have to revise its financial and

economic set-up both drastically and swiftly, and will for the first time be made to feel that there is a war. It is bad luck that the blow should come so late in the day and so near the winter season, for there is no doubt it will cause hardship among the shopkeepers and merchants and unemployment among the local coloured population. . . . However, these are only local hardships and easy to bear as compared to the lot of most other countries. . . .

Amidst all the worry of the situation, the Duke cannot have failed to experience a certain grim satisfaction. Ever since his arrival in the Bahamas he had tried in vain to persuade the House to take measures (*a*) to make the Colony productive, and (*b*) to relieve local unemployment. Now at last they would be forced to listen to him. As he wrote to a friend: 'It is now my difficult, but at the same time interesting, task as Governor to help these people save what they can from the ruins of a policy whereby the welfare of a large portion of the population was sacrificed to the benefits accruing to a few illicit and fickle industries. However, I am confident that once the local bosses realise the seriousness of the unemployment situation, and its possible consequences, I shall be able to convince them that a long term policy based on greater self-sufficiency, and even some exports, will be sounder in the end. . . .'

Before December was out he had set up a Government Board of 'all the talents', known as the Economic Investigation Committee, which was to search for every possible means of employment and production, relief and revenue. (It was, incidentally, the first official body in the Bahamas on which coloured men were substantially represented.) What he himself most wanted was to set up something along the model of Roosevelt's CCC camps which he had seen on his recent trip to America – government farms which would both alleviate unemployment and teach the skills of the land. After a few weeks, with the aid of land and buildings donated by local worthies, the services of an agricultural expert lent by the Colonial Office, and £10,000 begrudgingly voted by the House, Windsor Training Farm came into being, employing a few hundred men at three shillings a day. It was a beginning.

Then, in the early spring of 1942 and quite unexpectedly, something in the nature of a miracle arrived which promised to save the Colony from the disaster which threatened it. After Pearl Harbor the British Air Ministry in consultation with the Americans had decided to construct a series of Operational Training Units all over the Atlantic: these would both train RAF crews and play an active role in the convoy system and anti-submarine warfare. It was now decided that one of these units – 'RAF OTU III' as it was to be known – would be situated in Nassau, and that alongside it would be an important base of RAF Transport Command, ferrying men and materials across the Atlantic. The second base would be shared with the Americans, and both bases would be constructed by American contractors using local labour. The constructions (which would involve about three thousand unskilled and one thousand skilled labourers, about half the working male population of the island) were meant to be completed in six months and to be top-secret. Thus the unemployment problem would be solved, and the Colony promised a busy future as a war base. Instead of tourists, a steady stream of service personnel would keep the shops, bars and hotels of Nassau permanently busy. The American constructors arrived; on 8 May 1942 the Duke poured the first bucket of cement at 'the Project', as it was known for security reasons; and the recruitment of labour began immediately.

At the end of May, with the Project under way, the Windsors returned to America. The circumstances were very different from their previous visit eight months before, for now they went on the Duke's urgent official business (defence, supply and trade) and their journey caused little sensation or even comment, the papers having other things to write about. The moment for the trip was deliberately chosen, for the Duke wished to be absent during the elections for the new House of Assembly which were due to take place in the middle of June. Only a few hours after his arrival in Washington on 1 June 1942, however, he was astonished to receive a series of telegrams from his deputy in Nassau, Leslie Heape, reporting serious rioting by the workers on the Project, with looting and fatalities. This news was wholly unexpected. The Duke conferred with President Roosevelt and General Marshall, and the following morning returned alone to Nassau by air to sort out the situation.

The riots of June 1942 amounted to a spontaneous uprising of Nassau's black population against the rule of Bay Street; but their immediate cause lay in a misunderstanding. Under the Anglo-

American Lend-Lease treaties, projects in British territories were to be constructed by American contractors using local labour at the prevailing local rate. In the Bahamas, the standard rate for unskilled construction work had been laid down by statute in 1936 at four shillings a day. By 1942, with the wartime increase in food prices and tariffs, this was no longer a living wage, and the Duke had tried repeatedly but in vain ever since his arrival to secure either a reduction in tariffs or an increase in wages. Nevertheless, the labourers recruited for the Project would probably have been happy to accept almost any wages to be in work, except that the Americans who worked alongside them belonged to a different scale of pay entirely, and spread the rumour that the American construction company had offered to pay Bahamians the same higher wages but had been prevented from doing so by the Bahamas Government.

Still nothing would have happened, but for the fact that the Bahamas were in the midst of a general election campaign. The black candidates in the eight New Providence constituencies addressed meetings of workers, suggesting they had been cheated of their rightful pay. These men were respectable citizens, whose aim was not to cause unrest but to win votes; when on Sunday, 31 May there occurred an alarming mass demonstration for higher pay at the site of the Project, they assured the authorities that there would be no further trouble and that the men would return peacefully to work the next morning. By the time the morning came round, however, passions had been inflamed among the hungry and resentful workers, who were no longer willing to listen to their leaders. Two thousand of them decided to go on strike and march to the govern-ment offices in the main square of Nassau to put their grievances to the Colonial Secretary Leslie Heape – the genial official responsible for day-to-day administration whom the blacks regarded as their friend. They failed to realize that Heape was not there, for he was now acting for the absent Governor and had moved his office up to Government House a mile away. When the mob, armed with scythes and sticks, arrived in the square, the other officials were too terrified to come out and confront them. After half an hour, having been met by no one in authority except for the distraught police chief who shouted at them to go home but otherwise had not the faintest idea what to do, the striking workers suddenly went berserk. But they did not attack the government offices in the square. Instead, knowing who their true enemies were, they surged into Bay Street which they proceeded to sack completely, smashing every window, looting shops and offices, overturning cars. The Bay Street bosses fled for their lives, many of them heading for the open sea in boats.

Although Nassau's small and unarmed police force was inadequate to deal with the situation, a company of Cameron Highlanders was stationed two miles away and the local defence volunteers could be called out at a moment's notice. But the administration was momentarily paralysed by events which seemed incredible. The people of Nassau were renowned for their sleepy and easy-going ways, and nothing remotely like this had occurred in living memory. It was almost an hour before Heape, in response to desperate appeals from citizens, summoned the nerve to call in the troops, at the appearance of whom the mob abandoned Bay Street and fled 'over the hill' to Grant's Town – Nassau's black shanty town.

Back in their own quarter, the mob continued on the rampage, breaking into the bar rooms and getting drunk. A party of Camerons arrived on the scene, to meet with a hail of stones and rocks. A Cameron fell in a pool of blood; his comrades opened fire; seven of the crowd were hit, one fatally. The soldiers retreated. Grant's Town was now a no-go area, and the policy a desperate one of containing the mob within it. One man was killed in the curfew that night, and two the following day, when the rioters invaded the eastern suburbs of Nassau before being driven back. Meanwhile trouble of another kind was brewing, for the Bay Street Boys, confronted with the wreckage of their properties, vowed terrible vengeance not only on the blacks but also on the colonial officials, whom they blamed for allowing the outbreak to occur and for not crushing it with bloody and ruthless determination.

After a long and difficult flight marked by engine failure, the Duke returned to Nassau on the evening of the second day of the troubles; and as soon as it was known that he was back in Nassau all disorder ceased and the men returned to work. This was evidence of his awesome prestige among the black population, who had always regarded him as a saviour. He was now in a most difficult position, however. The riots had broken out because the workers had been frustrated in their search for someone in authority to whom they could express their grievances; and now that the Duke was back they expected him to deliver miracles. On the other hand, the Bay Street Boys who had suffered from the riots expected him to be brutally tough and to concede nothing.

After a week's close study of the situation and consultation with all parties, the Duke delivered, on 8 June, a masterly broadcast to the Colony. His aim, he told the Colonial Office, was to take account of the just demands of the workers and so prevent a recurrence of violence, 'without giving the impression of weakness but emphasising that further outbreak of disorders cannot be tolerated nor the way to bring grievances to my notice'. His tone was paternalistic, addressed to unruly children. 'The prospect of obtaining work for two thousand men at four shillings a day would, a few months ago, have seemed too good to be true. But this has come to pass – and yet the advent of your good fortune has been made the occasion of an *outburst* unprecedented in the history of the Bahamas in our time.' Emergency measures would remain in force, and lawbreakers would be ruthlessly hunted down and prosecuted. Contrary to what the strikers had believed, his administration had had no say in fixing wages on the Project, which had been set 'in accordance with a high policy far beyond the power of this Government to control'. Yet he saw the men's point of view. 'In the course of my preliminary investigations, I have discovered that the job is heavy and arduous and that the contractors, in view of its urgency, require it to be pursued with unremitting energy.' He had therefore decided to give the men a free meal on the job, and would return to Washington to try to negotiate a wage rise with the Anglo-American authorities. 'I have good reason to believe that I will not return empty-handed.'

This address, which conciliated the workers while announcing a tough stand on law and order, seemed to satisfy everyone for the moment – except for the Colonial Office, who criticized the Duke for making a policy speech without consulting them, vetoed his proposal to try to obtain an increase in the men's wages, and ordered him to stay where he was. After a furious exchange of telegrams, however, he obtained a free hand to deal with the troubles, and was able to procure an increase in the men's pay from four to five shillings a day. week.

There was to be no more unrest in Nassau in the 1940s. But the other trouble was about to begin. When the new House of Assembly met in September, it prepared to take its revenge on the Government. It set up a Select Committee to conduct an inquiry into the riots, summoning the Duke's officials to appear before this Committee with a view to pinning the blame on them and impeaching them. The Duke – who was now in a position of strength, since his handling of the post-riots situation had rallied both black and white public opinion to his side – refused to allow his officials to attend the House, which he upstaged by getting a reluctant Colonial Office to send out a distinguished retired judge, Sir Alison Russell, to chair an independent inquiry. When the Russell Commission reported in November, it identified the real culprits – the Bay Street Boys themselves, whose attitude and policies had been the root underlying cause of the outbreak. To the Duke's satisfaction, the report vindicated his own policies, and endorsed a programme of gradual reform.

By the beginning of 1943, the Duke could be well pleased with his achievement in the Bahamas. He felt he had won the constitutional struggle with the House of Assembly: although they went ahead with their own inquiry into the riots, the report they eventually published was little more than an apology, and even admitted the need for new labour laws. The Project had been completed just before the New Year, and the Royal Governor, always popular with the British and American armed services, presided over Nassau's smooth trans-formation into a busy war base. He had also finally solved the Colony's unemployment problem by negotiating a treaty with the United States whereby Bahamians could volunteer to go to the mainland, at unheard-of wages, to make up wartime shortages in agricultural labour, remitting part of their pay to their families back home. The Bahamas Labour Scheme, as this became known, was entirely his own idea; like many of his original efforts it had met with resistance from the Colonial Office, and only been adopted as a result of American pressure.

In May 1943 the Windsors made another visit to the United States, where they met Winston Churchill, who was in Washington as the guest of the President, for the first time since 1939. They were present when Churchill addressed Congress on 19 May – and the press noted that the Duke received more applause when he appeared than had the Prime Minister, who seemed annoyed by the fact. The Duke had two long talks with Churchill, suggesting that after three difficult but successful years in the Bahamas he was entitled to a change of post. Churchill seemed to agree, and promised to see what he could do. The Duke was probably hoping for the Governor-

Generalship of Australia, which had recently become vacant; but when he next heard from the Prime Minister on 10 June it was only to be offered the Governorship of Bermuda.[4]

This presented him with a difficult decision. Bermuda was higher in the colonial pecking order and therefore represented promotion. It also had a better climate than Nassau and was more important in the war, being the key staging post in the middle of the Atlantic. After three days of reflection, however, he turned the offer down. As he wrote to George Allen, 'Winston does not seem to have got my meaning of a move'. It was hardly worth starting afresh for so small an advancement. Besides, while Bermuda was over five hundred miles from the mainland, the Bahamas had 'the immense advantage of close proximity to the United States, which . . . constitutes one of the distinct benefits of life in this otherwise lousy little island upon which we have been marooned for far too long'.

'I am convinced the Duke was perfectly correct to refuse,' wrote the Duchess to her aunt. 'I can't see much point in island jumping. I'm for the big hop to a mainland.' In her memoirs she afterwards wrote of the episode: 'It was now clear beyond question that David's family were determined to keep him relegated to the furthermost marches of the Empire.' To the Duchess it was always evident that they had the Court, and in particular her sister-in-law, to thank for their difficulties and frustrations. In an exasperated letter to Aunt Bessie of March 1941 she had cursed their banishment, attributing it to 'a woman's jealousy and a country's fear his brother wouldn't shine if [the Duke] was there!' But in one sense the Duchess was mistaken. The Queen had in no way been responsible for sending them to the Bahamas, for she had in fact disapproved of the post, thinking it too good for them. In July 1940 she had written to Lord Lloyd, Secretary of State for the Colonies, protesting that the Duchess was unfit even to be a governor's wife.

During his five years in the Bahamas the Duke had virtually no contact with his family in England, who behaved as if he did not exist. The closest he came to seeing any of them was in September

---

[4] The Windsors would have been less than flattered had they known that this post had first been offered to, and refused by, David Bowes-Lyon, Queen Elizabeth's brother.

1941, when his favourite brother Prince George, Duke of Kent, who was also the member of the Royal Family to have known Mrs Simpson best before the Abdication, was on a drum-beating trip to the United States. The Windsors were then about to leave on their own first American tour and hoped to meet him there: but this was not permitted, and the Windsor tour was deliberately delayed by the British authorities in order that the two brothers should not coincide. Indeed, they were never to meet again, for in August 1942 the Duke of Kent was killed in an air crash in Scotland while on active service.

'It is a most tragic death,' wrote the Duchess to her aunt, 'and I think his services will be greatly missed by Great Britain. He was the one with the most charm left at the job – and they made a couple more up with the advances of this world – in spite of the "turn coat" to us. We are both greatly shocked and distressed and it is so sad for her and the 3 little children.' At the memorial service held in Nassau cathedral, the Duke (as one of his aides remembered) 'broke down at the beginning and wept like a child all the way through – the only time I saw him lose his self-control like that'. He was plunged for a time into the blackest depression – but managed to shake himself out of it in order to confront the House in the great constitutional battle shortly afterwards.

Earlier that same year, some conciliatory but futile words had been written from Government House, Nassau, to Queen Mary – not by the Duke but by the Duchess, using as her courier the retiring Bishop of Nassau, John Dauglish, who had connections to the Royal Family since he had confirmed the future King George VI at the Royal Naval College at Osborne. The letter, which contained nuances, read:

Madam,

I hope you will forgive my intrusion upon your time as well as my boldness in addressing Your Majesty. My motive for the latter is a simple one. It has always been a source of sorrow and regret to me that I have been the cause of any separation that exists between Mother and Son and I can't help but feel that there must be moments, however fleeting they may be, when you wonder how David is. The Bishop of Nassau is leaving in a short time for England, having been appointed by the Archbishop of Canterbury, Dr Lang, as Secretary to the Society for the Propagation of the Gospel, an advancement over his post here. . . . He is a delight-ful man and has been of the greatest help to us here, not only through his understanding but his knowledge of local conditions on this tiny isle. He can tell you if all the things David gave up are replaced to him in another way and the little details of his daily life, his job, etc., the story of his flight from France leaving all his possessions behind. The horrors of war and the endless separation of families have in my mind stressed the importance of family ties. I hope that by the end of this year we will be nearer that victory for which we are all working so hard and for which England has so bravely lighted the way.

I beg to remain

Your Majesty's most humble and obedient servant,

WALLIS WINDSOR

Back in England, Dauglish was eventually summoned to Badminton in Gloucestershire, where Queen Mary had been living since the outbreak of war with her retinue of fifty-five. The old Queen listened with interest to the tale of the Duke's life and work in the Bahamas, but when the Bishop began to talk enthusiastically of the Duchess and her endeavours there was (as he wrote to her) no response, just 'a stone wall of disinterest'. In her next letter to her son, however, Queen Mary included the surprising line: 'I send a kind message to your wife', prompting the Duke to exclaim: 'Now what do you suppose has come over Mama?' He knew nothing of the step his wife had taken – and would remain in ignorance until the Duchess was writing her memoirs some twelve years later.

As for George VI, there was no direct communication whatever between him and his elder brother for three years. When Churchill saw the Duke in Washington in May 1943, he brought a message from the King – but it was not one calculated to please the Duke, who was moved a few days later to draft a letter (possibly never sent) to the sovereign

. . . in an attempt to bring you to your senses with regard to your attitude towards my wife and myself.

Winston told me that you and he lunched together once a week and he described you as unhappy over this family estrangement and that I had not replied to your last letter of July 1940 and asked me whether there was anything I could do towards improving relations between us.

Now I must say that I was *amazed* at this information and especially his enquiring as to what part I thought *I* could play in this shake-hands-forgive-and-forget act, for no one knows better than you and Winston that I have taken more than my fair share of cracks and insults at your hands and that notwithstanding your belligerence I suffered these studied insults in silence on the supposition that they were a necessary part of the policy of establishing yourself as my successor on the throne.

Granted that the first year or two cannot have been too easy for you – I can see that – but ever since I returned to England in 1939 to offer my services and you continued to persecute [me] and then frustrate my modest efforts to serve you and my country in war I must frankly admit that I have become very bitter indeed.

The whole world knows that we are not on speaking terms, which is not surprising in view of the impression you have given via the F.O. and in general that my wife and I are to have different official treatment to other royal personages. . . .

The Duke returned from America and his meetings with Churchill on 30 June 1943, to find himself at once plunged into two local crises. First, he received an astonishing letter from the Secretary of State for the Colonies, Oliver Stanley (who was a personal friend of the King and Queen), ordering him to have a showdown with the local politicians and force them to accept without delay the whole programme of reform recommended by the Russell Commission. Unless the Bahamas introduced modern labour laws, secret voting in elections, and an income tax, it would receive nothing in development aid and its constitution would be abrogated by the Imperial Parliament. What was remarkable about this ultimatum was that, up to this point, it had always been the Duke who had been pressing for reform and the Colonial Office, desirous of keeping things quiet during the war, that had proved cautious and discouraging. Now that the Duke had embarked on a course of gradual change, here was London proposing a violent political offensive against Bay Street which promised to bring local odium upon the Royal Governor and make the Bahamas ungovernable.

As he was wondering how to respond to Stanley's demands, a

frightful event occurred. On the night of 8 July, Sir Harry Oakes, the Canadian gold millionaire who was the richest and second most famous man in the Bahamas and upon whom much local enterprise depended, was murdered in his sleep at Westbourne, his mansion outside Nassau. Oakes was a personal friend of the Duke and Duchess; they had lived at Westbourne when they first arrived in the Colony, they admired his bluff character, and the Duke closely relied upon him in his local economic schemes. The murder caused a vast sensation, not only locally but in the United States; and Nassau found itself flooded by American reporters, crime writers and private detectives. The case was beyond the local police, discredited as they were after the riots; and the Duke, in a desperate effort to get it cleaned up quickly, took the understandable but ill-fated step of calling in two senior criminal detectives of the Miami City Police, Melchen and Barker, whom he had got to know on his visits to Florida when they had efficiently organized his personal security. As all the world knows, these two policemen, in their anxiety to deliver the goods, 'cooked' the evidence against the principal suspect, Oakes's unpopular and dissolute son-in-law, de Marigny, and the inept manner in which they did so ensured that de Marigny had little difficulty in proving his innocence when the case was heard in October. It has remained unsolved to this day.

Following his unfortunate decision to call in the American detectives, the Duke distanced himself from the affair; he and the Duchess took care to be in America at the time of the court proceedings. 'The whole circumstances of the case are sordid beyond description', he wrote to the Secretary of State, 'and I shall be glad when the trial is over and done with.' One of the worst results was to intensify the air of gangsterism which, harking back to the age of the pirates, had never been far away in Nassau throughout its history. 'We are endeavouring to keep as clear from this awful case as is possible,' wrote the Duchess to her aunt. 'I am afraid there is a lot of dirt underneath and I think the natives are all protecting themselves from the exposure of business deals – strange drums of petrol etc. – so I wonder how far it will all go. Most unpleasant as I do not think there is a big enough laundry anywhere to take Nassau's dirty linen. . . .'

The year 1943 had begun on a note of triumph for the Duke, with his constitutional victory over the Bay Street gang, the implementation of his cherished economic schemes, and the transformation of

New Providence into a war base. Thanks to the Oakes affair, by the end of the year the atmosphere had turned sour. The administration had been discredited by the police fiasco. A mood of fear and suspicion prevailed in the wake of the unsolved murder. It was the most inauspicious possible moment to begin the political offensive which the Colonial Office demanded; and the Duke, as he saw in his fourth new year in Nassau, felt at the end of this tether.

WITH BEST WISHES FOR

CHRISTMAS AND THE NEW YEAR

1947

Bertie

Greetings from George VI

Arriving in England after the death of the King, February 1952

Walking at the funeral of George VI, between his brother the Duke of Gloucester and nephew the Duke of Kent

New York, March 1953: the
Duke with his sister Princess
Mary, with whom he is about to
sail to join their ailing mother
Queen Mary, and the Duchess,
who is to stay behind

Crossing the Atlantic in the early
nineteen-fifties

Fort Belvedere

La Cröe

The house in the Bois de Boulogne

The Duke's garden at the Mill

Sir Walter Monckton

Sir George Allen

Sir Alexander Hardinge

Sir Alan Lascelles

Faces of Exile

Chapter Eight

The Quest for a Post
1944–46

*B*y the beginning of 1944, it was clear that the Allies were going to win the war; and henceforth the thoughts which naturally filled the Duke of Windsor's mind were of what was going to happen to him once the war was over. As he pondered the matter, he found himself torn between two conflicting reactions. The first – reflected in much of his wartime correspondence – was the bitter personal feeling that, after the way he had been treated by the Court and the British authorities, he no longer wished to see any member of his family, to accept any other position under the Crown, or have anything further to do with England. He and his wife would resign themselves to their status as outcasts from Great Britain and retire to a quiet life abroad, and that would be that. This was a philosophy of defeat and hopelessness, but had the Duke followed it he would undoubtedly have spared himself much unhappiness and frustration. His other reaction, however, was that of a patriotic Englishman who loved his country and wished to continue to serve it and who, after a third of a century of strenuous work in the public interest, could not contemplate the idea of a life of inactivity. (He was, after all, still short of his fiftieth birthday, which he celebrated in June 1944.) This side of the Duke refused to accept the hopelessness of his position; it caused him to yearn for – and fight for – family reconciliation, further and more important official posts, and eventual return to live in England.

For two years, between the summers of 1944 and 1946, it was the second of these opposing reactions which prevailed. Believing he had reason on his side, and eternally optimistic in the face of every indication that his family would never welcome him back, allow him any work or honour, or accept his wife, he battled away for recognition. He battled especially for a respectable postwar job. Even if he were not to return to England, even if his family continued to ignore him, he wanted a post which would enable him to serve his country and give him and his consort a dignified status abroad. Above all he wanted to help the cause of England in America, for she had urgent need of good representatives there and the Duke was without question the most popular Englishman in the United States. Again and again he tried and failed to secure such an appointment. It is possible to regard him as a man who refused to face realities, engaged in perpetually banging his head against a brick wall; but in fact he came nearer to his goal than is often supposed, and in the end it was only the hostility of key courtiers and members of his family which stood between him and the realization of his dreams.

In 1944 the Duke was still Governor of the Bahamas, but this was a post he had become desperate to relinquish. On 3 May he wrote a long, confused and introspective letter to his faithful solicitor George Allen in which he brooded upon his predicament. As regarded local politics he was 'at the end of my rope', and had threatened to resign 'in the event of Colonial Office policy requiring a show down and dissolution of the Bahamas House of Assembly'. That March he had in fact drafted a letter of resignation to Winston Churchill; and although he had decided not to use it he now sent a copy of it to Allen 'as an indication of what has been in my mind for some time past'. It read:

My dear Winston,

. . . By August 17th next I shall have completed no less than four years in the appointment of Governor of the Bahamas, a post I have conscientiously filled notwithstanding my lack of experience and training in colonial administration.

But he who is wise senses when he has outgrown his usefulness in any given job, official or otherwise, and without any claim to great wisdom, I am fortunate in being able to detect that this has happened in my own case. It has been a gradual process and whilst I can say that I have been proud to serve in the novel role of colonial administrator, and that I can look back on the four years I have spent in the Bahamas with some degree of satisfaction in the light of having done one's best for the people of this Colony under the difficulties of wartime conditions, other considerations now enter the picture.

Although still reasonably active in my fiftieth year, so long a spell of official responsibilities in a tropical climate has taken considerable toll of my energy, and your offer of another island governorship last year was further proof, if it were needed, of the limitations placed on my capabilities. These limitations I do not seek to challenge in any way; that is entirely a matter of opinion. Nor do I wish to refer to the circumstances created by my family, which make it impossible for me to return to Great Britain.

In tendering my resignation which will be forwarded through the usual channel of the Secretary of State for the Colonies, I have one request to make of you. That is that the United Kingdom Exchange Control Authority be directed to allow me sufficient US dollar funds in order that I can live in dignified simplicity in America until such time as I have been able to make some arrangements for the future.

The Duke explained to Allen: 'You will notice that I have scrupulously avoided any mention of the Duchess in this draft letter, but it is largely her state of mind and health after four years in the tropics that has brought things to a head; that and the difficulties of explaining to the outside world the "whys and wherefores" of our continued exile on these islands. She should just not have to take it any longer, and you know me well enough to understand that when I say I am reluctant and fearful to I have very good reasons.' This last remark was almost certainly a reference to the sinister atmosphere in Nassau following the Oakes affair.

Although anxious to give up his existing post, the Duke was perplexed by the problem of what he would then do with himself, and here we see the mass of contradictions. 'With my experience of official treatment since 1936,' he continued to Allen, 'which includes five years re-enlistment in the British service and ample proof of the continuation of the hostile official attitude towards myself, my one desire is to return to private life.' Yet it was unthinkable 'to retire at this most critical juncture in the war, with the most momentous military operations in history impending'. He longed for 'an appointment worthy of my experience'; yet he had 'become more or less resigned to the fact that family jealousy would oppose any suggestion of such an appointment'. What he wanted most of all was

> ... a created job in America, which is the assignment for which I consider myself best qualified. We spent a total of four months there last year ... and were able to make very useful contacts, both official and private. And I could make many more which would be of value to Anglo-American relations were I given a whole time job to do so, a sort of roving commission, in close cooperation with the British Ambassador of course, but not resident or tied down to Washington. The job would have to be defined, but I would insist on handling it in my own way. ...

The Duke wondered if Allen might start a sort of campaign for him in London, rallying his friends and supporters with a view to influencing the authorities to grant him such a post. Allen did his best. He consulted friends in the Colonial Office, who admitted that the Duke was 'widely regarded as the best governor in the service'; he went to see Beaverbrook, Monckton, Ulick Alexander and Bernard Rickatson-Hatt. It was not an auspicious time for such an initiative, for the Normandy invasions, launched on 6 June, claimed all attentions. Nevertheless, it was not entirely without effect. The papers of Anthony Eden indicate that the Foreign Office seriously considered making the Duke an ambassador that summer, much to the concern of the Palace who saw to it that the idea was promptly shelved.

Throughout the first half of 1944 the Duke, in spite of frustrations, continued to work hard as Governor and to advance his various schemes; but his main preoccupation, as he had indicated in his letter to Allen, was the state of health and mind of the Duchess, who was visibly exhausted and ill. She was overworking herself: in addition to her charitable endeavours and ordinary duties as a governor's wife, she personally organized the canteen for the services stationed in New Providence and ran Government House as a hotel for the many senior officers who passed through. Her letters to Aunt Bessie at that time show her increasingly nervous and irascible.

15 January 1944: I really feel that neither of us can stand this place either physically or mentally for another year. . . . I do not think the Duke would hesitate to throw his hand in for this is no place for him and to think he is dumped here solely by family jealousy. . . .

6 February 1944: This is still an awful place and some days I feel I can't resist slapping everyone in the face. . . .

5 April 1944: There is no sign of getting elsewhere and some days we feel we simply cannot carry on any longer but everything presents a problem nowadays and it is hard for us to know best what to do. . . . The war looks to be longer now than it seemed in the autumn. . . . I doubt if we will ever see our things again. What a really good mess it all is and it will never become straightened out in our time. How one longs for liberty once again! Being shut up here is like being a prisoner-of-war only worse, as there are trying responsibilities whereas it is the host's responsibility if you are a captured prisoner-of-war. Who would have believed that it could have gone on so long and what will we have got in the end? When you read the war books of those who have seen the horrors, one prays the sacrifices are not in vain. I hope you can read this scribble and will not think I have entirely lost my sense of humour. I am rather tired and I use up a lot of energy hating the place. . . .

23 April 1944: The Duke is anxious for me to go [to America on her own] next month . . . but I can't bring myself to leave him alone in this awful hot depressing hole. . . . You see 4 years is really too long – no one can take it – how to get out is the question. We are in correspondence with Allen over what course to pursue. . . .

13 May 1944: I dislike this coral rock more every day – but the Duke's patience with the [local] community and England's treatment is really inspiring and I should not complain in the face of such a good example. . . .

5 June 1944: We had a nice party here to celebrate our seven years of bliss – just think 5 of which have been war years and 4 in the Bahamas – *not* as planned! . . .

The Duchess's nervous state had a deep-rooted physical cause. In July 1944 the Windsors left the Bahamas to spend the rest of the summer in America; and a thorough medical examination in New York revealed that the Duchess was suffering from cancer of the stomach. On 31 August she was operated on at the Roosevelt Hospital. It was a moment of great anxiety for the Duke; but the operation was a success, and they went off to recuperate at the Hot Springs resort in Virginia.

They were still at Hot Springs in late September when the Duke unexpectedly heard from Winston Churchill, who was staying with the President on his estate at Hyde Park following the Second Quebec Conference. Churchill suggested the Duke join him there, which the Duke proceeded to do, afterwards reporting to Allen 'a long and satisfactory talk – in so far as it went, which was not very far'. Churchill agreed that the Duke had done well in the Bahamas and that there was little more for him to achieve there, that he should be allowed to give up his governorship as soon as he wished and return to his home in France as soon as this was practical. (Paris had been liberated the previous month, though German armies remained in France which was in a state of utter chaos.) But when the Duke asked if he might serve in another and more responsible post until the end of the war the Prime Minister became evasive and switched to another subject. As the Duke wrote to Allen:

> The only thing he did say of interest, which amused me a whole lot, was to emphasize the alarm and discomfort it would cause at the Palace were I to indicate any intention of taking up residence in Great Britain. While assuring him that the Court need have nothing to fear on that score, I did express surprise at his remark and that, after nearly eight years absence, I was still considered so formidable a menace to the solidarity of the monarchy; especially so because hardly a day passes by that British propaganda does not stuff us with the extent to which the King has established himself in the hearts of the people.

In effect, the Duke had obtained a release from his post, on condition that he stayed out of England and did not expect alternative official employment of any kind. But a part of him never ceased to hope that he would one day be offered the kind of job for which he longed. In October he tried again, writing to Churchill from Hot Springs:

Whilst I realize that the German war has yet to be won before the situation in Europe can crystallize into anything recognizable, and that it is still too early to visualize which job, if any, there might be for me on that continent, I would not wish to remain unemployed if there was any sphere in which it was considered my experience could still be appropriately utilized.

He even offered, through Allen, to do undercover work for the Foreign Office in liberated Europe, work which would not have brought him any reward or public recognition; but this offer did not receive so much as an acknowledgement.

Although the Duke now had to resign himself to the fact that he would be given no other post so long as the war continued, he continued to harbour one cherished hope. At some point, probably during 1945, he and the Duchess would be passing through England on their way back to Europe. It was too much to expect any general change in the attitude of his family, but he did look (as during the summer of 1940) for some small, symbolic gesture – a minor, formal act of recognition – which would allay scandal and dispel the idea in the public mind that the Windsors were outcasts. As he wrote to Churchill:

> Were the King and Queen to behave normally to the Duchess and myself when we pass by England, and invite us merely to tea at one of their residences, a formality which as a matter of fact is pre-scribed by Court protocol in the case of Colonial Governors and their wives, it would avoid any division of feeling being manifested. . . . It could never be a very happy meeting, but on the other hand it would be quite painless, and would have the merit of silencing, once and for all, those malicious circles who delight in keeping open an eight-year-old wound that should have been healed officially, if not privately, ages ago.

The Duke hoped the Prime Minister would agree that this was 'the best cure for an evil situation', and that he would persuade the King and Queen 'to swallow "the Windsor pill" just once, however bitter they think it is going to taste'. But Churchill replied on New Year's Eve that, while he had tried to intercede with the King over the single meeting, both Queen Mary and Queen Elizabeth remained 'inflexibly opposed' to receiving the Duchess. 'I do not see any prospect of removing this difficulty,' wrote Churchill. 'I have not concealed my regret that this should be so.'

Although in September 1944 the Duke had obtained Churchill's agreement to his relinquishing the Governorship of the Bahamas at his convenience, he in fact remained at this post for another seven months. This period, indeed, was among the busiest he spent in Nassau, for he worked strenuously to bring to fruition all of his political and economic schemes which had not yet been realized. He persuaded the House to vote almost half a million pounds for the agricultural development of the Out Islands; he induced them to accept the principle of secret voting in elections; and he brought about another reform that was to earn him the gratitude of all the Colony's future administrators – he got the House to agree to pay the travelling expenses of officials in getting out to the Bahamas, thus removing one of the outrageous factors which had contributed to making Nassau the most unpopular post in the Colonial Service.

His resignation was announced on 15 March 1945, to take effect at the end of April. Had he not resigned, his five-year term would have come to an end on 9 July; his slightly premature departure caused relief to the British Government, who were thereby spared the embarrassment of announcing that his appointment had terminated and there were no plans to give him any other. The official reason given by him for the resignation was that 'having directed this British Colony's war effort, it is only practical that I should hand over to my successor, who will be responsible for post-war policies, before those problems descend upon him'. But he admitted in a letter to his friend Roy Howard, owner of the Scripps–Howard newspaper chain, that it

> . . . all derives from the fact that the Court and Cabinet in London won't let bye gones be bye gones, even in the greatest crisis that has overtaken mankind. I have a perfectly clean record in the matter, for I have done everything in my power to heal the breach, but to no avail.

Any immediate future official war activities of mine therefore must be determined by the value the British Government places on my services which are always available. On the other hand, I see no reason why I should continue to rot indefinitely on a semi-tropical island or accept some other exiling job, just because the British may not offer me a worthwhile appointment. . . .

Once the announcement had been made, the Duke was resolved to end his governorship on a conciliatory note, with past political struggles forgotten. Addressing the House for the last time on 3 April, he generously remarked: 'Under present disturbed world conditions there must be times when the Legislature finds it difficult to appreciate the full implications of certain measures which are laid before them. Such occasions have, fortunately, been very rare during my administration, and for my part I shall carry away with me only recollections of harmony and understanding.' These words were addressed to an assembly which had done its best to frustrate his every reform. But, as the Duke wrote to Allen, in spite of the

. . . difficulties I have had to contend with owing to the attitude of the reactionary white element who rule the local House of Assembly, and their stubborn opposition to the progressive measures I have invited them to adopt . . . it would be most unfortunate if my final bow to Nassau should be tainted with any hint of recrimination. As a matter of fact, although this reactionary white element has often proved itself an irritating obstacle in my administration, they have actually voted funds for most of the important schemes I have initiated, even if they have voted them reluctantly and with bad grace.

In other words, the Duke had won, and wished to be magnanimous in victory.

Given his anxiety to depart in a harmonious atmosphere, he was pleased by the local reaction to the news of his going. The Duchess recalled in her memoirs: 'We were astonished and stirred by the genuine regret with which our imminent departure was viewed.' Many were the local testimonials of gratitude and devotion. It was the general view that the Windsors had done very well in the

Bahamas. The next Secretary of State for the Colonies to visit Nassau, Arthur Creech Jones, stated in public that the Duke had given the Colony its 'best administration in modern times'; while Brigadier Daly, Officer Commanding North Caribbean Defence Area, thought the Duke the best of all the governors he visited. In spite of all discouraging indications, it was difficult for them to believe that there would not be some reward for five years of patience, successful hard work, and discreet behaviour.

The Windsors left Nassau without ceremony on 3 May 1945. Although the war in Europe was over and they were anxious to return to France to find out what was left of their houses and possessions, Churchill advised them to spend the summer in America: France was still in a state of turmoil, and passages across the Atlantic were difficult to secure. They therefore established themselves at the Waldorf Towers in New York, and during the four hot and idle months they spent there the Duke was given ample opportunity to brood on his predicament. Faced with a life of nothingness, and aware again of his great popularity in America, his thoughts once more turned longingly both to family reconciliation and the idea that he might do a job in the sphere of Anglo-American relations. The election that July of a Labour government in Britain under Clement Attlee encouraged him in his hopes: the new regime, which included several men he considered to be his sympathizers, would be freer of the establishment and court influences which had been so unfriendly to him. By the time he sailed for France with the Duchess on 15 September, he had resolved to approach the new political chiefs in London as soon as possible and at the same time to make a serious attempt at resolving family differences.

Arriving in Paris, the Windsors were at first relieved to discover that their rented residence in the Boulevard Suchet, on which the Duchess had worked so hard before the war, had remained untouched by the Occupation and its aftermath, only to receive the shattering news that the house had been sold during the summer, and that the new owners required them to leave by the end of the year. The prospective disappearance of their principal home lent an urgency to the private visit to England which the Duke made that October, unaccompanied by the Duchess.

He spent five days in London, staying with Queen Mary at Marlborough House, her residence next to St James's Palace. It was the first time he had seen his mother since the Abdication, and he was hoping that at this emotional moment of reunion he would finally persuade her to receive the Duchess. In this he failed completely. But he had two reasonably cordial talks with his brother, and a series of encouraging meetings with members of the Government – the Prime Minister, Attlee; the Foreign Secretary, Bevin; and the Colonial Secretary, George Hall. On his return to Paris, he wrote the following important and conciliatory letter to the King, which significantly contains no reference to the Duchess.

24 Boulevard Suchet,
Paris XVI

18 October 1945

Dear Bertie,

I was very glad to see you again in London after so long an interval and to find you looking so well and vigorous after the strain of the last six years of total war.

No one realizes better than I do all that you have had to endure along with the people of Great Britain in the front line against the Germans, and my admiration for your fortitude knows no bounds. On the other hand, although in another sphere and under quite different conditions, my life has not been easy-going either, and without any desire to seek praise I am satisfied that the job I undertook as your representative in a third-class British Colony was fulfilled to the best of my ability.

I was also glad for the first opportunity you and I have had of a frank discussion of personal and family matters with special regard to the future. Now that all the shooting is over and postwar problems emerge in all their complexity, it is only natural that I should want to place my experience at the disposal of any organization that could use it rather than retire to a life of complete leisure. My desire therefore to offer my services to you and British interests . . . is sincere and genuine.

I suggested the field of Anglo-American relations . . . because, along with many others, I am convinced that there can be no lasting peace for mankind unless the two countries preserve a common approach to international politics. Having spent more than one year at intervals out of the last five in America I have made many useful contacts in that country and I believe a number of converts among convinced isolationists.

It is a difficult and subtle subject and one that requires a realistic approach as well as a thorough knowledge of the two peoples and their ever-changing political reactions. As a long-term policy, I advocate exchange educational schemes along the lines of the Rhodes Scholarships and the Harkness Fellowships in order that many more Britishers and Americans gain a first-hand knowledge of each other's countries during their college years, the most impressionable period of their lives. I know of many responsible people – both in Great Britain and America – anxious to help in this important field who are only waiting for concrete proposals and someone to coordinate their efforts. . . .

While I am frank to admit that I was sorry when your answer was in the affirmative to my question as to whether my taking up residence in Great Britain would be an embarrassment to you, I can see your point of view and am therefore prepared to put your feelings before my own in this matter. On the other hand, don't forget that I have suffered many unnecessary embarrassments from official sources uncomplainingly during the last nine years, but I have reason to believe from the spirit of your recent two long talks with me that it is now your desire that these should cease.

The truth of the whole matter is that you and I happen to be two prominent personages placed in one of the most unique situations in history, the dignified handling of which is entirely your and my responsibility, and ours alone. It is a situation from which we cannot escape and one that will always be watched with interest by the whole world. I can see no reason why we should not be able to handle it in the best interests of both of us, and I can only assure you that I will continue to play my part to this end.

I spent a very interesting week in London and accomplished a great deal in a short time. I saw Winston, Attlee, Bevin and George Hall in that sequence and found odd spare moments to visit old haunts in the West End or what is left of them. It was wonderful to find Mama looking so young and well, and she took me for a long drive through the bombed areas of the East End docks' section and back across the Thames through Kensington on the Sunday. . . .

Yours ever,
DAVID

Something which encouraged him in his hopes for an Anglo-American job was that he now appeared to have the support of Winston Churchill, who spent a day with the Windsors in Paris on 14 November. As the Duchess wrote sardonically to her aunt, Churchill promised to be far more friendly and helpful to them in opposition than he had ever been as Prime Minister. 'The Duchess and I were very pleased to see you again yesterday,' the Duke wrote to him on the 15th. 'We were also very interested to hear your views regarding our future and the plan by which I could be most usefully employed in the service of my country, and wish to thank you for your efforts on our behalf with the present powers in Great Britain.' At Churchill's suggestion, he drew up an account of the work he felt he might accomplish in the United States.[1]

The King replied to the Duke on 10 November in a letter that was brief. He too had been glad to see his brother after so many years, and what had pleased him particularly was the news that the Duke did not propose to return to live in England. He entirely agreed that it would be a good idea for the Duke to move permanently to America in order to 'lead the kind of useful life which is in your mind', and he would be happy to facilitate this project in every way, even to the extent of writing a letter of recommendation to President Truman. On the other hand, he did not think there was any question of an official post there 'which would appear to be invented for you alone'.

The Duke was not discouraged by this letter; he believed that all would still be well thanks to Churchill's intervention. He wrote again to his brother on 15 November:

> . . . While I appreciate your suggestion of writing to the President to inform him of the project under discussion, I do not understand the difficulty of actually creating an official post for me which . . . would appear to have been invented for me alone. As it is agreed that my position is unique, why should a unique post not be created for me?
>
> If you will see Winston on his return to London, he will explain how I could be appointed to work in America 'within the ambit of the British Embassy in Washington', or phraseology to that effect which he has devised in his own inimitable way. Most of my

[1] Reproduced in Appendix IV.

activities would, of course, be of a private and personal nature, but any efforts of mine would be fruitless and the American press puzzled and derisively critical were my return to America not accompanied by an official statement from the Foreign Office that I was accredited to the British Embassy in the form Winston suggests. . . .

The Duke was undoubtedly correct in his surmise that his efforts on behalf of Anglo-American relations would be held up to ridicule unless he had some official support. He also (as he frankly admitted to the King) required diplomatic status in order to retain across the Atlantic the tax privileges which he enjoyed in France: otherwise his means would not allow him to live in the United States. 'I hope', he concluded to his brother, 'that you will make arrangements for me along these lines in the same spirit that I am willing to respect your feelings with regard to my living in Great Britain. Be assured that I appreciate your interest in my future activities, but it is not so easy to embark upon a fresh venture at the age of fifty-one and it is important to start off on the right foot.' Life in France at that moment, he added, was 'really quite impossible for a foreigner who has no official job'.

❧

In Paris, the Duke waited and waited for a reply to his proposals. While he remained hopeful of the outcome, he suffered keenly from postwar blues that autumn and winter. For the first time in his life, he found himself with virtually nothing to do and no one to see. A year after the Liberation, Paris remained grim with its food shortages, electricity cuts, and political tensions and reprisals. With the Duchess preoccupied by the problems of household management under these conditions, the Duke had little company to cheer him apart from a few British and American diplomatic and service personnel: his English friends were prevented from visiting him by travel and currency restrictions. The only good news was the presence of their old friends the Duff Coopers at the British Embassy, and a temporary reprieve from the problem of having to seek a roof over their heads when the new owners of the house in the Boulevard Suchet allowed them to stay on until the following April, by which time the Duke hoped his future would be decided.

The Quest for a Post

The Duchess's letters to Aunt Bessie give a fascinating picture both of their lives at this time and the atmosphere of postwar Paris.

22 October 1945: Everyone was very efficient at Havre – army lorry to take our things and the Embassy car for us. . . . I found the house looking really lovely and after five years away I would not have changed a thing. . . . The great blow fell when we were informed that the house had been sold. . . . House prices are such that I cannot describe and hotels are the top and scarce as the U.S. army is all over Paris so . . . we have to move from here. . . . (I must now continue by candle light. The electricity is on for half an hour and off for half an hour – quite an irritant to the nerves. I had a dinner of 18 for the Duff Coopers under these conditions – not too good – but luckily we have our pre-war candles here to help.) We have to start packing December first. You can imagine how I hate to leave and feel I shall go mad if we do not finally settle somewhere. . . . The Duke's London visit passed off most pleasantly even though their attitude regarding me remains the same and they prefer we do not live in G.B. as it would be too much competition for the brother – which seems weak. Also they do not want him to find work outside as the idea is you can't give a King a job. Wonderful people aren't they. . . . I would not feel so down about the future if we could remain here in this lovely house – but it is finding a place and beginning again which is so dreary. . . .

5 December 1945: . . . We are always waiting results of the Duke's visit to London which though won't be anything very grand (if anything at all) would be better than having nothing to do for the moment. In any case nothing can develop until the late spring. Winston lunched here on his way to Brussels. He is more helpful now that he is out of power! Walter Monckton arrives Saturday also Allen for discussions and so it goes. We have persuaded the buyer of this house to let us stay until April first – and we will then go to pack La Cröe staying at an hotel. That will take about 3 weeks or more. Then we have to go to England to look over our things there. By then we should know if Britain is going to give the Duke anything. . . . The cost of running the house is so awful. I cannot see how foreigners are to continue to live here unless the exchange improves. We seem to have plenty to do if not very exciting in comparison to NY! Max Beaverbrook comes to dinner tonight. He is always interesting if not always loyal. . . . It is not too cold in the house and of course Pinaudier[2] finds food. We live a lot on venison sent by either British or US army in Germany. The most annoying thing is the lack of electricity – sometimes every half hour cut – or 5 hours on end. It is unpleasant when caught under the dryer! For the ordinary civilian living here I think it's hell but military & embassies do not fare too badly and we have the same or nearly the same privileges.

The light has just gone so this is continued with the aid of 2 candles. . . . I have done all my official duties and asked all my French friends – even to a cocktail for 100! . . . We have no Xmas plans and with cost it seems hardly worthwhile to make an effort for a party for there is no-one exciting. . . .

3 January 1946: . . . We had a little party here with a G.I. thumping out on an army piano and a few French, English and Americans all trying to be gay. The house looked pretty – the wine was plentiful – though the black market turkey was tough alas. Then Lord Forbes gave a large party for his sister Friday night and I had a dinner for the Coopers beforehand and so it goes. Only the Duke thinks everything is dull after the American parties. . . . The clothes here are much prettier than at home. My eye is trained now to less straight line and all the women look so feminine. I feel quite like an old umbrella case in Mainbocher's straight lines. Have bought 2 evening dresses and one afternoon. The Duke is for pulling up all stakes here as there is really nothing for him to do and no men who would be congenial to him. The Riviera has such cheap permanent residents that he thinks it is a place to rent a house for the summer if one wishes to go there. I don't know how I feel: I am always tempted by places where servants are cheap and fairly easy to get. I am afraid you are wrong about England. That is just what his brother doesn't want or the Govt – they admit they are scared of that. Anyway that's frank and I suppose can be construed as a compliment. Now the game is how attractive will they make it elsewhere under those conditions – plus the fact that they really do not want him to have any official recognition anywhere – so you see the impasse we are in at the moment. We hoped for an answer before W.C. went to the US as he was talking for us – but of course he has little power now and when he did have took the same line as the King & Govt. The Duke goes to London tomorrow for another crack at the Court and the powers that be. . . .

---

[2] The outstanding French chef who had been in the Windsors' employment throughout their marriage and had accompanied them to the Bahamas.

25 January 1946: I had a fine cold for only 2 days. The Duke was not so lucky for he developed an attack of virus pneumonia. . . . Very irritating – he is not a good invalid. I seem to survive the chill houses in silk stockings and wool dresses night and day whereas the Duke has lined shoes, wool socks and endless pullovers. I also wear no underwear to look thin as I have an appetite like a horse and am gaining madly. I am sure it is a result of the way mother drove me out in socks and never wrapping up my throat in winter. I had quite a party here last Tuesday – 17 for dinner – French, British American etc – then 50 in after dinner. I then had a well known French cabaret woman singer at 11 and then Maurice Chevalier came at 12 after his theater. He was divine and I think everyone was cheered up. Funnily enough it coincided with De Gaulle's departure – so people needed a light touch. We had a buffet of hot dogs from the US, ham mousse from tinned ham, salade russe from tinned vegetables, sandwiches of cheese & cresson and black market eggs stuffed – our only extravagance. They got away with 30 bottles of champagne and 3 of whiskey. . . . What a mess France is in and the country is certainly having a super 'crise de nerfs'. One does not really know what is wrong – but nothing works but party politics. Soon I fear the people will be really fed up with that if they do not get fed in any other way. We start to pack Feb 25th. I have had a good winter . . . in spite of the difficulties to live and certain discomforts – the greatest of which is the mentality that the Occupation has left. . . . I am now glad to be getting rid of our things in this country – but the question of the future is not clear. The English are determined not to give the Duke a big or important job for the reason they think it would take from the King – this in high circles is frankly said. The belief is that 2 Kings can't operate therefore the Duke having made his decision should eliminate himself. In the meantime they search for some camouflage type of position. We definitely have refused any colonial governmentship [*sic*]. What is the use to bury ourselves away for nothing? If a camouflage can't be found I think there are 2 things to do – either decide where we can best live a private life taking taxes into consideration – or go to England for six months privately naturally and see what the effect would be. . . .

8 March 1946: We are in the midst of the great packing problem which is going quite well considering the difficulties here. I have felt very sad about giving up the house but now that it is a mass of crates and dirt etc I have become hardened to leaving here for it really was the ensemble not the house itself. The expense of moving is awfully high due to the scarcity of materials. . . . I have sold all the curtains and carpets and some pieces of furniture to the new owner getting a good price. We have 3 sealed vans going on the railroad to Antibes. . . . We will keep La Cröe running until August then pack and be in Paris in September or go to England and then come to the U.S. We still have no news from G.B. I do not think they will give anything to us and the opinion seems to be a certain number of visits so that the people in upper and lower classes can get used to the idea of us. . . . Everyone here is very depressed about the world situation – but I suppose it will clear up. . . . I have had a nice winter and people have been most hospitable and kind – and I have met many exceedingly nice French people – young and gay and not so hectic as my American friends – but I have enjoyed entertaining them here – the house ran so well. I am taking all the staff to La Cröe. . . . All love. . . .

⚜

The Duke's second postwar visit to London in January 1946 – for the purpose of sounding out his job prospects – brought him little comfort. He had another anodyne meeting with his brother; he had further discussions with Attlee and Bevin; and again he stayed at Marlborough House – though his mother was in the country. He had been looking forward to accepting a private invitation from his old friend General John Marriott, the Officer Commanding the Guards Division, to visit the British Army in Germany: he was now told that he must refuse this. As regards the proposed job in America, nothing had yet been decided; Bevin explained that all would depend on the attitude of the new British Ambassador to Washington who was shortly to be nominated to succeed Halifax.

He was therefore immensely excited, in Paris later that month, to learn from the newspapers that the man chosen by the Labour Government for the Washington post was an old friend of his – Sir Archibald Clark Kerr, a veteran diplomatist who during the past ten years had served as Ambassador both in China and Russia, and was now raised to the peerage as Lord Inverchapel. On 28 January the Duke wrote hopefully to the royal private secretary Sir Alan Lascelles that

> . . . it would be my judgment that Archie would personally place no obstacles in the way. Although I have not see him in several

years, I have known him on and off all my life and he was
Minister in Stockholm during my visit there in 1932. Of course,
people change, but I would be surprised if he and I could not
make a success of the experiment. . . . I can go to London to see
Archie as soon as he returns from his mission to the Far
East. . . .

The Duke begged that a decision be made one way or the other
before he had to give up his Paris house at the beginning of April; and
he ended his letter with the reflection that he did not think he could
face going to America again unless he had a proper position.

A month passed. On 23 February the Duke had what he
described to Allen as 'a perfectly amicable telephone conversation'
with the King, who promised to call him up with some news 'later in
the week'. But yet another month passed, and the Duke, now about
to leave Paris, had still heard nothing. 'There are limits to what one's
pride can take,' he wrote to Allen; and on 21 March he wrote to the
King (it was one of the last letters he wrote from the Boulevard
Suchet):

Dear Bertie,

I am very surprised not to have had any word from you since our
telephone conversation on February 23rd when you said you
would call up again later in the week after you had seen Bevin with
whom you had an appointment the next day.

Your silence is discouraging and hardly in the spirit of our two
talks in London. . . . It is difficult for me to believe that the
appointment in America really does hinge on the feelings of Halifax's successor in the matter, for your command in this personal
instance would be obeyed. . . .

Although no-one realises better than I do the strain that present
world political conditions impose on Heads of State and their
Ministers, I have been waiting more than five months for a decision on the question of my employment. . . . I will continue to bear
myself in patience until I hear that Archie Clark Kerr has returned
to London from Indonesia. If you then still remain silent on the
subject, I can only conclude that you and your advisers have
turned down the offer of my services. . . .

Wallis and I have packed up this house and leave Paris next week for La Cröe, Cap d'Antibes. . . .

Yours ever,

DAVID

Still the Duke heard nothing, and was forced to draw the bitter conclusion.

The attitude of the Palace is summarized in a remarkable letter from Lascelles to Halifax written on 10 March 1946, just before Halifax's departure from Washington. The King and Lascelles both 'strongly' believed that America was the only place for the Duke, and that the sooner he went there the better. For him to return to England was out of the question (as he fortunately seemed to realize); France was 'no place for him'; and there were 'obvious difficulties' in sending him to any part of the Empire. The Duke had therefore been 'strongly' advised by the King 'to pack up and go to the United States as soon as possible'. He seemed to want to help the cause of Anglo-American relations, and this was fine so long as he did so '*in an unofficial capacity*'. He might, for example, buy out of his own resources a mansion in the Southern States and 'make it a centre of private hospitality, like a great English country house in the nineteenth century'; and he might send reports on issues and perso-nalities to the British Embassy – 'so long as they were private'. Unfortunately Churchill had butted in, mesmerizing the Duke with the word 'ambit', with the idea of an official job 'within the ambit of the British Embassy in Washington'. This 'pleasant-sounding phrase', like so many in history, had 'proved will-of-the-wisp, raising false hopes'. For nine years, wrote Lascelles, using another pleasant-sounding phrase, it had been impossible to discover a way of getting the imperial machine to accept the 'extra wheel' of an ex-King and make it go.

On 1 April 1946 the Windsors left Paris, where they no longer possessed a residence, and installed themselves at La Cröe, from which they had fled in June 1940 following the fall of France, but on which they had continued to pay rent to its English owner, Sir

Pomeroy Burton, throughout the war. From November 1942 until June 1944, Antibes had been occupied by the Italians, who had littered the gardens and shore of the villa with mines; the area remained part of an American military zone. Fortunately it had been possible to clear the mines over the winter, and the villa itself was found to be intact apart from the theft of the curtains and a few oil paintings.

Hoping that the new year would bring him important news about his future, the Duke had originally planned to spend no more than a few weeks at La Cröe: indeed, as the property was up for sale, the trip was at first conceived with the purpose of packing up their possessions. But no good news had come, and since the villa was now the only house they had anywhere (apart from their ranch in Canada) they persuaded Burton to let them go on living there. It was to remain their principal home for the next three years; and although their existence at the villa was (thanks to the Duchess) far from uncomfortable it was strange and isolated, food shortages and transport difficulties lending the Riviera a peculiar remoteness in the postwar period. La Cröe became in effect a kind of distant and enchanted island on which the Duke awaited the call that never came.

Once again, the Duchess's letters to her aunt give a tantalizing picture of their first months there.

24 April 1946: We packed from Feb. 25th until April first – it wasn't too bad and we remained until only the bed left the day after we did. . . . We sent the staff down a few days ahead in relays. . . . After two weeks of the Duke and I practically unpacking and arranging everything ourselves and speaking French continually I was pretty exhausted. . . . After I had thrown things together we had the Baron and Baronne de Cabrol who stayed ten days leaving Easter Monday, also Mr Allen and the Comte de Castéja. It was my first experience with French house guests and came off very well. Noel Coward has been here and we spent a week-end in Monte Carlo with him. There are more people here than I expected – tired from the war etc – so it is not too lonely but not Paris which I adore. Nothing but adverse news comes from London, so we must plan our future independent of any chance of the British Gov't doing anything for us. It is certainly a tough problem, for where to live today is not easy – taxes to be considered first of all and then the mounting costs everywhere. There are 28 people employed here, not counting the 2 secretaries. As you can imagine there is always something. No-one wants such a large house today – endless basements etc. – and the cost of food is breaking us. Wages are ten times pre-war – but not up to America – but then the food is so expensive that it comes to the same thing. I imagine outside of embassies it is the only house run in this fashion in France and probably England today. We will have to make a survey of the cost of living in the U.S. . . . The Duke is very restless for a job. I think he would like to do something with Bob Young[3] but I do not know how that would appear. Everyone in Europe is searching for the answer to the future and nearly everyone wants to leave France – there is much property for sale – the elections[4] will decide a great deal. The grounds here are very messed up – we haven't lost too much considering the moves and the furniture not badly banged about. I have got everything in place again and we can continue here apart from a faded shabby look but everything and everybody looks that way in Europe. I have replaced the stolen curtains with a sort of lining material. Food is very scarce here and the prices double Paris. . . . The Duke is still reluctant to have an A.D.C. . . . The Princess Maria of Italy lives here with her husband Prince Louis Bourbon. They seem to have no money and a rather miserable existence. . . .

11 May 1946: I am delighted about the idea of the parcels and if you tell me what they cost I can send you a cheque for them. Food is really quite a problem. If you get off in different parcels a couple of Virginia Hams it would be perfect – cheese is welcome – canned butter – olives – olive oil – really anything – tinned fish (even though we are on the sea not many people fish because of the mines). . . . I have Mrs Bernadotte coming to stop for the first three days of June! She is the one who married Prince Carl Johann of Sweden who has given up 'everything'.[5] They live in N.Y. but he

---

[3] The railway tycoon, who had become a friend of the Windsors during their years in the Bahamas.

[4] Probably a reference to the coming referendum on the proposed constitution of the Fourth Republic, due to take place in May.

[5] Prince Carl Johann, Duke of Dalecarlia (b.1916), the fourth son of King Gustaf VI Adolf of Sweden, was obliged to give up all his styles and titles and his rights to the Swedish throne upon his marriage to a Swedish divorcée in February 1946. He thus became plain 'Mr Bernadotte' – though some years later he was to be created a count in the Luxemburg peerage. His wife Kerstin thus joined the club of morganatic wives of which the Duchess of Windsor was the most notable member. Another was the Princess de Réthy, whom King Leopold of Belgium had married during the war, and who was to become a close friend of the Duchess.

wrote the Duke to know if she could come to see us – as she is coming to Europe for something. It will be quite amusing! Time is simply flying by – we always seem to have someone here. Tuesday we go to Marseilles to visit British units there and in Toulon – also to try to pick up some army rations. . . . I am thinking of you always and wish I could have your advice on the many problems we must face in the future. However I do not think we can make a definite decision until after our trip to the U.S. and I will have the chance to talk to you there. I dread facing up to the press once again in that country. . . . Kenneth de Courcy has been staying with us for a few days – you remember the Hunters' friend who writes the Review of World Affairs letter. . . . I am very short of candles for the table. Could you sent 6 dozen of the long ones? . . . Keep gay and don't let the Russians get you! . . .

12 July 1946: . . . We have been quite busy here getting ready for the guests that seem to be calling up from all parts of the world wanting to come all at once to La Cröe. . . . We have also had quite a few people passing through for lunch, dinner etc. – a great drain on the pocket book in this country. . . . We have taken this place for another year – it is too hard to move and I think we should have some place to come to in an emergency – this is of course always subject to its being sold. Our plans are to leave here around the end of August, be in Paris for about 2 weeks, go to England for about 2 weeks, and sail [for New York] on the first trip of the Queen Elizabeth. . . . We have written to the [Waldorf] Towers and had a reply that the rates are much higher. I am afraid the U.S. will not be a great improvement on the cost of living here. There is no change in the attitude across the Channel. So now the question is what to do and where. Also I feel the time has come when the Duke should write a book. It is no use going down in history with Mr Winchell[6] as our historian. And it is fair that everybody should now know the truth. . . .

---

[6] Walter Winchell, New York social columnist who regularly disparaged the Windsors.

Part Three

Postwar Life and Letters

Chapter Nine

Ex-King's Story
1946–51

*T*he next few years, if not exactly unhappy, were restless and rootless ones for the Windsors, who had no permanent home and little idea of where or how they were going to live. By the summer of 1946 there was clearly no immediate prospect of the Duke's being welcomed back to England by his family or given any kind of position by the powers that be; but he did not cease to hope that this state of affairs would eventually change in his favour, and this made him reluctant to establish himself too firmly elsewhere. Until September 1949 he clung uncertainly to La Cröe in order to maintain his French residence with its tax advantages; but while the Duchess came to love the villa and the life she had created around it, and they varied their Riviera existence with occasional hotel visits to Paris, it proved a far from ideal temporary solution to their problem. It was a rented house whose owners constantly threatened to sell over their heads; France was in economic and political turmoil; they had no proper Paris base; and the fierce United Kingdom exchange control regulations of the austerity period made it almost impossible for their English friends to come out to visit them. Meanwhile they examined various possibilities of constructing a life elsewhere.

One solution was simply to turn up in England for a period and live there quietly, accepting the chill winds of austerity and swallowing the bitter pill of official ostracism. In the autumn of 1946 they experimented with this idea, staying for a month at Ednam Lodge, a country house near London lent to them by the Duke's old friend Eric, Earl of Dudley: apart from the unhappy trip of September 1939, it was the Duchess's first stay in England since the Abdication.

They received a heartening welcome from their friends; but the visit was spoiled by a distressing event – the spectacular theft of the Duchess's jewels (many of them inscribed love tokens from the Duke) from Ednam Lodge on 16 October, only five days after their arrival. They were pleasantly astonished, however, by the hundreds of letters of support they received following this loss, many from influential people. 'It really is too bad,' read a typical note from a Member of Parliament whom they had entertained in the Bahamas. 'An abominable incident, when you and HRH were entitled to expect a warm welcome and a peaceful and happy stay in England. I'm sure the whole country sympathises with you and hopes you may quickly get back your property. . . .'

From England they sailed that November to try another experiment – that of five months' stay in America, during which they based themselves at the Waldorf Towers in New York but also visited Palm Beach, Nassau and their ranch in Canada. The Duke enjoyed this trip immensely. In February 1947, as we have seen in Chapter 4, the Duchess wrote to George Allen from Palm Beach to say that the Duke would be happy to retire to America for the greater part of the year, if only the King would allow him the use of Fort Belvedere in the autumn and spring. 'It is a waste of time being homeless on the face of the earth and most disturbing. . . .' The Windsors seem to have been fairly optimistic that this favour would be granted, for in the spring of 1947 they returned to England, renting a house in Sunningdale near the Fort. On 19 July that year the Duchess wrote to Aunt Bessie reporting that their visit had been quite enjoyable:

> We saw all the old gang and had week-end guests etc. The Great Family were the same – the Duke made the usual visits – no job from any direction of course and I really feel we have been away from England for so long that it would be difficult to take up the customs and ideas again. So again the question of where to live which is really spoiling our days and nights. . . .

In spite of the Duchess's doubts, the Duke would certainly have grasped at the opportunity of living again at the Fort had the King honoured his promise and put it at his brother's disposal as his English residence. But this was not to be.

Further confirmation, if such were required, of the intransigent attitude of the Duke's family was provided by the fact that they received no invitation to the wedding of Princess Elizabeth to Philip Mountbatten in November 1947. Later on, the Windsors' exclusion from such occasions would be taken for granted; but this was the first significant royal event since the Coronation of George VI, and their absence from it excited much press comment on both sides of the Atlantic. On 11 September the Duchess wrote to Aunt Bessie:

> I think the answer to the question 'were you invited to the wedding' should be the plain truth 'no' and then refuse to comment, don't you? Naturally the English do not want this so definite and the Duke has been told he should avoid answering! Why should we go on protecting their rude attitude after ten and a half years? I can't see how any sane person should think I would be asked after all this time and I don't think it hurts to answer the truth, do you?

Before the wedding took place, they were off on another extended winter tour of the United States. This time they experimented with rented houses there – in Florida during February and March, and on Long Island during April and May. Once again the Duke was tempted to make their permanent home in America: but there were fearful obstacles. Life would be expensive, and he would lose the tax privileges he enjoyed in France. He hesitated cutting himself off from all prospect of return to England by interposing the Atlantic. The Duchess, oddly enough, was not in the least attracted by the prospect of returning permanently to her native land, though her principal concern was for the happiness of her husband. She felt her people had let her down in 1936 by sensationalizing her dilemma, and dreaded the attentions of the American press. She had also fallen in love with France, which in spite of political disorder was on the way to becoming a land of gracious living once more. They returned to Europe in the summer of 1948 with little better idea of how they would organize their future.

Their arrival back in France coincided with two developments: the outbreak of the Cold War in Europe with the start of the Berlin blockade, and an illness of the Duke. In a moment of nervousness, and much to the dismay of the Duchess, he had the majority of their belongings at Antibes packed up and sent off to storage in New York. They vaguely planned moving back to Long Island, and thought of taking Baron Eugene de Rothschild's house there for two years. But, as it ironically turned out, they did not feel rich enough to return to America and rejoin their paraphernalia, and remained in Europe for the next eighteen months.

For the first year of that time, between the summers of 1948 and 1949, they lived a curious existence at La Cröe, occupying a small suite of rooms in the great villa surrounded by their few remaining possessions, entertaining modestly and seeing occasional friends. One couple they saw frequently were the Winston Churchills, who were much in the South of France at this time: the Duke renewed his friendship with his old supporter. But there was another spectacle which cast a gloom: the slow death of Katherine Rogers from cancer of the larynx. She and her husband Herman, who had sheltered the Duchess in the dark days of December 1936, had remained the Windsors' best friends on the Côte d'Azur. With their disappearance from the scene, the Windsors decided to take the plunge and move their principal home back to Paris. In the spring of 1949, after boring negotiations and numerous hesitations, they took a year's lease of No. 85, rue de la Faisanderie, a somewhat lugubrious town house in the sixteenth district of the city belonging to their friend Paul-Louis Weiller. It was let to them fully furnished (their own furniture still being across the Atlantic) and intended to be no more than a short-term base while they continued to work out their future: but they were to stay there for more than four years. In September they finally let go of La Cröe, to the Duchess's regret.

Once again, the Duchess's letters to her aunt provide revealing glimpses of their life at this time – a picture of worry and confusion as they strove to make the best of their circumstances.

La Cröe, 16 August 1948: We have had a disturbed time – you remember I was not looking forward to this journey to Europe [*sic*]. . . . The Duke has had colitis and when he is sick as you know he becomes the real invalid. Also the Russians have him down and he wants to get everything out of this country at once. So you see what the situation is. . . . The Duke is in a strange mood – upset over the world and plans which are hard to adjust for us around taxes. . . . We will picnic here until after Christmas. . . .

La Cröe, 15 September 1948: We got most of the silver and furniture off today. I am sure it's the right thing but I do hate breaking up a home. . . . After the Churchill visit which ended Monday after lunch we told the chef he was to leave and what a scene! . . . The Duke will go to London next month to stop with 'Ma' and attend to business while I try to hunt a 'Home' in Paris . . . hoping later to get the wherewithal from England to purchase away from this disturbed continent.[1] . . . What a mess everything is and people here are quite resigned to war in a year or two. . . . Winston thinks the Duke's mother has not behaved well – which isn't news, is it? There is a lot to be said against as well as for royalty – there is no doubt their upbringing makes them hard with no understanding. The Churchills could not have been nicer or more friendly. . . .

La Cröe, 27 September 1948: We are packing away – very sad but the news gets no more reassuring. We have decided to keep our rooms, the white salon and the dining room for the moment. . . . Winston is at Monte and I have become his favourite opponent at Oklahoma. . . . The weather is wonderful – still swimming every day. . . .

Montpellier, 2 October 1948: I motored over yesterday to be with Herman and Katherine as K is having her throat operated on this morning. . . . She has great difficulty breathing. . . . It is all heartbreaking and their courage you could not believe – and naturally there is no fooling K with her medical knowledge. Nobody really knows about this dread disease. I spent 3 hours with her yesterday and she is as though a tooth were coming out – so wonderful and he must suffer even more to see her. I feel so upset over the poor things. . . .

Ritz Hotel, Paris, 20 October 1948: We arrived here a week ago and since then have been trying to find a residence. . . . I am thinking of taking Mr Weiller's town house. It is not what one would select as decoration but as we will not be in it much we can survive with some of our things added. . . . The Duke is in London for ten days with Mama and I seem to have plenty of friends to prevent me from being lonely. The coal situation means electricity cuts and a cold winter. . . . I have a new maid – a Belgian who seems excellent and was found for me by the Princess de Réthy, King Leopold's wife.

[1] It was a ludicrous fact that the Windsors, who were effectively prevented from making their home in Great Britain, were unable, under the existing currency restrictions, to remove their capital from that country.

Herman writes that Katherine is recovering and suffers no more discomfort. I am afraid all this is temporary and that it will break out again in another spot. They are both wonderfully brave. I think we shall have a very sad Xmas with them. . . .

Ritz Hotel, Paris, 5 November 1948: We are all sunk over the election[2] which is a great help for the socialists. Europe is of course delighted to see Santa remain. No-one here can be convinced that Republicans are anything but anti-Britain and Europe. R[oosevelt] is still the great hero over here. . . . Can you beat the world today and capital levy in G.B. Only HRH's family seem to have everything. . . .

La Cröe, 1 December 1948: I am writing on the terrace in beautiful sunshine and this makes it harder to pack up. I am so confused by our plans that I do not know whether it is a mistake to give up this nice place where we can afford to live in comfort to pursue the Duke's desire to live on Long Island which I know we can't do in the same comfort. There is nothing to do here and no-one to see except the Rogers – and Katherine is speechless for all this month and must live the life of an invalid. The Weiller house in Paris is gloomy and I must find something else as soon as possible. Most of the furniture is now in N.Y. – shouldn't be surprised if it all came back again! . . . I don't see how my friends live in the grande luxe and pay those taxes. Americans are certainly rich and have the opportunity of making money – whereas the Duke has none and [investment] incomes nowadays are not much good and we can't bring capital out of G.B. We must be unique, unable to spend capital. The King's illness is too bad.[3] The Duke spoke to his brother on the telephone. . . .

La Cröe, 18 December 1948: I am struggling to get up a gay Christmas. My bag for Christmas night consists of General and Madame Catroux,[4] the Aga Khan and the Begum, Princess Glinka and her granddaughter,[5] Rory Cameron[6] and Charles Murphy the writer

---

[2] Truman's re-election as President of the United States.

[3] On 23 November it had been announced by Buckingham Palace: 'The King is suffering from an obstruction to the circulation through the arteries of the legs. . . . Complete rest has been advised and treatment . . . has been initiated. . . .'

[4] General Georges Catroux, the colonial administrator and Gaullist wartime hero who had served as French Ambassador to Moscow from 1945 to 1948.

[5] The mother-in-law and daughter of Paul-Louis Weiller.

[6] An American-born travel writer, decorator and landscape gardener who lived at Cap Ferrat.

boy.[7] . . . Katherine has had a relapse – rather puts the gloom on Xmas for us, we were to have lunched with them etc. Anyway if anyone can win this fight she has the real guts. . . . Winston and Mrs Churchill are coming to Monte after Xmas and we hope to spend New Year's eve with them. . . . I leave here 7 January for Paris [to get the house ready] the Duke remaining behind with Murphy to work. I think I should go down in history as Wallis the home maker. I am fed up with my movie star and his house decisions. . . .

The Duke at La Cröe to the Duchess in Paris, 16 January 1949: The weather continues to be wonderful here and I have ordered lunch to be served on the porch for the Rogers. I have been playing golf with Liliane and Leopold[8] at Mandelieu. Otherwise I'm lashed to my desk or rather my card table and the work goes on apace. 'Faisanderie' sounds the end and unless it complicates the movement to Paris too much I 'humbly submit' keeping this house on. . . . It would be far better for our health and for writing the book at this stage. But you will see and only YOU shall decide my darling one. It is very sad and lonely here without you. . . . God bless WE. More and more and more my sweetheart. . . .[9]

Duchess to Aunt Bessie, La Cröe, 26 February 1949: Here I still am sitting in the most heavenly sunshine. . . . The coast is deserted, 'the Kings have departed', but the weather remains divine. . . . The Duke has stayed on because of the book he is undertaking and this is a perfect spot for concentration. . . . Tomorrow I am having 17 officials to lunch to say goodbye – all in French! We dined with Katherine and Herman last night – so sad to see them. We are complete slaves to the book and therefore future plans depend on how that goes. . . . I am really so twisted around that I make very little sense on plans any more. . . . I really think I must have been temporarily out of my head when I rented rue de la Faisanderie – it is just a servants' hotel. . . .

Ritz Hotel, 1 May 1949: We had a very nice visit to England, saw all the old friends, enjoyed the usual treatment from the Great Family. . . . We have to move next week-end into rue de la Faisanderie – but I dread it. Never was there such a gloomy dark spot

---

[7] See p. 243 below.

[8] King Leopold of the Belgians and his morganatic wife the Princesse de Réthy, friends and neighbours of the Windsors on the Côte d'Azur.

[9] This is the first postwar letter from the Duke to the Duchess to be preserved among their papers in Paris.

and I can do nothing to cheer it up. We will still be here when you arrive and can go off to La Cröe shortly afterwards. It will be lovely to see you darling and I hope you won't be too uncomfortable in a half closed house. . . . All plans depend on the temperamental author. . . .

⚔

The Duchess's letters show that, although they were no nearer to finding a life which suited them, the Duke had at last found an absorbing occupation – the writing of his memoirs.

Ever since the end of the war, the Duke had been under pressure to begin a work of autobiography. He was especially pressed by two great newspapermen who were friends of his – Lord Beaverbrook, owner of the *Express* group in London, who had been one of his principal supporters during the Abdication crisis, and Henry R. Luce, proprietor of the Time–Life magazine empire in New York, whom he had got to know on wartime visits to America. Though sympathetic to the Duke, these two magnates were principally motivated (as he was well aware) by the realization that his story would be a magnificent scoop for their titles. Of the Duke's advisers, the ever reticent George Allen was against the idea; Walter Monckton, realizing that it would give the Duke a necessary chance to justify himself, was in favour of it; and his New York lawyer Henry G. ('Hank') Walter – who offered his services as literary agent – was strongly in favour. The Duchess also encouraged him in the project, which would have the triple advantage of earning him substantial sums, enabling him to express his own point of view and at least temporarily solving the problem of what he was to do with himself.

The Duke proceeded cautiously. In New York in February 1947 he accepted a lucrative proposition from Luce to write a series of four long articles, under the general title 'The Education of a Prince', dealing with his career up to the end of the First World War. The writing of these uncontroversial pieces brought him much pleasure and presented few difficulties, and caused a mild sensation when they were published in *Life* and the *Sunday Express* in December of the same year. During the early months of 1948, Luce and Walter worked assiduously on him to go further and write his own account of the events surrounding the Abdication: but he hesitated to embark on this potentially explosive project. He sought the advice of Beaverbrook, who wrote to him that July:

It is clearly of high importance that such a work should be prepared without delay. If there is any postponement, the facts will inevitably become blurred and distorted.

Such a book must be a historical document of the first importance. It should shape the work of all the historians of that era for all time. It is imperative that you should write the record yourself. No-one else can do it with such authority. . . . What you wrote last year produced a response which must have gratified you. . . . The British people have never really understood the story of the Abdication. . . . If your account is given to them, you may be sure you will get an overwhelming response. . . .

'I am both interested and gratified by your comments,' replied the Duke from La Cröe in August 1948. 'The telling of the events of 1936 will be difficult and will require all the tact and skill at my command. . . . The unsettled state of the world and the war clouds which hang so heavily over us hardly create an atmosphere conducive to quiet thought and reminiscing. . . .' Eventually he agreed to proceed, on the basis – possibly unique in the annals of publishing agreements – that *Life* would provide him with all necessary editorial, secretarial and research assistance, along with an advance of $25,000, without there being any obligation upon him to produce any particular manuscript by any particular date. Had he wished, he could have dabbled at the project at Luce's expense for the rest of his life.

In the summer of 1948 a combination of illness and anxiety at the world situation had contrived to plunge the Duke into depression; but as the weeks passed, and he relived the dramatic events of twelve years earlier, his mood turned to euphoria, and the work began to proceed with astonishing speed. Many old intimates – Monckton and Allen, Beaverbrook and Churchill, Aird and Metcalfe – came out to see him at La Cröe to share their memories of 1936 with him, and these visits stimulated the Duke to the point where he forgot about the Cold War and did not even think of leaving Europe that winter. His correspondence reveals his growing excitement in the task.

To Dan Longwell, editor of 'Life', 28 August 1948: Sir Walter and Lady Monckton are with us now for a ten days visit and he has contributed valuable and fascinating details with regard to the story of

1936. As soon as I can arrange to get my records from Great Britain, I shall have a unique and comprehensive collection of material. . . . Of course the dangerous international situation to which one is much nearer in Europe makes long-range planning impossible. But if there's no shooting the Duchess and I will remain here until New Years as it's a fine and peaceful place for writing. . . .

To George Allen, 8 September 1948: Any details from your own records would be very useful and valuable additions to the material I am collecting. I have not yet asked the Duchess to talk and reminisce of those eventful times, but her contribution will of course be essential and invaluable. Winston and Mrs Churchill are arriving here tomorrow to stop with us and I am hoping to get him alone and clear up some points that are confused in my mind. Max Beaverbrook is also on this coast and I know I shall have no difficulty in getting him to talk. . . .

To Walter Monckton, 2 October 1948: The 1936 file is growing ever bulkier. . . .

'Round robin' to Sir Godfrey Thomas, 'Jack' Aird, 'Fruity' Metcalfe and others, 7 December 1948: With the thought that you might be interested to continue reminiscing, I was wondering whether you would like to come south for a few days in January. We can take care of any franc expenses you might incur and the sunshine could be appealing. . . .

To 'Hank' Walter, 16 December 1948: The work goes on apace, and this is the ideal location for writing – not even the proverbial 'cat' on the Côte d'Azur, and the weather is pleasantly warm. I hope to have 1936 finished, at least as a rough draft, by New Years. . . .

Though the forecast that the Abdication chapters would be in draft by the end of 1948 proved somewhat optimistic, the Duke was sufficiently encouraged by his progress to sign a contract with the well-known New York publishing firm of Putnam for the delivery, within two years, of a book of memoirs covering his life up to the end of his reign, to be entitled *A King's Story*.

❖

Something must be said about how the Duke went about his literary task.[10] It has been alleged, unfairly, that *A King's Story* was not his own work. It is true that he had no training in writing for publication: on the other hand, he had (as his letters show) a lively and characteristic written style, and also possessed a talent for grasping the detailed facts of any subject that absorbed him. What he lacked was a mastery of the technique of historical research, and the ability to give structure to his writing. He needed assistants to help him assemble his material, which would then be woven into the form of a draft chapter or article by a ghostwriter. When presented with these ghosted drafts, however, he rewrote them completely, often in longhand, using his own language and incorporating his own thoughts. This would be only the beginning of a painstaking process of revision, one version after another being dictated to a secretary.

From July 1947 to December 1950, the 'ghost' assigned to the project was Charles J. V. Murphy, a senior journalist on the staff of *Life* whom the Duke had inherited under his contracts with that publication. He spent much time with the Windsors, living in their houses and even accompanying them on holidays to such resorts as Como and Biarritz. Over the articles on the Duke's early life written in the second half of 1947, the collaboration between the two men seems to have proceeded smoothly; but after that their relations were often stormy. As a journalist, Murphy sought to sensationalize the Duke's story, whereas the Duke himself was concerned to present a sober recital of events. Increasingly, Murphy found his contributions relegated to the waste-paper basket. Murphy was also unpopular with the Duchess and the staff; and this animus eventually rubbed off on the Duke who, although he respected Murphy as an experienced professional, was increasingly irritated by his arrogance and unpunctuality. Possibly Murphy felt himself to have been slighted and snubbed: if so, he amply avenged himself thirty years later by writing a grotesque book about the couple whose hospitality (and a large share of whose literary earnings) he had enjoyed, a book full of scandalous untruths which presented a picture of the Windsors which others who had known them at the time found unrecognizable.

---

[10] For the information that follows, I am particularly grateful to Miss Anne Seagrim, who was the Duke's secretary from August 1950 to August 1954 and closely involved in the last stages of work on the memoirs. Miss Seagrim, who is contemplating writing her own memoirs of the years she spent with the Windsors, has kindly allowed me to quote in this chapter from a series of letters which she wrote at the time to her family in England.

The difficulty of working with Murphy was not the only problem the Duke encountered as the work proceeded. Churchill, who began by co-operating in the Duke's research, quickly became fearful that his association with the book might affect his political standing in Great Britain and his personal standing with the Royal Family. He was still leader of the Conservative Party and hoped again to become Prime Minister. He begged the Duke not to use their private correspondence at the time of the Abdication, and to ensure that the book did not appear before the forthcoming British general election (1950), to which the Duke reluctantly consented. Beaverbrook, on the other hand, who had been the arch-enemy of Stanley Baldwin in the British politics of the thirties, was only too happy to help the Duke with a flood of dramatic reminiscence, and in particular to encourage him in the idea that Baldwin had conspired at his destruction in 1936 – a seed which fell on fertile ground, for the Duke had long believed Baldwin to have been his principal adversary. Allen begged the Duke not to follow this line:

> It seems to me to be the worst of tactics to slang S.B., and to accuse him either directly or by innuendo of double-crossing, and of exploiting your terrible problem for his own personal political advantage. I do not myself believe that this has any basis in fact, and . . . I am sure there will be a storm of denials from well-informed quarters, such as his cabinet colleagues. . . .

Alas, the Duke ignored these wise warnings, and most historians would agree that the role assigned to Baldwin is much the weakest part of his book.

The very fact of the Duke writing his memoirs also enraged his brother and his mother, as well as his former private secretaries Hardinge and Lascelles (who deserved far more than Baldwin the distinction of having been his enemies in 1936). The Court refused to co-operate in the project in the slightest way: even a mild request to let Murphy visit his childhood home at York Cottage, Sandringham, was curtly refused. On the other hand, although his book closed with the end of his reign, the months of reflection on the past filled the Duke anew with dismay at all that had happened to him since the Abdication, and in particular at the continuing refusal to accord equal status to his wife. As we have seen, 1949 was the year in which he made his last great attempt to obtain a royal title for the Duchess – to no avail.

The series in *Life* finally appeared in June 1950. The last stages of work, which took place during the Windsors' winter tour of America, had been marked by particular disharmony between the Duke and his principal assistant. 'The Duke has really worked like a slave on these articles,' wrote the Duchess to Allen from Canada on 12 April 1950. 'Every a.m. at Palm Beach he was up at 8, left all dinner parties at 11. Murphy was extremely difficult, and I think impertinent, writing many stupid things as well, which has caused the Duke double work. I cannot see how the Duke can stand him, much though his patience is something to admire. I hate to think that he has to spend more months in Murphy's company, because of the book.' Murphy's employer, however, was well satisfied with the finished result. 'My sincere congratulations on what is a really superb piece of literary history,' Luce wrote to the Duke on 28 April. 'If all history could be so well told, there would be no trouble in getting schoolboys, and their parents, to read it. . . .'

The latest articles had earned the Duke $100,000 from *Life* and £32,500 from the *Sunday Express*, with all the book royalties still to come. Even allowing for agents' commission and Murphy's cut,[11] these were substantial sums; and it was with a slightly greater sense of financial security that the Windsors addressed themselves yet again to the question of where to live. Back in Paris in the late spring of 1950, reinstalled in the rented gloom of the rue de la Faisanderie, they hunted for a house of their own and very nearly purchased La Clairière, a large villa with a park in Garches, a fashionable rural suburb to the south-west of the city. It was a short walk from Saint-Cloud where the Duke played his golf; and nearby residents included their friend the Aga Khan. As the Duke agonized over whether to buy, he drafted some random handwritten reflections attempting to express his thoughts to the Duchess:

---

[11] He took 21 per cent of all earnings – except for the payments from *Life*, since he was on the magazine's payroll.

The choice confronting us is whether we want a home in the country (there is no other kind of home to my way of thinking), where we can enjoy our possessions, our garden, our dogs and our property.

As it appears to be impossible to establish a country home in America, the alternative is France where we have exceptional tax advantages. La Clairière appears to be the best compromise between the country and Paris and its amenities. But it is a very expensive property. The house will cost a great deal to fix. It is in land we don't like and where we would be committed to spending at least 6 months of every year.

La Clairière might prove to be a ball & chain round our ankles during our lifetime & a white elephant to the one who survives who won't want to live there but would never be able to realise all the capital sunk in the property.

The whole point of La Clairière as I see it is that it would provide an all round home with secluded amenities in the country. But it would restrict travel & isolate us from our friends. . . .

The alternative form of life would revolve around cities, travel, the Ranch. A small house or apartment in Paris: *no country*. A hotel or apartment in New York: *no country*. Travel, boats, hotels: *no country*. The E.P. Ranch would provide the only form of country life. A lovely place, but only habitable from July to September and very isolated from all comforts and amenities and social life.

But this schedule would be less binding in these uncertain times. On the other hand, it would mean disposing of the bulk of our possessions for which there would be no room in Paris, NY or the Ranch.

It all boils down to how to get the most out of our untaxed income to give us BOTH the greatest pleasure & happiness. Although you like the country, it means more to me than to you.

I am the one who is a mass of indecision. I have not taken the question of staff into consideration. That would depend on the size of the establishment we bought or rented in Paris.

Do we want to live in the country as most oldies of our class are doing? I say yes – but not further out than La Clairière for your sake. . . . One could spend longer in America by breaking the duration of our stays with trips to Canada, Mexico, Nassau, South America etc.

These random notes are the result of my thinking & puzzling for many months past. I hope they are not too incoherent and may help us make up our minds. But I'm still puzzled to death.

The Windsors went so far as to obtain an official exemption from the French tax which would have been due on the purchase of the property; this was one of the first important services performed for them by their new French legal adviser, Maître Suzanne Blum. But at the end of June 1950 the Korean War broke out, and the Duke, unwilling to risk his capital 'in these uncertain times', withdrew from the transaction.

It remained to fill in the gaps among the mass of articles and chapters and so round off the book. The Duke hoped to complete this task with Murphy by 16 November 1950, on which date he and the Duchess planned to sail in *Queen Mary* for New York; but as the date drew near it became clear that they would not be finished in time. 'Our plans change like the weather due to this wretched book,' wrote the Duchess to Aunt Bessie in October. The new plan – to which the Duke had agreed – was that she should sail on her own on the 16th, and he would follow with Murphy in *Queen Elizabeth* on the 30th. 'This leaves Murphy and himself here for 2 weeks without any interruptions of people and dinner parties. . . . I get 2 weeks away from it all if I can keep NY quiet. So the idea is that you would spend those 2 weeks with me at the [Waldorf] Towers. Does that appeal?'

By the beginning of November the Duke was already regretting his decision. 'HRH is pretty miserable about her going on ahead,' wrote Miss Seagrim, the Duke's new secretary, in a letter to her sister, 'and wishing he hadn't said he'd stay till he'd finished the book.' But it was too late to change arrangements yet again, and on 16 November the Duchess duly embarked without him. It was an error of judgement. Throughout the thirteen years of their married life, the Windsors had never been separated for more than ten days at a time; and their annual arrival in New York was always a big news event. The Duchess's sudden appearance on her own was likely to encourage the story for which the scandal columns of the newspapers had been longing for years – that their marriage had run into difficulties.

No sooner had the Duchess departed than the Duke began to pine for her. The day after her departure he wrote to her:

'On the Street'![12]

Paris 16e

November 17th 1950

My Sweetheart,

Oh! dear Oh! dear. It was terrible watching the train take you away from me and I feel so desperately lonely without you. Please don't ever do this to me again. . . . Take care of yourself my precious darling one and I hope the voyage has been smooth and restful and the press not too difficult upon arrival in NY. Cable me please and give my love to Aunt Bessie. God bless WE. I miss you and love you more and more and more.

DAVID

He tried to devote himself to the book, but Murphy's behaviour was becoming intolerable to him. On 20 November he wrote to her:

. . . Hank[13] has just called from New York and asked how the book was progressing. I told him as slow as molasses and that I couldn't get it into Murphy's head that there is any hurry to finish the writing. Murphy's attitude is confirmed by both Miss Seagrim and Waddilove.[14] They say he has told them that the book can't be completed in a hurry and that although he has to go back to work for LIFE in January it is his intention to return at intervals to work with me on the book![15]

It's all so unsatisfactory that I believe Hank's suggestion that Ken Rawson[16] fly over to Paris to needle Charlie is the best solution. Under the circumstances I may decide not to have Murphy return to New York with me for if he won't play ball I'll have to

---

[12] The rue de la Faisanderie.

[13] Henry J. Walter, the American lawyer who acted for the Duke in his writing activities.

[14] Victor A. Waddilove, the Duke's English major-domo and financial secretary, 1946–59.

[15] In one of her letters home, Miss Seagrim recalled the scene: 'HRH nearly blew up, he gasped and spluttered, and said how – and when – and God! – and he supposed when he was out of the room – God what a man! – and he didn't know how he'd not quarrelled with him – and he wouldn't get another cent out of him. Poor HRH, it really was a day of disillusionment for him, but at least it is just possible now that Murphy won't be making the trip to New York. Which would suit us just fine!'

[16] Kennett L. Rawson, the Duke's editor at Putnam's.

find someone else to help me put my material in grammatical and readable shape on time. And I don't believe that presents any problem and Murphy should pay his percentage of the cost.

I wish I could get into the envelope with this letter. . . .

Though the Duke and Murphy had been due to sail for New York on 30 November, the slow progress of the work caused the date of departure to be put back to 9 December. When 30 November came round, however, the Duke suddenly decided to leave then after all. Miss Seagrim described the events of that and the following days in a letter which is worth quoting at length: first, because its account of events is so completely at variance with that published by Murphy; and, second, because of the picture it gives of the Duke's personality at this time.

Cunard Line

R.M.S. Queen Elizabeth

Monday 4th Dec. 1950

. . . I ambled up the rue de la Faisanderie on Thursday in all innocence & was met at the door by Bowyer [the Duke's chauffeur] saying I was needed urgently as HRH had decided to leave that day. . . . Waddilove said not to worry, that I should be following HRH next week with the baggage, but . . . no sooner had I got into the office than HRH rang down to say he'd changed his mind & wanted me to come too. Could I be packed in time? He had been having a terrible time with Murphy – and that morning when the car went to fetch Murphy he sent it away saying he'd had a late night & would HRH mind if he didn't appear till after 11.30. This was too much for HRH who after all had given up all the things he likes most – especially being with the Duchess – to work on the book. So at 9.15 it was action stations. . . . I trotted off and packed in less than an hour & was back again packing the secretary's trunk before HRH was down. He looked piercingly at me & said 'OK?' & I said 'OK, Sir'. 'Packed?' 'Packed, Sir.' & he was delighted. . . . In good time at the station, dogs tucked under our arms. Murphy arrived after us, distraught, almost raving, & HRH said that the one thing he didn't want was Murphy in his carriage for the whole journey. So Waddilove & I sat firmly there & talked idle nothings to HRH. We had tea in the restaurant car – just the three of us – & HRH was in wonderful form, making us roar with laughter over the business, just like a naughty boy. When we talked of rigging up the cabin for working with Murphy, he said he hoped the table would be a very big one so that he would be a long way away from Murphy! We had dinner together too – we had to have Murphy with us then, & he further blotted his copybook (literally) by spilling a glassful of wine over HRH's place! We had great fun, & I made HRH simply screw up his face with laughter once with some nonsense over a roll. He really was sweet, and terribly nice to me all the time.

We arrived at Cherbourg – way cleared by police – civic reception – the press. . . . Waddilove came back saying we were in trouble, that the *Queen Elizabeth* couldn't get into the harbour & that we wouldn't leave that night. HRH, poor dear, looked so upset. The Cunard said they'd got rooms for our party at a hotel, & in pouring rain & raging wind we dismally bundled off in taxis. . . . We got HRH up to his room but hadn't a clue which case his pyjamas were in so he said he'd sleep in his shirt. He was so uncomplaining, & kept thinking with compassion of people with children, realizing how awful it would be – how they would have planned to put them to bed as soon as they got on board, & so on.´ . . . By 8.30 [the next morning] we realized we were not going to get away even then. . . . The whole day we sat in the station, HRH being perfectly marvellous & putting up with everything without a murmur. . . .

We finally boarded that night. I flew around, saw HRH installed with tables, & he settled down instantly & started working. He was as happy as anything & said we'd done wonders. . . . Woke at 8 the next morning feeling sick. I was appalled, but when I told HRH he was terribly sympathetic & said I'd had a very hard time, & just to rest the whole day & worry about nothing. I emerged again about 5 & HRH was very pleased to see me, but wouldn't let me do any work. The next day I was as fit as a fiddle & ever since have been working furiously. . . . HRH couldn't help grinning at me this morning, nor could he resist asking me how I was, because I looked so blooming bouncing! Murphy is just like a sour grape, & being incredibly objectionable both to me & HRH. He is the most horrible man to have around, & I just long for the book to be finished to have shot of him. . . .

. . . We arrive in NY at 7 a.m. He's so excited there's no holding him. . . . I still feel as if I'm in a dream. . . .

Ex-King's Story

. . . At 6.15 a.m. [on board ship] HRH phoned me excitedly & told me to look out of my porthole. As I hadn't got one he said, well then, get on deck quickly, we are in New York. So I dressed like lightning & tore up – & what a sight. We were slowly steaming up the Hudson River, & dawn just breaking. . . . It was quite a confusion, when the Duchess & the lawyers & the press came on board. I managed to do a decent curtsey for once, & she seemed really pleased to see me. We had already waved through HRH's porthole. He was of course quite wild with excitement. The press were very well behaved, apart from taking photographs of their first embraces – but that seems to be the thing over here. . . .

. . . As soon as we arrived I started typing & haven't stopped since. . . . HRH pranced into the room saying: 'There you are you see, same clothes, same work, same everything – just New York instead of Paris, that's all.' The Duchess said she didn't know how I'd managed. . . . HRH gave me a photo – he was so funny & shy about offering it to me! He's been very nice. Yesterday he said that when he's finished the book he would return to normal. 'Of course you've never seen me normal – I'm a very efficient & orderly person really. . . .'

By the New Year, Murphy had vanished from the scene, and the Duke completed *A King's Story* with Miss Seagrim's assistance. 'Nearly finished now I think,' she wrote on 13 January 1951. 'HRH is crawling all over the floor, saying five, six, seven – and other things – as he tries to sort out the chapters.' And on 11 March she finally announced:

. . . We really did finish this damn book yesterday. He had to write the whole of the author's note and acknowledgements in his own hand, as they are going to print from that. . . . At the last moment HRH thought up this travelogue – a schedule of every journey he ever made – which is something terrific. We've been working like slaves on it because no-one else could be bothered to do it accurately. He's very proud of it. . . . He excelled himself by not getting dressed till after the first guest arrived for cocktails. He went roaring into the salon with: 'Hullo all. No I haven't just got up. I've been working on the damn book all day. . . .'

The final effort on his book had exhausted the Duke, but a further trial awaited him. During February 1951, while he was correcting his proofs in New York, the Duchess fell ill and had to go into hospital. The nature of her condition was kept secret even from the staff. 'The Duchess is in hospital having a check up,' wrote Miss Seagrim to her sister on 20 February.

> At first the intention was to say she had flu, but some low hound at the hospital seems to have talked, and the papers are full of it. We have had the most awful time with the reporters ringing up third degreeing us (mostly me) every two minutes. When the fiftieth or so woman rang me up this morning she asked if the Duke and Duchess were on the point of separation! And one has to be polite to them. . . . Poor HRH is very miserable, he's so tired with working so hard, furious about the press, worried about the Duchess, though there can't be much wrong with her as she's been looking splendid lately.

Appearances were deceptive: the Duchess was suffering from cancer of the womb, and had to undergo a hysterectomy. 'She really is an astonishing person,' wrote Miss Seagrim in her next letter home on 11 March.

> She's certainly had quite a big operation, and at present walks slightly bent, as one does when one has had stitches – but she's been to a dinner party, and been out already. She is not allowed to go away, because she has to go up to the hospital every morning for some treatment. I had to entertain her nurse on Friday evening, and she said she's never known such an amazing person in her life. She says the Duchess just throws illness away. . . .

The Windsors had been due to go to Palm Beach for a week in the second half of March; and the Duchess insisted that the Duke, who badly needed a rest, make the trip without her. They spoke every day; but on 20 March he wrote to her from his hotel there:

Sweetheart,

It would be lovely here if only you were too. I'm very lonely, although everybody is very kind and it's good to get off the sidewalks of New York. My golf was naturally lousy the first three days but it's coming back eanum [a little] now. I've not been in swimming yet but I'm always in by midnight so am getting lots of 'driz'. I didn't realise how wacked [*sic*] I was until I got here and the book washed right out of my hair.

It's too bad Dr Watson has chained you to 'the Beast'[17] for all of April. But I guess he's right my darling one and the important thing is for you not to be made sick and sunk. We must get you quite well again and maybe the weather will improve and we can go away week-ends. . . .

God bless WE my sweetheart. I miss you terribly. Thomas sends his love to you and Mr Pick too.[18] More and more. Your

DAVID

One thing which caused him astonishment – and mild satisfaction – was a letter from his mother which almost unprecedentedly mentioned the Duchess. 'I feel so sorry for your great anxiety about your wife, and . . . we must hope the improvement will continue. Do write me a short account of what has really happened. . . .'

The Duchess continued to make a good recovery; and April was a month of triumph for them both. *A King's Story* was published by Putnam amidst great fanfares on the 14th. 'HRH in terrific form,' wrote Miss Seagrim, 'very happy about the book, which has had a wonderful reception, and the reviews have been too marvellous – completely beyond our wildest expectations. . . . He spends most of the day signing his name.' The long task was at last over; and as the Duke and his secretary spent a wistful evening in their office, clearing away the years of paperwork and 'packing the tin boxes', he remarked to her – 'with a look that meant a thousand things' – that

[17] A radium treatment machine.
[18] Thomas and Pookie, the Duke's Cairn terriers.

he might one day write a sequel volume relating all that had happened to him since the Abdication. 'And I dare say', he added, with a repetition of the confidential look, 'it will be a great deal more inter-esting than this one. . . .'

The Windsors duly returned to Paris and the rue de la Faisanderie that May; and on 4 November the Duchess wrote to Aunt Bessie to describe their life during the intervening months. The Duke had been 'all in after the book', but over the summer they had enjoyed a delightful boating trip and taken a house in Biarritz, where they had both managed to have 'a real rest'. Since their return in September, their time had been taken up house hunting, which had been 'very discouraging. We cannot find the one unit near Paris, and the Duke must have the country. So now we are looking for a small house or flat in Paris and something small in the country for week-ends.' In spite of the success of *A King's Story*, they were still having to cut down their expenses and were planning to sell numerous possessions for which they had no room. The Duchess looked forward to seeing her aunt in New York before Christmas, and closed with the injunction: 'Don't pay any attention to those vile US papers. There never has been a cross word between the Duke and myself and we laugh at all their nonsense.'

Strangely, the Duchess said nothing about the British general election which had taken place only ten days earlier, and returned Churchill and the Conservative Party to power after six and a half years of Labour government. During his period of opposition Churchill (in spite of his disinclination to help the Duke with his memoirs) had seen much of the Duke and they had renewed something of their old friendship;[19] and the new cabinet contained several of the Duke's good personal friends – notably Walter Monckton as Minister of Labour. The Duke had not yet settled down in France; he continued to keep his options open for the future; and while the attitude of his family showed little sign of change he nevertheless hoped

---

[19] Churchill had, however, provided the Duke with the last line of his book: 'Though it has proved my fate to sacrifice my cherished British heritage along with all the years in its service, I today draw comfort from the knowledge that time has long since sanctified a true and faithful union.'

that the new political regime might signal an improvement in his fortunes. It was therefore in a mood of cheerful optimism that, as had now become his custom, he sailed with the Duchess to spend the winter in America in December 1951.

Chapter Ten

A Change of Sovereign
1952

*I*n the early hours of Wednesday, 6 February 1952, while the Windsors were wintering in New York, King George VI died suddenly in his sleep at Sandringham. He was able, however, to delivery a final posthumous snub to his elder brother, who was not given any early information of the news either from Buckingham Palace or the British Consulate-General in New York. The Duke had to endure the humiliation of learning about the King's death from the newspaper reporters who flocked to the Waldorf Towers where he and the Duchess were staying, clamouring for a statement.

The news came as a great surprise to the Windsors, as to almost everyone. Although the King had not been at all well for some time, and had undergone a serious operation for the removal of a lung the previous September, he had appeared to make a good recovery and only recently had begun to appear again in public. He was just fifty-six. Only his closest family and advisers knew that his condition was such that his heart might fail at any time in 1952 and that the end was likely to be sudden – and this inner circle did not include the Windsors.

'Profound shock' was the phrase used by the Duke in the state-ment he issued to the press that morning; and he used the same expression in his telegrams of sympathy to his bereaved mother and sister-in-law. He declared his intention of departing immediately for Great Britain, and the following evening he sailed from New York aboard *Queen Mary*: this would arrive in England on 13 February, and the funeral was due to take place on the 15th. In a statement which he read to the press at the quayside he spoke of the sadness of the journey ahead of him – which would be all the greater since he would have to undertake it alone, without his wife.

Unable to be with him, the Duchess wrote him a series of letters over the next two weeks which reveal much about both her own state of mind and his. They are consoling and encouraging letters, letters of love, and they show that the Duke's feelings at that moment were made up of three elements – grief, embarrassment and hope. The grief was genuine brotherly grief which transcended the bitterness of their relationship; the embarrassment was provoked by the idea of being with his family again after years of coldness; the hope was that the moment of reunion would also be a moment of reconciliation, that his relations would at last let bygones be bygones. The Duchess was concerned that her husband should be a model of dignity and good behaviour at this decisive hour.

Her first letter was written immediately after his sailing.

Thursday [7 February 1952]

My own darling one,

I hate not being with you at this time when you need me most and when my place is by your side. I will be thinking of you every minute and holding your hand very tight and giving you all the courage I have to go through *gracefully* with this ordeal. Take care of yourself in every way – and the famous charm must come out. I hate, hate having you go away alone – but you are not really alone because I am so much a part of you. Maybe one telephone call or even two just to hear your beloved voice – we must however be careful. Be canny with Dickie [Mountbatten] – we do not want any favours through the young Prince Consort because he doesn't know how *nice* we are. Darling I shall miss you each second and you know that I love you more than anything in the world for always my dearest darling David.

WALLIS

Friday [8 February]

Darling One,

I have just completed all the wires and a few more that came in including one from Alba.[1] Thomas[2] is miserable and takes it out on

---

[1] The Duke of Alba, former Spanish Ambassador to London.
[2] The Duke's Cairn Terrier.

Dizzy.[3] You see he won't sit in the same room as Dizzy here – he is very sad like all of us. I am sending by air all the clippings: the photos are pretty good and the statement reads well. I hope you can make as graceful a statement upon arrival in Southampton as you did on your departure.

Sunday the 10th. Darling – I am enclosing what you cabled Cookie[4] – also 2 other cables as I thought through the Spanish Embassy you could get their addresses in Madrid. Don't neglect this my darling. The papers and radio talk of nothing but Bertie and the girl – very, very sentimental. I hope everything won't be too hard and that for once a few decent things will come your way after the long, sad journey and the difficult relationships. You have jumped many obstacles in your life and this is just one more. I am dealing with everything that comes in – mostly fan mail. I am thinking of you always and love you darling.

WALLIS

Tuesday [12 February]

My Darling One,

Well, tomorrow is the big day[5] and I shall be thinking of you and praying for you. I wish you could wear uniform. I am really scared to breathe. The memorial service[6] is to be Wed the 20th at 8 p.m. in the Cathedral. I hope you can make some headway with Cookie and Mrs Temple Jr.[7] Thomas is very bad because now that you have gone he thinks I am his property and thus Dizzy comes in for a lot of attacks. A few cracks have been made in the papers that you did not fly. I knew there would be. Goodbye and I love you and keep your chin up.

WALLIS

[3] Disraeli, the Duchess's pug.

[4] Windsor nickname for the widowed Queen Elizabeth.

[5] Of the Duke's arrival in England.

[6] The service in New York in memory of the late King.

[7] In their correspondence during the months before their marriage, the Duke and Duchess had used the code 'Mr and Mrs Temple' when writing of King George VI and Queen Elizabeth. Now 'Mrs Temple Senior' (or 'Cookie') referred to the Queen Mother, and 'Mrs Temple Junior' (or 'Shirley') to the Queen.

The Duke arrived in England on 13 February. It is indicative of his mood of depression that, during the voyage, he had only sent the Duchess one telegram.[8] Before proceeding to London (where he was to stay with his mother) he issued the following statement at Southampton.

> This is indeed a sad arrival in my country. I have crossed the Atlantic for the funeral of a dear brother and to comfort my mother, Her Majesty Queen Mary, in the overwhelming sorrow which has overtaken my family and the British Commonwealth of Nations.
>
> Ever since our childhood, the late King and I have been very close. We knew each other well. The outstanding qualities of Kingship he possessed made easier for me the passing on of the uninterrupted succession to the throne.
>
> And my brother drew strength in his heavy responsibilities from what I once described as 'a matchless blessing . . . a happy home with a wife and children'.
>
> So as we mourn a much beloved monarch our hearts go out to the widowed Queen Mother and her two daughters in their grief.
>
> The eldest, Elizabeth, has by God's will been called upon to succeed her father. His well known attributes will I am sure descend to the young princess. . . .
>
> God save the Queen.

In London, the reception the Duke received from his family was at first rather better than he had expected. So much may be deduced from his uncompleted draft of a letter to the Duchess, which dates from this moment, and even more so from an excited letter which the Duchess wrote to him after hearing his news over the telephone, encouraging him to strike while the iron of forgiveness appeared to be hot. Particularly interesting is her insistence that he should *not* bring up the matter of her royal title.

---

[8] This was dispatched on the 11th and read as follows: 'Winston Cables "I thought your words indeed well chosen". Smooth voyage is giving good if lonely rest. Hope digglets better. All love your D.'

The Duke to the Duchess (draft)

My own darling Peaches,

At last I've a moment to write you and there's more room on one of these familiar yellow blanks[9] than on the narrow, thick, black-edged M[arlborough] H[ouse][10] stationery.

Officially and on the surface my treatment within the family has been entirely correct and dignified. I haven't seen all of the visiting foreign royalty but a good many – Uncle Charles of Norway[11] & Ricco of Denmark[12] & I insisted on meeting President Auriol of France[13] at the door [of Marlborough House] & being present when he called here. We have a foot in the door of the Elysée!!

But gosh they move slowly within these palace confines & the intrigues & manoeuvrings backstage must be filling books. . . . [draft ends]

The Duchess to the Duke

Thursday [14 February]

Darling One,

It was lovely to hear your voice and so clear, because you know how hopeless I am with a bad connection. I am so glad that for once things have been done properly regarding you – and this is my advice to you (which I hope you will not leave around the room for all and sundry to read). Now that the door has been opened a crack try and get your foot in, in the hope of making it open even wider in the future because that is the best for WE. I suggest that you see the widow and tell her a little of your feelings that made you write the offending letter.[14] After all, there are two sides to every story. I

---

[9] The lined yellow foolscap used by the British civil service and also in American legal offices, which remained the Duke's favourite form of stationery.

[10] Queen Mary's London residence opposite St James's Palace.

[11] King Haakon VII of Norway (1872–1957), who was twice related to the British Royal Family. He was a nephew of Queen Alexandra, and had married his cousin Maud (1869–1938), George V's youngest sister.

[12] King Frederick IX of Denmark (1899–1972), the Duke's cousin and nephew of the above. He had come to the throne in 1947.

[13] Vincent Auriol, President of France 1947–54. Whether the French President should be met by English royalty 'at the door' or at the top of the staircase was an old and absurd problem of official protocol.

[14] The letter in question appears to have been written by the Duke to his mother. No copy of it has been found among his papers in Paris.

should also say how difficult things have been for us and that also we have gone out of our way to keep our way of life dignified which has not been easy due to the expense of running a correct house in keeping with your position as a brother of the King of England. And leave it there. *Do not mention or ask for anything regarding recognition of me.* I am sure you can win her over to a more friendly attitude. I would also try and see the Queen and Philip casually just so they will know what you are like etc. You should also talk to your mother. I know how you hate being there but this is a golden opportunity and it may only knock but once. I am writing quickly in the hope that this will reach you Monday. I am OK and everyone is more than kind. All my love and do try to do what I suggest.

All my love my Sweetheart,

WALLIS

So anxious to see you walking at the funeral.

Following the promising beginning, however, the Duke had a nasty shock. He was informed that the allowance he received from the Palace – which, as we have seen, amounted to a little over £10,000 per annum – would be discontinued, since it had been a personal favour of the King who was now dead. This was, of course, a violation of the original financial agreement between the two brothers, which was that the Duke should give up everything he had inherited in return for a pension which was clearly meant to be for his own life, not that of his successor.

Learning this news on the day of the King's funeral, the Duchess gave vent to her feelings. She had also been incensed by newspaper reports (inaccurate, as it turned out) that the Duke would not be allowed to walk in uniform in the procession behind the coffin.

The Duchess to the Duke

[Friday, 15 February]

Darling,

I can hardly believe this can go on at this time. I hope you have not taken the expensive trip to lose the £10,000 and to be insulted. When you get this I will know what you did at the funeral. I hope you walk

262

and wear uniform. Why shouldn't you? Love, love and fight for WE. Your

WALLIS

The Duke to the Duchess (telegram)

[Friday, 15 February]

Bless you for letters. Funeral passed off well but am foot weary. Never any question of my not having correct place in procession and wore naval uniform. Am pursuing all our problems relentlessly but tactfully. Missing you terribly more and more. D

The Duchess to the Duke

Sunday [17 February]

Darling One,

I did feel so distressed hearing your voice last night. You sounded so sunk and discouraged. They are beasts to continue to treat you the way they do. Anyway do the best you can my darling but I am afraid Mrs Temple Sr will never give in – all due to that letter which your mother should have kept to herself. I am writing notes today. Friday nearly everyone sent flowers. People have been too kind to both of us. I am afraid Mrs T. Senior won't see you as she may feel she would lose the stand she has taken. Naturally you can't storm the Palace. You will however be able to work on some of the girl's advisors I imagine. Everything the same here. Thomas misses you so much. Hope they won't put me under the pew for the [memorial] service [in New York] but the papers have emphasized my not having been received so much that I think the British will be embarrassed to even have me there. One paper – Daily News – says they could not give you a job because of me. I am so sorry darling one that you are having such a hurting time. All my love goes out to you and is with you. One more question. If the boat gets in at dawn shall I come down? Because of the press I think I should, don't you?

Much, much love
WALLIS

The Duke to the Duchess (telegram)

[18 February]

Your good suggestions in letter fourteenth being carried out. Have asked to see Cookie but general atmosphere frustrating. Am growing long grey beard in snowstorm so cant wait here too long. Glad you well. All repeat all love. D

One senses that the Duke was not much in the mood for writing. It was not until one week after the funeral that he finally completed a letter to his wife, the first sentence of which summed up his lonely and depressed feelings.

Marlborough House, S.W.1.

February 22nd, 1952

My own darling Sweetheart,

Your letters and cables and our telephone talks have been my only props on this difficult, painful and discouraging trip. I'm making notes of all incidents and conversations for when we meet so won't sit up too late writing them to you now.

Cookie was sugar as I've told you and M[ountbatten] and other relations and the Court officials correct and friendly on the surface. But gee the crust is hard & only granite below.

George Allen has some sensible and convincing arguments over the £10,000 if only they'll play at Clarence House.[15] But I'm afraid they've got the fine excuse of national economy if they want to use it. We shall see & anyway we won't know anything for sure until the new Civil List. It's hell to be even this much dependent on these ice-veined bitches, important for WE as it is.

I hope to see Cry Baby[16] again before I sail and have been invited to lunch at Clarence House next Tuesday when I get back from Paris.

I'm sorry I haven't written before, Sweetheart, but I've not had a minute. I'll call you from Paris Sunday afternoon N.Y. time and

---

[15] The residence of the new Queen and her husband, pending their move to Buckingham Palace.

[16] Winston Churchill. See the Duke's *notes* below.

make a report. You'll never know how much I miss you, Peaches, and just can't wait to get back to you and out of all this here. . . .

There has of course been no adverse comment over my walking in uniform in the funeral procession. On the contrary, my huge British fan mail of close on 1,000 letters has been very favourable. So don't give that bunk a thought.

Good-night my darling one. I love you love you more and more and more. God bless WE and take care of your precious self for your

DAVID

My love to Aunt Bess.

These are the handwritten notes to which the Duke referred in his letter.

Nobody cried in my presence. Only Winston as usual.

Cookie & Margaret feel most.

Lying in State. 800,000 for Papa. 300,000 this time. But one day less.

Funeral. Police took extra control precautions from experiences of 1936 & 1937. But streets empty in comparison.

Mama as hard as nails but failing. When Queens fail they make less sense than others in the same state.

Cookie listened without comment & closed on the note that it was nice to be able to talk about Bertie with somebody who had known him so well.

Clarence House was informal & friendly. Brave New World. Full of self-confidence & seem to take job in their stride.

Economy is the slogan in G.B. I don't believe the Civil List will be cut but they are all talking poor which is bad.

Cookie might not support both Royal Lodge & Clarence House. Lilibet has 3 of the largest houses in GB and will organise a flat in Windsor Castle for week-ends.

Mountbatten. One can't pin much on him but he's very bossy & never stops talking. All are suspicious & watching his influence on Philip.

Edwina – apart from India, hard to nail too, but Walter Monckton watched her register facial disapproval of Winston's speech at Guildhall.

Although the Duke had described his funeral visit as 'difficult, painful and discouraging', he was nevertheless sufficiently reassured by it to imagine that he might attend the Coronation of his niece the Queen in June 1953. A page would then be turned with the investiture of a new sovereign, and he retained a lingering hope that his family would be prepared to bury the past. What greater symbol could there have been of family reconciliation than his presence in Westminster Abbey together with that of the Duchess? But while the world's press waited to see if an invitation would be issued the Court left no doubt that they regarded the Windsors' attendance at the solemnization of the new reign as unthinkable.

The Duke of Norfolk, who as Earl Marshal was responsible for all the Coronation arrangements, told journalists in October 1952 that, although the ex-King was technically entitled to be present as a Royal Duke, such entitlement would not be extended to his wife. He 'did not believe the Duke would come', and hoped the Duke would soon make a statement to this effect 'to ease the situation from every point of view'.

The Duke asked his solicitor George Allen to discuss the question with the royal Private Secretary, Sir Alan Lascelles. Lascelles, as we know, was no friend of the Duke of Windsor, whose disapproving aide he had been in the 1920s and again in 1936. He wrote to Allen on 10 November 1952 that the presence of the Duke with his wife would be 'condemned . . . as a shocking breach of taste'. The attendance at this sacred ceremony by 'one who, however good his reasons, did not feel able to undertake its obligations himself' would strike a 'distressing and discordant note' which would be deeply upsetting to his niece. Allen argued strenuously that sixteen years was a long time, long enough to soften memories of the Abdication; but Lascelles replied that some things could never be forgotten or forgiven. 'Have you or I, for example, forgotten the Somme?'

Unhappily, the Duke accepted the verdict of what he described to Winston Churchill as 'my uncompromising family'. He asked only one price for his absence – that none of the other ex-Kings should be invited, such as Leopold of the Belgians or Umberto of Italy. (By tradition, reigning monarchs are never invited.) The authorities agreed to this, but refused to issue a statement; and it was left to the Duke himself to explain to the press that the Coronation would not be attended 'by the sovereign or ex-sovereign of any state'.

He had other reasons to feel bitter. He had imagined that his Palace allowance would be restored as soon as the new Civil List had been voted; but the Civil List Act became law in the spring of 1952 and, in spite of Allen's constant argument with the Court, there was no sign of the money. Not only did he regard this as a breach of faith, but he also needed the extra funds. In the late summer of 1952 the Windsors had finally bought, from their friend the artist Drian, the Moulin de la Tuilerie ('The Mill') at Gif-sur-Yvette. The business of restoring, converting and decorating this near-derelict property into a country house where they could live and entertain would be a long and expensive business.

Apart from his financially disastrous ranch in Canada, where he had lately been prospecting unsuccessfully for oil and of which he would eventually rid himself, the Mill was the only real property which he owned anywhere in the course of his married life. Its purchase – only six months after the Duke's unhappy reunion with his family in England – may be regarded as a symbolic act whereby the Windsors committed themselves, after seven years of hesitation and hope of better things, to remaining in exile in France.

In the autumn of 1952 the Duchess wrote what turned out to be almost the last of her many hundreds of newsy letters to Aunt Bessie, and summed up their situation in her characteristic style.

85, rue de la Faisanderie

Paris

October 3 [1952]

Darling Aunt B

If you can stand this yellow stuff[17] you can have one of my great efforts. I am sorry not to write but I really do not seem to be able to do it any more. Our summer was very upset by the Duke becoming ill and also the boat was not a success – bad crew and most things

---

[17] See note 9 above.

did not work. Anyway Biarritz was good and the Duke put back the lost pounds and had lots of golf. He has had his check up in London and told me last night that everything was fine. The [oil] well they were drilling on the ranch turned out a dud so that is very discouraging news and we could use a little cash as the *new regime* has cut the rent on Balmoral and Sandringham in half[18] and just when we have taken a Mill a half hour from Paris with everything to be done to it. It is not a place for all the time but for long week-ends etc. Now we are looking for a flat in Paris as we can reduce the staff and the upkeep is less than a house – but everything here is so expensive and hard to find. We do not know about coming over as yet. It is hard to leave the Mill with work starting Nov 1st – but decorating can't commence until April. Also finance enters in. I will know more about that when the Duke returns as the reason for his trip [to England] was to review the entire situation. The family are certainly charming, aren't they? We will also have to take a lot of Coronation cracks – and Winston though very friendly won't interfere in what he calls a family matter. I wish the world and particularly the U.S. press would forget the Windsors. Such an old story.

I have tried to bring you up to date in a sketchy way with our life – which seems more complicated in old age than in youth – this world with taxes etc. is difficult to handle. But it is heaven living with someone with the disposition of an angel and a rubber ball quality to bounce over British rudeness.

All my love
WALLIS

---

[18] This is a rather muddled and inaccurate way of expressing the arrangements described in Chapter 2. The Duke had been promised a pension of £21,000, half of it coming from the sale money of Sandringham and Balmoral held in trust, the other half from an allowance. It was the second of these sources of income which had been suspended.

Chapter Eleven

The Death of Queen Mary
1953

*I*n spite of financial doubts and the work to be done on the Mill, the Windsors sailed for New York before Christmas 1952 to spend the winter in America. Soon after their arrival, the Duke received an intriguing proposition from his lawyer Hank Walter – that he should write a long article for wide syndication, giving his reflections on the meaning and future of the British monarchy at the time of the Coronation. He grasped enthusiastically at the idea. Certain to be read by millions and to command large sums from newspaper publishers, it promised to make up not only for his humiliating absence from the ceremony itself, but also for the royal allowance which was being held back from him. Contracts were quickly signed and the Duke got down to work, staying on in New York while the Duchess went off to visit friends. By the end of February 1953 he had written 12,000 words – enough for the piece to be published eventually as a small illustrated book entitled *The Crown and the People*.

Now a collector's item, it is a curious little work. The Duke saw no irony in writing about the Crown that had been his. Great Britain, he began, was the last of the great monarchies; but the Queen's would not be the last Coronation, for the British monarchy had demonstrated 'an outstanding capacity to adapt itself to social change' and his young niece could be relied upon to carry on the process 'of continuous and enlightened evolution'. On the other hand, the sovereign's role had not become easier since the two Coronations the Duke had himself attended – those of his grandfather Edward VII and father George V. In particular, the old landed aristocracy on which the Court traditionally depended had been 'impoverished by a confiscatory taxation', its decline threatening to leave the monarchy 'more or less marooned'.

The Crown and the People showed that the Duke, who was fifty-eight, had abandoned the radical views he had once held and now had the outlook of a conservative and a traditionalist. He lamented the passing of empire, made wary remarks about the advance of socialism, and even referred to 'Soviet aggression'. Such political allusions risked getting him into trouble. On the other hand, there was only a single, fleeting reference to the Abdication. Writing of 'the constant strain' to which King George VI had been subjected by his constitutional duties, the Duke went on to say: 'And I am not insensible to the fact that through a decision of mine he was projected into sovereign responsibilities that may at first have weighed heavily upon him. . . .'

No sooner was the ink dry on the first draft of his manuscript than the Duke received a letter dated 28 February from Sir Horace Evans, the royal physician, reporting that Queen Mary had 'not been well for the past week'. She had returned in good form from her holiday at Sandringham – but then had suffered abdominal pains as a result of a deformity in the colon, upon which it was impossible to operate because of the state of her heart. She was telling everyone that she did not wish to go on living as an 'old crock'. (She was eighty-five.) 'I cannot help feeling that she wants to see you,' Evans continued, 'though She has not said so.' The letter ended with a reference to 'the great uncertainty of the situation'.

The Duke had only just been rejoined by his wife in New York, and it was with a heavy heart that he decided to return at once to England to attend his mother's sickbed, sailing on 6 March aboard the liner *Queen Elizabeth* along with his widowed sister Princess Mary, who had been wintering in Trinidad and, now arriving in America to catch the boat, became the first member of the Royal Family since the Abdication to meet the Duchess.[1] As with the Duke's return to attend the funeral of King George VI the year before, the family nature of the journey made it impossible for the Duchess to accompany him. This was another of the few occasions during their married life that the Duke and Duchess were totally separated for a period of several weeks; and in the course of it they

---

[1] With the sole exception of the Duke and Duchess of Gloucester, who had spent a day with the Windsors in Paris in November 1938. See Chapter 5.

exchanged letters which are of great interest: first, because they show how strong remained the bonds of love and protection after sixteen years of marriage; and, second, because they illustrate the Duke's now total estrangement from his family and country.

The Duke wrote his first letter three days out to sea.

R.M.S. 'Queen Elizabeth'
At sea
March 9th 1953

My Sweetheart,

Fate certainly can be tough taking me away from you after two weeks of separation with my nose to the grindstone to repair the loss of income my very wealthy niece withholds. And what I think of having to make this ridiculous and costly trip instead of our being together in Palm Beach is nobody's business.

I can't of course judge the situation in London until I reach the wretched place or how soon I can return to you. The *Queen Mary* sails Saturday March 21st and this ship not until ten days later April (fool) 1st! Maybe the Q.M. will be too quick a turn round but gee! I'd like to make it. Anyway we shall see and in the meantime the bulletins from Marlborough House proclaim the old lady's condition to be slightly improved! Ice in place of blood in the veins must be a fine preservative.

At least the weather has been good to me & we are having a wonderfully smooth voyage. Mary seems to have become more human with age and has revealed a few interesting family bits of gossip. . . .

Socially speaking it's been dull. I've taught Mary to play Samba which helps pass the boring evenings after dinner in the Verandah Grill with the incredible old Colonel Balfour.[2] Unfortunately he has to eat with us although he's had the tact to stay away otherwise. As WE already judged him in New York he's an insufferable stuffed shirt who tries to conceal a hypocritical British self-satisfied names-dropping make-up by trying to be genial. The only funny thing about him is that he never says no to a drink. The last two evenings he's come to dinner feeling no pain at all[3] while admitting

---

[2] Princess Mary's equerry.

[3] A private expression of the Windsors, meaning the worse for drink.

that he'd been to two cabin cocktail parties. I've been as polite to him as possible and hope to land before I'm rude. . . .

I've screened the Coronation Article and like it better all the time. It's now in shape for George Allen and Walter Monckton to read and I must try to get Charles Eade[4] and Young Max[5] bidding against each other.

But gee I miss you my darling one. I cabled you again because I thought economy had gone too far and the word from you which I got this afternoon comforted me more than I can say.[6]

I hope the dogs are well and that Thomas isn't pining too much. I'll write as soon as I get to London and in the meantime 'God bless WE' and please take care of your precious self for your

DAVID

who loves you more than life

The Duke landed at Southampton on 11 March. At Marlborough House he found three letters awaiting him from the Duchess, the first of which had been written only just after his sailing.

. . . I did hate to see you go away from me and you must not pine and be thin. I worry so much about you because you are such a child when you are alone. I am sure you did the right thing – and hope that from now on we can do the wrong thing! . . . All my love goes with you and I long for April.

The main purpose of the Duchess's letters was to keep her husband's spirits up, and to suggest all kinds of absorbing and useful things with which he could occupy himself when not attending his mother's bedside. She asked him to look around for furniture which would be needed at the Mill, and if possible to make a brief visit to Paris to see

---

[4] Editor of the *Sunday Dispatch*, one of the Rothermere group of newspapers.

[5] Max Aitken, the son of Lord Beaverbrook, who had negotiated the rights in *A King's Story* for his father's *Express* newspaper group.

[6] The Duke's telegram to the Duchess following their ship-to-shore telephone conversation that afternoon read as follows: 'HE wants to tell HER that HE was very sad it could only be "hello" and "goodbye" and that HE loves HER more and more too.' Those who have read their published correspondence of the 1930s will recognize the characteristic third-person style.

how the work was progressing. She gave him news of their dogs. 'Thomas [the Duke's Cairn Terrier] and Trooper [the Duchess's pug] had a slight fight which the latter won. It was not serious.' Her tone throughout is of an anxious mother concerned about her little boy. 'Please eat and take care of yourself,' she concluded in her letter of 7 March. 'Don't fetch and carry for everyone including servants. Work [for the restoration of the allowance] on Cookie [the Queen Mother] and Shirley [the Queen]. All my love goes to you.' And again on the 9th:

> I hope things won't be too unpleasant for you my darling and you know I am thinking of you every second. We should think of a title for your article. Don't forget your date line, April 6th. So much love my darling and keep your chin up and your tummy full.

Another of the Duchess's themes was the need to economize in view of their uncertain financial situation. She asked him not to bombard her with his usual torrent of cables and telephone calls, and to avoid the expense of a hotel. Following this advice, the Duke went to stay with his old friend Eric Dudley at his country house Great Westwood near King's Langley in Hertfordshire. From there he commuted to London, sometimes spending a night in town at the house in Regent's Park of Lord Dudley's son Lord Ednam. The Ednams were in New York at the time, and the Duke, appreciative of their hospitality, telegraphed the Duchess to look them up at the Sherry Netherlands Hotel and make a fuss of them.

On his third day in England he wrote to the Duchess from Great Westwood.

March 14th, 1953

My Sweetheart,

> Bless you for your three sweet letters and all your news. You can't be more lonely than I am my darling one though our few friends in London are being kind and sympathetic.
>
> Although Mama doesn't look quite as badly as the doctors warned me she is very sick indeed and it's just a question of how

long she will last. I have seen her twice with Mary for fifteen to twenty minutes. The hour is 4.15 and while she notices if you are one minute late and talks coherently she repeats herself a lot and has one or two theme songs upon which she harps all the time. Our arrival seems to have done her good and although she gives us no indication we are told she got quite a kick out of seeing us again.

I have had two long talks with Horace Evans and Lord Webb-Johnson, the surgeon who can't operate because of Mama's age. They paint a very black picture indeed. . . . But the most agonizing part of this condition is the way it drags on, agonizing for poor Mama and all concerned. As the doctors point out, she could die any night in her sleep or any moment for that matter and yet she might linger on for some weeks. I'm desperate over being stuck here away from you my darling and living on a day to day basis according to what the doctors say. . . . Gee! it's all hellish.

Coronation Article. Walter Monckton and George Allen have both read and like it but think the political parts need toning down a bit. . . .

I must dress for dinner now my Sweetheart and expect there'll be Canasta or Samba after dinner. . . . Good night my darling one. I miss you and love you more and more. Your

DAVID

The days passed, with little change in the Queen's condition. The Duke passed his time fulfilling the Duchess's various commissions – buying a long oak table, inspecting a Humber motor car – and revising his manuscript. But his next letter, dated 21 March, shows that these activities had not been enough to keep him from becoming restless.

Great Westwood

My Sweetheart,

I was so busy working on the Coronation Article the last two days in London that I never had a moment to write you. . . . George Allen had first crack at the manuscript and slashed ruthlessly at the meaty pieces! Walter Monckton has read it superficially but on the plea of being too busy and a member of the Cabinet washed his hands of any responsibility editorial-wise. So I suggested I call in Harold Nicolson[7] and the weak-kneed Minister of Labour agreed. Harold couldn't have been more helpful[8] and was of course far less drastic cutting-wise than George and more constructive in softer and alternative ways of saying the same thing. Hank [Walter] flew back to New York with an amended copy of the article from Heathrow last evening and I'm well satisfied with the changes which don't bother the general theme and eliminate all the passages that could offend in this charming country and lay me open to criticism beyond the usual line that Windsor shouldn't write or raise his head at all!

At Marlborough House the same condition prevails with not daily but hourly changes. I go to see Mama every day I am in London at 4.15 and Horace Evans calls me to report after his 6.30 bedside visit. The background of the illness always remains the same: there can be absolutely no hope of Mama ever getting dressed or going into circulation again. It's all just a question of how long her heart lasts out and can take the strain of the periodical treatments she receives which keep her alive. It's one of the most trying situations I've ever found myself in and hanging around someone who has been so mean and vile to you my sweetheart is getting me down.

The Duke had now virtually made up his mind to return to New York in *Queen Elizabeth* sailing on 1 April.

. . . Of course, if there is a rapid deterioration for the worse in the meantime I'll have to think again. But I just can't take this hanging around any longer and anyway as I have no part in the Royal Family beyond Burke's Peerage or Who's Who and don't stand to benefit from Mama's will I'm off back to *you* my beloved where I belong.

[7] The writer, politician and social figure (1889–68), husband of the novelist Vita Sackville-West, whose official biography of King George V had appeared the year before. He had met the Prince of Wales and Mrs Simpson in the salons of Lady Cunard and Lady Colefax in the early 1930s, and had remained on terms of casual friendship with them since. In 1947, to the surprise of his friends, he had joined the Labour Party.

[8] Nicolson's biographer, James Lees-Milne, writes: 'Harold was embarrassed by the subject of the article, and urged the Duke to drop an unflattering reference to the Labour Party, which would do him much harm if the article were to appear in this country. Finally he took the manuscript away, made certain corrections and deletions, and returned it to Lord Ednam's house where the Duke was staying. . . . Harold was ever more distressed by the fading charm of the Duke and the aimlessness of his life in exile.'

I'm glad the dogs get on OK now and hope Trooper is developing our taste for good rare meat.[9]

HOLD EVERYTHING!! As I write in Eric's library you have just called me out of the blue without the usual notification. It was a wonderful surprise my darling one and I'm sorry you were worried over my silence cablewise. But it's all the fault of your 'economy drive' or you know I would have phoned or cabled every day! It was wonderful to talk to you and to know everything is OK. Still I won't call you unless there is an urgency. . . .

We went to the Hertfordshire Hunt point-to-point yesterday afternoon and I gave the cup for the Brigade of Guards Race and got quite a good hand from 20,000 spectators. I enclose a picture. I'm trying to eat all I can but the uncertainty and loneliness of this wretched trip has got me down. Goodnight my beloved sweetheart. I miss you and love you more and more and more. Your

DAVID

Queen Mary died at Marlborough House on the night of Tuesday, 24 March. The Duke's first act was to send a telegram to the Duchess: 'Mama died at 10.15. All love and more.' She replied to him: 'All my sympathy and love. Only wish I were with you.'

His next letter to her was written three days later from their house in Paris, where he had gone to make a brief inspection of the work in progress at the Mill.

85, rue de la Faisanderie,
Paris 16e

March 27th 1953

My own darling Sweetheart,

I was so happy to find your letter of March 22nd when I got here yesterday and all your news.[10] I will deal with that later.

Well, thank God the nightmare of watching Mama die is over. I

---

[9] On 14 March the Duchess had written: 'The dogs are well and get on perfectly. Trooper still prefers liver or chicken. The vet says to give him his fill of these and the meat appetite will suddenly come.'

[10] Discussing their plans for the summer, the health of their dogs, the need for economy, and servant problems. 'Please eat darling. I will be so happy to have you back again. A big hug and a bigger kiss from me.'

couldn't have taken it for much longer, for her sake or for mine. Mary and I were with her for a few minutes Monday afternoon and she talked of other topics than her illness and how miserable and wretched she felt which was her daily theme song. Then during the night she had a haemorrhage and from then on it was only a matter of hours. I was at Marlborough House most of Tuesday afternoon and peeked into Mama's bedroom although she was unconscious by then with the doctors and nurses around with dope and sedatives to prevent any suffering. While I was there the Archbishop of Canterbury[11] showed up to 'give Mama a blessing' as he called it and Mary and I had to kneel in the next room while he said some prayers. An unctuous hypocrite like all the rest I should judge and he reminded me of 'Auld Lang Swine'!![12]

I dined with Colin and Gladie[13] that evening, and when I called M.H. at ten for news was told to go there around eleven. Five minutes later I was called to hurry there urgently and Mama died five minutes before I arrived. Only Mary was there and none of the rest of the family showed up that night. Not even brother Harry[14] whom I found, glass of scotch in hand and feeling no pain, when I went to York House[15] for a few minutes afterwards. I guess it was emotion!

Wednesday morning the whole family gathered at M.H. for more archbishoply prayers and a last look at Mama. My sadness was mixed with incredulity that any mother could have been so hard and cruel towards her eldest son for so many years and yet so demanding at the end without relenting a scrap. I'm afraid the fluids in her veins have always been as icy cold as they now are in death.

That night I ferried across [to Paris] in the comforting knowledge that the funeral will be on Tuesday March 31st. The

---

[11] Geoffrey Francis Fisher, Archbishop of Canterbury 1945–61.

[12] Cosmo Gordon Lang, Archbishop of Canterbury at the time of the Abdication, had afterwards broadcast an ill-judged attack on the Duke of Windsor which had shocked public opinion. The following rhyme had circulated, playing on the title 'Cantuar':

> My Lord Archbishop, what a scold you are;
> And when your man is down, how very bold you are;
> Of Christian charity how very scant you are;
> You Auld Lang Swine, how full of cant you are.

[13] Commander Colin Buist, an old shipmate of the Duke, and his wife Gladys.

[14] Prince Henry, Duke of Gloucester (1900–74), third son of George V.

[15] A house in St James's Palace where the Duke of Windsor had lived as Prince of Wales, and which since 1936 had been the Duke of Gloucester's official residence. It was only a minute's walk from Marlborough House.

first rumour was Thursday and I was frantic, then it was Wednesday and I'd have had to fly from somewhere near Windsor to make the 'Q.E.' at Cherbourg. However now all is well and I'll soon be on my way back to you my darling one and I just can't wait to get aboard.

The Mill is a shambles and I'm glad you can't see it. Will tell you all when we meet and I took some of my wonderful pictures to show you how the work is progressing. Your room is going to be charming and you've no idea what a difference the extra windows and door onto the terrace have made. Old Drian brought a sketch of the screen he's going to paint yesterday and I'm bringing it over for your approval. I'm sure you'll like it too.

I'm swamped with letters, wires and cables of sympathy and shall probably find another batch at York House tomorrow morning. What strange things do happen for believe it or not I'm to be the 'Unknown Soldier's'[16] guest in London for the funeral ceremonies and until I sail! Maybe age has softened him a little like it seems to have done to Mary.

I'm sad to hear that Dizzy[17] isn't so well. He'll have to take it easy with the games for a while. . . .

We'll see about going to Palm Beach next month. Maybe we won't bother although it might be nice to get away from New York somewhere as we won't be able to go to theaters or night spots for a month at least, not that we frequent the latter.

You started the 'New Economy Campaign' by not cabling me on the voyage over my darling one! On the contrary we should be quite flushed this year from the Coronation Article. George Allen called me only this afternoon to report that not only does Max [Beaverbrook] want the article for the Sunday Express but will top any other bid with £1,000. I believe the price may go to £15,000! and I'm keeping my fingers crossed.

Oh! my sweetheart, I'm so excited to think that I'm going to be with you again so soon and that this agony is all over with. Thank God this is the last of these Royal Family passings that I'll ever have to leave you and cross the ocean for.

It's time to change and dine before making the ferry. God bless WE my Sweetheart and take care of your precious self. HE loves HER more and more too and can't wait either! (Hide face!) All all love from your

DAVID

---

[16] The Windsors' nickname for the Duke of Gloucester, who until the Abdication had followed a professional military career.

[17] Disraeli, another of the Windsors' pugs.

The Death of Queen Mary

The Duke's final letter to the Duchess before embarking was written on his return to London after the funeral at Windsor.

York House,
St James's Palace!

March 31st 1953

My own darling one,

Well, it's all over now thank God and I sail at 12.30 tomorrow. I've no time to give you details now. They can keep until Monday when if the weather is kind I should be with you again my sweetheart. I'll bring pictures with me too.

I took Mary over to Marlborough House this afternoon upon our return [from Windsor] to show her the kind of things I should like to have when they begin disposing of Mama's personal possessions other than the heirlooms which I am afraid will constitute the greatest proportion and will include the most valuable and interesting objects. I also told my niece I wanted some nice things but of course I'll be at a disadvantage being away when the division is made and the 'vultures' will have had first pick. Anyway I've done my best.[18]

What a smug stinking lot my relations are and you've never seen such a seedy worn out bunch of old hags most of them have become. Mary has been quite sweet and human on the whole and Harry and Alice [Gloucester] have been friendly hosts here. But of course they don't talk our language and never will and I've been boiling mad the whole time that you haven't been here in your rightful place as a daughter-in-law at my side.

But let us skip this rude interlude and enjoy our lovely full life together far removed from the boredom, the restrictions and the intrigues of the Royal Family and the Court.

You just don't know how much I love you my Sweetheart and although I'll be able to take it easy on the voyage I'll not relax until I can hold you tight again. God bless WE. All all love. Your

DAVID

---

[18] To the Duke's surprise, he learnt the following month that he had been briefly mentioned in his mother's will. Her legacy to him consisted of three small boxes and a pair of candlesticks in lapis lazuli. These were accidentally sold in 1973 along with the general contents of the Moulin de la Tuilerie.

Chapter Twelve

The Duchess Writes
Her Memoirs
1953–55

On 2 June 1953 the Coronation took place in Westminster Abbey. A year earlier the Duke had hoped to be invited to attend with the Duchess, but now his attitude was one of indifference. His letters written at the time of his mother's death show that he had become alienated from his family and the British royal scene. Such was his detachment that he cheerfully accepted an invitation from United Press to comment on the ceremony as he watched it on television in Paris, impressing his guests on that occasion by his familiarity with the details and protocol. As the Windsors had foreseen, their absence provoked some jeering articles in the press; the columnist Elsa Maxwell wrote a particularly unpleasant piece as a result of which the Duchess refused to speak to her for five years.

At the funeral of his brother the Duke had still harboured hopes of return to England and family reconciliation, but now there was little doubt that he and the Duchess would be spending the rest of their lives as exiles in France. In July 1952 they had bought the Mill at Gif as their country house there. For some years they had been looking for a city residence to replace the rented house in the rue de la Faisanderie, and the Duchess had become resigned to their moving into a flat. But in May 1953 they heard that a spacious turn-of-the-century villa set in two acres of grounds in the Bois de Boulogne was about to fall vacant. It was owned by the City of Paris, and such was the Windsors' local popularity that the city authorities agreed to grant it to them for a term of twenty-five years. They signed the lease on 22 June. The rental was low, though not 'peppercorn' as is sometimes alleged:[1] at the time of the Duchess's death in 1986 (the lease having been extended for her lifetime) it amounted to about £15,000 per annum.

The business of decorating, restoring and furnishing these two houses, and of creating an English garden at the Mill, was to occupy most of the time and interest of the Windsors during the next four years. But throughout this period the Duchess had another preoccupation – the writing of her memoirs. Ever since the success of *A King's Story* she had been under pressure to embark on a book of her own – but she had at first not been at all enthusiastic about the idea. While the Duke was in England attending his mother's sickbed, she wrote to him expressing her doubts.

[14 March 1953]

. . . Naturally the money is tempting to us, Hank, and all concerned. On the other hand, I am not sure that I think Hank's idea of keeping us in the public eye a good one. For you to write the Coronation Article was all right because it is serious and has a reason. But for me to go into my life when I was a figure in a very controversial subject only brings everything up again and I am bound to have criticism. If it were absolutely financially necessary that would force me to make the sacrifice. But with all the hurts I've had, do I want to stick my neck out deliberately? I do not agree with Hank that this is the only moment that will arise when there would be interest in a book by me. The story is always there. I am not shirking the work – it's the publicity I dread. . . .

But the Duke sought to reassure her and change her mind:

[21 March 1953]

. . . I told both George Allen and Hank Walter the reasons for your hesitation over going ahead with your writing project but they are

---

[1] All French domestic rents were abnormally low at this period, having been regulated by statute in 1949: as a result there was a chronic shortage of leasehold property. The rent at first paid by the Windsors, 800,000 francs per annum, was the same as that charged to the previous tenant, M. Pierre Renaud.

both in favour of your doing so. Of course they both stand to do well out of it but I believe they have your interests at heart as well. It seems for some strange reason which I don't understand that at least one if not two more unpleasant people contemplate writing your life. Well, it's not strange actually because unfortunately anything about WE sells. The lawyers say that it's important you go ahead with your story to kill any others which are bound to be inaccurate if not in bad taste.

I couldn't understand more how you feel about it my darling one but I do see the lawyers' viewpoint. I also think it vital to get the material [on family history] from Aunt Bess and Cousin Lelia[2] before it's too late. I don't think there is too much time to waste. . . .

Eventually the Duchess agreed to proceed. The enormous cost of doing up their new Paris house and of hiring the extra staff it required was the deciding factor.

The writing of the memoirs turned out to be a saga beset by dramas and problems. Needing editorial assistance, the Duchess was at first attracted by Cleveland Amory, a young American author who had impressed the Windsors in Palm Beach. The publishers, however, insisted that she use Charles Murphy, the ghostwriter who had been employed on the Duke's memoirs. Contracts were signed in 1953 involving huge sums (the American serial rights alone were sold to *McCall's* magazine for $250,000) but little got done in 1954 owing to Murphy's absence on other assignments and the Duchess's absorption in decorating her houses. It was not until 1955 that Murphy presented his first chapters – and the Duchess was not pleased with what she saw. She wrote to say that she simply did not recognize herself in Murphy's prose. Murphy was paid off and Cleveland Amory was hired, working with the Duchess in France in the summer of 1955. This time it was the publishers who complained; they found Amory's writing inadequate and unacceptable. Amory blew up, protesting in public that the Duchess had been impossible to work with. The story soon filled the scandal columns of the American newspapers.

The Duchess was now in a fix; large advances had been paid, and

[2] Mrs George Barnett, a cousin of the Duchess's mother, a formidable figure who lived on a large country estate in Virginia.

a publishable manuscript had been promised by early 1956. Reluctantly she was obliged to turn once more to Murphy, whom she personally disliked but whose writing was able to satisfy her publishers. Murphy, who had been threatening to sue the Duchess, agreed to return but demanded a price, and also insisted that he would not go to France and that the Duchess would have to come to New York. Indeed, if the book were to be completed on time she would have to come immediately and get down to hard work.

And so the Duchess sailed from Le Havre for New York on Thursday, 20 October 1955. She persuaded the Duke to remain behind to look after the restoration and gardening work at the Mill: his absence was indeed essential if she were to concentrate totally on the book. She planned to return in good time for Christmas, which they would celebrate with their guests at the Mill, and after which they would sail together for New York at the end of December, where she would resume her work.

This was the fourth time during the fifties that the Windsors were separated for a period of several weeks, and indeed the last time during their married life that they were to be parted for so long a period. As before, they wrote to each other regularly, she telling of her progress with the book, he of his progress at the Mill. As ever, he is lost without her, and she full of maternal worries over him.

These letters – the last substantial letters exchanged by the Windsors – are also of interest for what they show of the Duke's reactions to the Margaret–Townsend affair, which came to an unhappy end at this time. Princess Margaret and the divorced Group-Captain Peter Townsend had wished to marry in 1953; but in the face of stern opposition from within the Royal Family, the Court, the Church, and a section of the Government and the press they agreed to postpone their decision for two years, Townsend leaving the country to take up a diplomatic post in Brussels. They were reunited in London on 13 October 1955, and spent two heart-searching weeks considering their future. Given the widespread continuing hostility to the proposed match (which was denounced with particular vigour in *The Times*), and the fact that it would require legislation which would certainly deprive the Princess of her royal status and Civil List pension, they reached the unhappy decision to give each other up – a decision which was made public on 31 October. There can be no doubt that one of the principal causes of this tragedy was the feeling, in royal and establishment circles, that to allow the Princess to marry Townsend and keep her royal status would make inevitable the rehabilitation of the Windsors and the granting of a royal title to the Duchess.

The Duke to the Duchess

[The Mill]

[Sunday, 23 October 1955]

My Sweetheart

I'm still quite dazed by all that happened on Thursday. And although seeing you off at Havre gave us a few more hours together, it made the last moments aboard all the harder to take.

Maybe I should have gone with you to N.Y. to be at your side if the press & Amory get tough. But you are well protected, so I'm not worried on that score. Still the sad loneliness of here without you is hard to take & it's taking a little while to readjust to the W having temporarily left the WE combine. Even the elements have been crying their eyes out too since that grim night to the extent of one & a half inches of rain.

Anyway that's good for the garden & the place in general as it was very dry. And after all, it's only on account of the building & gardening projects I have remained behind. It won't be my fault if you don't see a big difference when you get back – and please make it soonest end of November. . . .

I cabled you my O.K. arrival after four and a half hours from Havre in pouring rain. No word from you but I guess from the barometer readings your first day or two at sea were not too hot. I hope Mr Trooper and Davy Crockett were not too unhappy. Dizzy and Peter Townsend miss them both but are settling down well together. . . .[3]

I attended the Guinness–Furstenberg wedding reception[4] at the Ritz yesterday in tail coat & with my best manners & believe it or not never yawned once although there were plenty of bores to make

---

[3] The Windsors' family of dogs now consisted of four pugs – Trooper, Davy Crockett, Disraeli and Peter Townsend. The first two had accompanied the Duchess to America while the others remained with the Duke in France.

[4] This was to celebrate an unusual union between stepbrother and stepsister. Patrick Guinness, son of the Windsors' friend Loel Guinness by an earlier marriage, had wed Dolores Furstenberg, daughter of Loel's Mexican wife Gloria by her previous marriage.

me. I had an interesting exchange with Seymour Camrose[5] over the Margaret–Townsend romance. He made some quite sensible comments which I parried with a tactful exposition of our attitude. I am watching the situation with interest. My guess is that it will reach boiling point any time soon.[6]

I have started sorting the photographs on the trestle table in the barn with a dust sheet to protect the green carpet. But gee it's a big job & I have to fight my way out of the sea of pictures & empty envelopes from time to time to get air! Still, I will send you a selection for the book before I go to London.

Must go to my lonely bed now & am missing & thinking of you so terribly my Peaches. Please take care of your precious self & don't let our friends keep you up too late or you'll not be able to work with Murphy which after all is the only reason for this wretched & stupid separation.

God bless WE my darling one & call me from New York after you have been there a few days. I am planning to go to London the night of Nov 6th. All all love & more & more & more your

DAVID

October 27th

My darling one,

I was so thankful to get your cable reporting your safe arrival in N.Y. . . . You have now been gone a week – a long week. Still, I have so many chores to attend to both inside and outside that these lonely days are passing reasonably fast.

Your dinner party at Neuilly[7] Tuesday evening passed off O.K. Needless to say you were greatly missed by all the guests too. There were no cards afterwards as everybody seemed to be enjoying each other's company & we all just sat 'yacking' in the library until around midnight. . . .

[5] The second Viscount Camrose (born 1909), chairman and principal shareholder of The Daily Telegraph Limited.

[6] Princess Margaret and Peter Townsend had by this date been discussing their future for ten days in the full glare of press publicity, the *Telegraph* being among the papers opposed to the marriage. They were to make their decision two days later, on the 25th.

[7] The house in the Bois de Boulogne, so called by the Windsors even though it was in fact just outside Neuilly, in Sixteenth District of Paris.

Work is progressing tolerably well. The terrassing [*sic*] of the bank along the river is almost thru' & the last stone wall will be completed tomorrow. Russell Page[8] was here this morning & we inspected every corner of the place with a fine comb. . . .

The Margaret–Townsend romance drags on & on. Walter [Monckton] says it has not been formally referred to the Cabinet yet so who knows what they are going to do. . . .[9]

I hope all goes well with you & the book & I shall look forward to getting a letter from you soon with all your news. All my love my precious one & come back as fast as you possibly can. Your

DAVID

who loves you more & more

The Duchess to the Duke

United States Lines

Friday, October 21st

Darling – It is not really rough but not really smooth. The cabins seem like empty ballrooms. Trooper misses Dizzy. Davy Crockett is fine and happy. . . . I hear you went to the Mill [after seeing the Duchess off] which was very naughty. I had changed the chefs orders 3 times[10] and Robert and Edouard were kept up all night. You can't have a happy house like that and if the servants leave I will too! Hope your drive wasn't too awful. Have had no cable from you which is worrying. Much love and do take care of yourself.

WALLIS

[8] The celebrated landscape gardener, who was then forty-nine.

[9] Princess Margaret had in fact made her decision two days previously but had so far announced it only to the Prime Minister, the Archbishop of Canterbury, and members of her family.

[10] Presumably the Duchess means to say that the Duke had changed his mind three times as to which of his two houses he would return to after seeing off the Duchess – and having left her had changed it yet again.

The Duke to the Duchess

[The Mill]

October 30th

My Sweetheart,

I have just returned to find your letter written from the boat. . . .
I returned here from Le Havre instead of to Neuilly simply to avoid
the sadness of finding myself alone in that big house which a girl
had left so few hours before. Far from being inconsiderate towards
the staff I am bending myself in two to make their service easy. I
had Hivet[11] type a schedule for Georges[12] and the chef indicating
when I would be in or out for meals, & when I would sleep here or
at Neuilly, & everything could not be running more smoothly & all
the staff are perfectly contented & smiling. So please don't fash
yourself over the way I am running the houses while you are away,
my darling one. I am doing very well indeed. Besides, with your
threat of leaving with the staff, I couldn't possibly have a greater
incentive. . . .

The Duchess to the Duke

[New York]

Saturday, October 29th

Darling darling one,

I do miss you so much and have had a most difficult time. There
were no contracts signed when I arrived and everyone fighting.
However I went to the charm school today and at last think I will
get something done without these legal battles. . . . I cannot alas
sail [for Europe] until the 2nd of December and I must return [to
New York] on the 28th of December. . . . At last we have the money
for the house. . . . Please do not sleep in your bedroom at the Mill.
It is the perfect *fire trap* – you could never get down the stairs. You
must sleep in *my* room. I never thought of this before and have had
night nerves over it. Papers not bad but always something to hurt a

[11] The secretary.
[12] The butler.

girl and Amory still spouting a bit. Ask chef if he found the chicken
spit, otherwise can bring one from here. . . . Darling this is a mixed
up letter but it has been an awful week. . . . Miss you miss you love
again

WALLIS

The Duke to the Duchess

[5 November]

My own darling one

I was so happy to get your letter of Oct 29th & all your news.
What a wretchedly difficult time you have had with those sharks &
so much time wasted. Anyway at last the contract with Murphy is
signed & I hope he is playing ball.

I just couldn't be more disappointed that you have to wait the
extra week & can't return to me here until December 7th. . . .

That 'Annie get your Gun' publicity must have been a headache
for you too. . . .

There is nothing new to tell you from here & my life is dull & oh
so lonely though luckily busy. . . . The Hall & Stables will look OK
for Christmas. . . .

Tomorrow night as you know I take the ferry to that hostile
island across the Channel. The unctuous hypocritical cant and
corn which has been provoked in the Times and Telegraph by
Margaret's renunciation of Townsend[13] has been hard to take. The
Church of England has won again but this time they caught their
fly whereas I was wily enough to escape the web of an outmoded
institution that has become no more than a government department & has more traditional than religious appeal. I have been
watching for tempting allusions to my decision in 1936 but have
found none in the British papers. There must have been some in
America. . . .

---

[13] Made public six days previously.

[a few days later]

Sweetheart,

Have just arrived [back from London]. Train one hour late &
noisy so didn't make enough driz.[14] Everything O.K. here
although some of the salon furniture still away being fixed. The
pugs are fine & Dizzy's eye almost well.

Now for the London report although it's not very interesting.
Socially I dined with the Buists, Baba [Metcalfe] and the
Moncktons who had some of the Cabinet in afterwards. . . .

Called at No. 10 Downing Street where Anthony Eden[15] was
cordial & friendly. When I touched on the Margaret–Townsend
episode he smugly declared how highly relieved he and his five
divorced cabinet colleagues were that my niece – Lilibet – didn't
seek their formal advice in the matter! Six sinners in one Cabinet is
not bad percentagewise. . . .

I sat for two hours to James Gunn[16] in his Hampstead studio. He
is as slow as molasses & won't have the picture finished until the
spring. Of course he is crazy to exhibit it in the Royal Academy but
I am against that after the way they refused your Brockhurst
picture in 1939. . . .[17]

It's terrible to return & find no you & the days drag endlessly
now even busy as I am. God bless WE my sweetheart and I only
hope you aren't getting too tired with the book. Missing & loving
you more & more & more your

DAVID

---

[14] Sleep.

[15] Who had become Prime Minister the previous April.

[16] The portrait artist Sir James Gunn (1893–1964), who the previous year had completed his
State Portrait of the Queen. He was a personal friend of the Duke and a regular visitor at the
Mill. The Duke had commissioned a portrait of himself in his Garter robes in a pose identical
to that in which he had been painted as Prince of Wales by Sir Arthur Cope in 1911. The result
was a tragic caricature.

[17] The celebrated pre-war portrait of the Duchess by Gerald Brockhurst.

Viking's Cove, L.I.

Sunday November 6th

Darling,

. . . I have missed you so much. Everybody has been too kind and I haven't had a night alone and won't have before I leave. . . . I have to have the first instalment [of the memoirs] ready the 14th so we are madly at work. I imagine it's as good as I can make it. But the great blow is that I can't leave N.Y. in January.[18] It's the Abdication chapter and you realize how much work I must put on that. It has to be right as that is what people want to know. Anyway, you will go. All this separation, but the book will be worth it financially I hope. . . . It is marvellous to think I will be arriving a month from tomorrow. . . . Aunt Bessie comes [to New York] on the 21st and will stay as long as she wants. Her memory is completely gone – rather a trial.[19] Darling I love you so very much and miss you every minute.

WALLIS

The Duke to the Duchess

[Saturday] November 12th

My Darling One,

Just a quick note to thank you for your letter of November 6th. You must be working very hard but it's a blow you can't make Horseshoe the last ten days of January. Still that's a long way off and it's terribly important to get the Abdication chapter 100% right. . . . This separation is unbearable but there's only three weeks more before that blessed day when I'll have you back with me. More & more & more my sweetheart. Your

DAVID

[18] In January the Windsors usually joined the annual duck shooting party of their friends George and Edith Baker on the Horseshoe Ranch at Tallahassee in Florida, an event to which the Duke particularly looked forward.

[19] She was ninety-one.

[weekend of 19–20 November]

My darling one,

Another dreary week-end is crawling along here. . . . Russell Page was here today & we planted all the stuff which luckily arrived this morning – Japanese maples and all kinds of pretty things and shrubs to flank the rock garden. There remain a few blank spaces on the new terrassing [*sic*] on the river bank under your window but these will be filled in the spring with plants from the Perry firm. So the whole place should be 'bustin' out all over' in June, at least Russell & I hope so or we know we'll both be in the dawg house!

It's icy cold & I direct operations in my short fur coat. I dine with Daisy Fellowes Wednesday and Margaret Biddle Thursday. Then back here to greet Gray[20] and Fruity [Metcalfe] who are flying over for the week-end. Fruity seems very gittery [*sic*] & a bundle of nerves & complexes. Still the change may do him good. . . .

The Duchess to the Duke

[New York]

Sunday, November 27th

Darling One,

Your letters have been wonderfully amusing and full of details re progress – a great help. I have had Charlie [Murphy] for the week-end and we did a lot of work. I am all wound up in the thing like you got. The first 5 chapters have been handed over. I saw Beaverbrook[21] Thursday. He was very nice in his fashion. We gave him the 5 chapters to read. I have done most of the Xmas shopping for the Paris staff and for our really good friends here. . . . Has the wall been started? Davy Crockett is a bad dog – chews everything and lamps and tables fly with his games – an amusing little personality but not up to Trooper's looks or affection. Maybe we should have stuck to the oldies. Never will I be away from you for

---

[20] Major Gray Phillips of the Black Watch, who had been the Duke's comptroller and private secretary 1939–45.

[21] He had bought the serial rights for the *Sunday Express* for £75,000.

so long again. Can't wait for Friday – we sail at 12 noon. Everyone has been too divine to me – we have good friends here in spite of the stinking press and Amory. I love you more & more and hope Fruity destroyed nothing at the Mill. Your

WALLIS

The Duke to the Duchess

[late November]

My Sweetheart,

It's so wonderful that this is the last time I can write you before you sail next Friday. Oh! it's been so long & lonely & it will be thrilling to have you back & running the place again. I will even welcome getting into the line of your machine gun fire at breakfast time. . . .

Postscript
1955–72

Many more years of married life lay before the Windsors; but at this point the story told by this book comes to an end. The Duke, who was now sixty-one, had given up all hope of returning to live in England, achieving a reconciliation with his family, having the Duchess recognized as his equal, and performing dignified and useful work in his country's service. Having installed himself with the Duchess in their country house at Gif and town house in the Bois de Boulogne, he settled down to a comfortable – but in many respects sad and lonely – life of exile. The stuff of his existence was henceforth to be his gardening and his golf, his dogs and his pipes, his morning correspondence and his periodic writing projects, a long annual winter stay in America and a summer holiday in the South of Europe. Above all his life revolved around the Duchess, towards whom his feelings of passion and devotion never changed, and with whom he never ceased to experience great domestic happiness. But he was unfulfilled, and suffered from

> The deep, unutterable woe
> That none save exiles feel.

The Duchess's memoirs, which were dedicated to him, were published in the autumn of 1956 under the title *The Heart Has Its Reasons*. At the last moment the English publisher, Michael Joseph, required her to remove some mild allusions to the unfriendliness of the Royal Family towards her. The book was a great commercial success in America and surprisingly well received in England; but its appearance was overshadowed by the international crisis which resulted in the Suez débâcle. With the departure from the political scene of Anthony Eden (and along with him Walter Monckton), there expired the Duke's last remaining hope of a British job. As late as 1954 there had been some talk of making him Ambassador to Brazil, though the idea was at once scotched by the Palace on the pretext of the embarrassment that would be caused to them by the Duchess's forthcoming book.

The late 1950s marked a low point in relations between the Duke of Windsor and his country. His disillusionment was now total, and he did not care to visit England at all except on urgent matters of business or for such events as the memorial service of his old friend Fruity Metcalfe. Though he no longer had anything to ask of the authorities in Great Britain, he was angered when Sir John Wheeler-Bennett, the official biographer of King George VI whom the Duke had gladly helped both with archives and reminiscences, was prevented by the Court from sending him those passages of the manuscript concerning himself for his comment and approval. He wrote to Allen in July 1956: 'Obviously that evil snake Lascelles and others have been working on Wheeler-Bennett to set my brother on a pedestal and to present me in as bad a light as possible. . . . I am incensed over this latest display of rudeness towards me from the Palace, and am determined that, unless my niece has the common courtesy to give me an opportunity of reading all references to myself in Wheeler-Bennett's official biography of my late brother, then no mention of me whatsoever shall appear therein.' Eventually, after a threat of legal action, the Duke was allowed to see the relevant portion of the text: as expected, it was found to contain a number of damaging inaccuracies which were duly pointed out and corrected.

In 1945 the Duke had given instructions that he and the Duchess were to be buried together 'in a country churchyard near Windsor'; but now he decided that he no longer wished his remains to return to England. While wintering in America in March 1957 he visited Green Mount Cemetery in Baltimore where most of the Duchess's relations were buried, and purchased a sizeable plot there to serve as their final resting-place. At the same time he drafted a statement to be published by his executors immediately upon his death:

I wish to set down in clear, unequivocal terms my wishes with regard to my burial and which I wish to be observed. I am aware that on my death many people, friends and well-wishers, may have strong views on this subject and it is with this in mind, apart from my wish to give clear instructions to my executors, that I am recording my wishes in this way.

For many years I have been domiciled in France and have resided there, but I have travelled much in America. At the time of my Abdication, I stated publicly that I was quitting public affairs and that it might be some time before I returned to my native land. I must confess that at that time I had it in mind that circumstances might permit the permanent return of the Duchess and myself to live in England; but I hope I will not give offence to anyone when I say that such a state of affairs was not encouraged by members of my family.

That being the case and because since my marriage I have enjoyed such happiness as can have been vouchsafed to few men, I have come to the conclusion that I would like to be buried in America, the country of my wife, and she in the full-ness of time likewise. Accordingly we have made provision to be buried in Green Mount Cemetery, Baltimore. This is my defi-nite choice and I wish it to be made public as soon as possible after my death to avoid any misapprehensions on this particular matter.

The plan for burial in America was supposed to be a close secret; but at the end of 1957 it leaked into the press. As the Duke had anticipated, he was deluged with letters from 'friends and well-wishers' urging him to reconsider his decision. Three years later, after a small gesture from the Palace had come his way, he relented. In 1959–60 he wrote, with the aid of the English author Lord Kinross, a small book of random reminiscences under the title *A Family Album*. When he had been working on his memoirs twelve years earlier, his brother had refused to give him or his assistants any facilities whatever; but now the Queen consented to Kinross using the Royal Archives. The Duke himself took the opportunity to make a nostalgic visit to Windsor, which he described in the first chapter of his new book; and it is clear from his account that, in spite of all that had happened, he found the ties with his country, and in particular with the places of his childhood, impossible to break.

There is one place . . . which hardly changes at all, and that is Windsor Castle. Here is a palace essentially English in character, because it is lived in. . . . I take pleasure in the way it broods, with an air of comfortable benevolence, down over the homely town of Windsor, while to the South spreads the spacious Great Park, with the Long Walk stretching three miles through the soft green English landscape and the meadows of the Home Park to the south, refreshed by the waters of the slowly winding Thames. . . .

Wandering through the rooms and corridors of Windsor, I opened a door and found myself in a dust-sheeted room. This was the room in which I made my Abdication broadcast in 1936. There in the window was the chair in which I sat on that occasion, and the desk on which I had placed my script. Outside the window the green English landscape spread away to the horizon. . . . Looking out at the view and reflecting on that historic occasion, I found I had no twinge of regret, leading, as the Duchess and I have since done, a very happy and contented private life. . . .

But one of my favourite haunts in the domains of Windsor Castle is Frogmore, a little-known Georgian house with a long Regency portico, only a few minutes' walk down the hill. Of this house, where my father and mother lived as Prince and Princess of Wales, I have childhood memories. . . . I rang the doorbell, to be answered by Bertha, for long the house's faithful caretaker. During the fifteen years which elapsed between the Duchess's and my marriage and our final acquisition of a home of our own in France, our furniture and silver and other possessions were stored at Frogmore in Bertha's charge, and she still takes care of my old uniforms, conscientiously laid away in mothballs. . . .

Frogmore has a romantic garden, well laid out, with undulating lawns and a winding lake, lush with water lilies, shaded by spreading cedars and weeping willows. . . . The general effect is one of peaceful beauty, far removed from the noisy world outside. . . .

After this visit, which took place in the summer of 1959 during the Royal Family's absence at Balmoral, the Duke asked the Queen if he and the Duchess might be buried in a private mausoleum in the gardens of Frogmore, following a simple funeral service in the case of each of them at St George's Chapel, Windsor. After careful negotiations conducted through the Keeper of the Privy Purse, Lord Tryon, this was agreed to in December 1960.

The mid-1960s saw a decline in the Duke's health and a slight thaw in relations with his family. In December 1964, when he underwent open heart surgery in Texas, the Queen sent him flowers; and when only three months later he had to undergo an eye operation at the London Clinic in Marylebone she sent him a present of wine and *foie gras* and eventually called to see him personally, thus meeting the Duchess for the first time since 1936. He asked if he might walk in the gardens of Buckingham Palace during his convalescence, and the Queen agreed to his doing so accompanied by his valet. Then, on 7 June 1967, only four days after their thirtieth wedding anniversary, the Windsors were for the first time allowed to take part in a minor royal ceremony as man and wife – the dedication of a plaque in memory of Queen Mary outside Marlborough House, at which they were seated in the front row together with the Queen and Prince Philip, the Queen Mother, the Duke and Duchess of Gloucester, Princess Marina and the Duke and Duchess of Kent. The proceedings lasted exactly fifteen minutes – and thus the Duke had at long last achieved the 'once only meeting of a quarter of an hour' for which he had pleaded in the summer of 1940 and again in the autumn of 1944, merely in order to dispel the public notoriety which surrounded the Duchess of Windsor's name.

If the Duke imagined that this event heralded a general reconciliation, he was to be disappointed; no further invitations of this nature were to be forthcoming during the remaining five years of his life, and even at this late hour there was no move to concede royal status to the Duchess. He did, however, have one other important family request to make. In August 1968 he attended (alone) the funeral of Princess Marina; she was buried next to her husband in the Royal Family's private burial ground at Frogmore, where all of its members apart from the sovereigns had been interred since 1928. He was impressed by the 'charm and seclusion' of this spot and wrote to the Queen asking if he and the Duchess of Windsor might be buried there with the rest of the family instead of in the planned mausoleum. After some consideration the Queen agreed to this in a letter to her uncle dated 7 August 1970.

During the Duke's last years, he and the Duchess were visited by some of the younger members of the Royal Family who happened to be in Paris. In this way they met Lord Harewood, Princess Alexandra, Prince William of Gloucester and Prince Michael of Kent. In the autumn of 1970 the Prince of Wales, who was then staying at the British Embassy in Paris, paid a surprise call one evening in the company of the Ambassador, Sir Christopher Soames. This gave the Duke much pleasure and, although he was not to see his great-nephew again except on his deathbed, they engaged in occasional correspondence over the next eighteen months, the Duke being able to share with the Prince some of the concerns which had been his own half a century before.

> I am glad [the Duke wrote to him on 8 February 1972] you are finding your stint at sea in the Navy rewarding, although the Fleet's spheres of action have become so drastically restricted that many of the old time honored [*sic*] stations and ports of call are now denied to its units.
>
> There are certainly plenty of problems and headaches confront-ing the British Government at this time. The insoluble Ulster crisis is the most tragic but is unfortunately the outcome of some three centuries of religious conflict. I was very young and away on world tours when partition was enacted in 1920–22 but I can recall how many of the responsible politicians of that time – not the die hard Protestant Ulster men of course – expressed the view that partition would never work.
>
> Unemployment and strikes are also unfortunate conditions that bring great hardship and despondency on the workers. The effects of inflation have of course much to do with the present troubles and I am sure you must be as concerned as I was forty years ago over the tragic plight of thousands of men thrown out of work by the closing of pits, ship yards and other industries. The Welsh mining valleys are especially hard hit for these men have no other source of employment and have become bound up in the tradition of their calling which is passed down from generation to generation. . . .
>
> Thank you again for writing and with all good wishes,
>
> your affectionate great uncle,
>
> DAVID

Another and frequent visitor during these last years was Lord Mountbatten; and while the Duke was always happy to see his old shipmate he was somewhat suspicious of Mountbatten's motives in extending the hand of friendship after so many years of coldness. These suspicions proved justified, for even while the Duke was still alive Mountbatten began scheming to obtain control of the ex-King's fortune, his archives, and his personal possessions.

In November 1971, a biopsy operation revealed that the Duke was suffering from a cancerous growth in the region of the tonsils, which it was impossible to remove owing to the proximity of the carotid arteries. A few weeks of painful cobalt treatment produced a brief respite; but by February 1972 he was clearly a dying man and knew it.

The last weeks of the Duke of Windsor's life may be described in the words of his French physician, Jean Thin.

Throughout the winter of 1972, the Duke's condition deteriorated. It became difficult to feed him, and new symptoms developed which meant that a fatal issue might occur unexpectedly at any moment. He was aware of this, but it did not affect his composure. His courage and resignation compelled general admiration. His only concern seemed to be that the Duchess should not be made too anxious. As he grew weaker, he was gradually confined to his bedroom. Apart from the Duchess, his principal companions there were his nurse and his favourite pugdog, who lay on his bed within reach of his caresses, remaining firmly in place when I sought to examine the Duke or administer treatment.

One day I was asked to go to see the British Ambassador to Paris, Sir Christopher Soames. He received me in his private office at the Embassy. He naturally knew in a general way about the state of the Duke's health, and he reminded me that the Queen was shortly to make a state visit to France. This visit, he explained, was extremely important. It was to improve the atmosphere for Great Britain's membership of the European Economic Community. Nothing could be allowed to interfere with the carefully planned schedule of official meetings. If the Duke's death occurred during the visit, it would upset this schedule and possibly affect the outcome of the Queen's mission. The Ambassador came to the point and told me bluntly that it was all right for the Duke to die before or after the visit, but that it would be politically disastrous if he were to expire in the course of it. Was there anything I could do to reassure him about the timing of the Duke's end?

I was very surprised at these remarks, and replied at once that I could give no such assurances. It was altogether possible that the Duke might die during his niece's visit. Moreover, the latest complications to his condition were such that he was liable to die quite suddenly, without warning. As a result of this interview, it was arranged that, during the royal visit, the Ambassador (who would be attending on the sovereign) would ring me every evening at six for the latest bulletin. It was also arranged that, all being well, the Queen would call upon the Duke in the course of her tour, accompanied by the Prince of Wales and the Duke of Edinburgh.

Finally the Queen arrived on her state visit. Wherever I happened to be, Sir Christopher rang me daily at the appointed hour to ask: 'And how is our friend today?' The monarch was due to see her uncle on her fourth day in France. The Duke remained lucid but was now extremely weak. He was bedridden, and depended on an intravenous drip that had to be kept going twenty-four hours a day. I asked him if he had any instructions to give me in connection with the visit of the Queen to his bedside. He replied that it was out of the question that the Queen should see him in his bedroom or wearing his bedclothes. She was his sovereign, and the least he could do was to receive her, properly dressed, in the adjoining sitting room which separated his room from the Duchess's. I tried to object that this was impossible because he could not be deprived of his drip, but he only answered: 'That's your problem.'

It was indeed a difficult problem but, thanks to the ingenuity of Dr Françoise Jacquin, we found the solution. This was to hide the drip underneath the Duke's shirt and attach it to a long tube, which would emerge from the back of his collar and lead to the fluid flasks, which would be concealed behind a curtain near which the Duke would be sitting. With much patience from the Duke, we managed to set all this up about an hour before the Queen arrived. When she entered the room, however, something happened which none of us had anticipated. Showing an effort of will that was remarkable, he rose slowly to his feet and gave the traditional bow from the neck. We were all terrified that the apparatus would come apart before our eyes. Fortunately it held in place, and I don't think anything was noticed. The Queen asked the Duke to sit down, and they chatted affectionately for about a quarter of an hour.

As soon as the Queen had left, we put the Duke back to bed. He was exhausted, but still remembered to ask me whether I had been presented to Her Majesty. When I replied that I had not, he seemed very annoyed. This was the only time I saw him display irritation throughout the whole of his long and difficult illness.

From then on he sank rapidly. I called to see him every evening. The faithful pugdog allowed me to examine my patient, but refused to budge from his place in his master's arms. On 27 May however – nine days after the Queen's visit – I was surprised to notice that the dog had left the Duke's bed and was sitting alone on the floor nearby, thus letting me know that the end was near. The Duke died in the early hours of the following morning.

Legal Opinion on the English Law Relating to Exile

Neither the King nor his Ministers have any power to exile a British subject. The liberty of the subject in this respect is secured by statute and by the common law. The strongest authority is to be found in old statutes and text books; at the present time the right is so secure that all mention of exile has dropped out of text books on Constitutional Law. The old authorities are as follows: –

        1. Statutes.
        2. Text books of authority.

1. *Statutes.*
  (i) Magna Carta Chapter 39 of the 1215 Charter
                       Chapter 29 of the 1297 Charter
                       (Halsbury *Statutes* Vol. 3 p. 29)
'No freeman shall be taken or imprisoned, or be disseised of his freehold, or liberties, or free customs, or be outlawed, or exiled, or any other wise destroyed nor will we not pass upon him nor (condemn him) but by lawful judgment of his peers, or by the law of the land. We will sell to no man, we will not deny or defer to any man outside justice or right.'

    (For commentary on this Chapter see W. S. McKechnie's *Magna Carta* 2nd Edition, 1914, at p. 384).

  (ii) Petition of Right, 1627 (Halsbury *Statutes* Vol. 3 pp. 127–130)
     . . . . . .

      (3) And here also by the Statute called the Great Charter of the liberties of England, it is declared and enacted, that no freeman may be taken or imprisoned or disseised of his freehold or liberties or his free customs or be outlawed or exiled or in any manner destroyed, but by the lawful judgment of his peers or by the law of the land.

. . . . . .

(8) They do therefore humbly pray your most excellent Majesty that . . . etc. And that no freeman in any such manner as is before mentioned be imprisoned or detained.

2. *Text books of authority.*
    (i) Coke: *Second Institutes*, p. 47 (1809 Edition) (Commentary on Magna Carta c29).

'By the law of the land no man can be exiled or banished out of his native country but either by authority of parliament, or in case of abjuration for felony by the common law; and so when our books, or any record, speak of exile, or banishment other than in case of abjuration it is intended to be done by authority of parliament; as Belknap and other judges etc. banished into Ireland. This is a beneficial law, and is construed benignly, and therefore the King cannot send any subject of England against his will to serve him out of this realm, for that should be an exile and he should 'perdere patriam'; no, he cannot be sent against his will into Ireland, to serve the King as his deputy there, because it is out of the realm of England; for if the King might send him out of this realm to any place, then under pretence of serving as ambassador or the like, he might send him into the furthest part of the world, which being an exile, is prohibited by this act.'

(ii) Blackstone *Commentaries*, Vol. I, pp. 137–8.

'A natural and regular consequence of this personal liberty, is that every Englishman may claim a right to abide in his own country so long as he pleases; and not to be driven from it unless by the sentence of the law. The King indeed, by his royal prerogative, may issue out his writ *ne exeat regno* and prohibit any of his subjects from going into foreign parts without licence. This may be necessary for the public service and safeguard of the commonwealth. But no power on earth, except the authority of parliament, can send any subject of England *out of* the land against his will; no, not even a criminal. For exile or transportation is a punishment unknown to the common law; and, whenever it is now inflicted, it is either by the choice of the criminal himself to escape a capital punishment, or else by the express direction of some modern act of parliament. To this purpose the great charter declares that no freeman shall be banished unless by the judgment of his peers or by the law of the land. . . .'

(p. 138) 'The law is in this respect so benignly and liberally construed for the benefit of the subject that, though *within* the realm the king may command the attendance and service of all his liegemen, yet he cannot send any man *out of* the realm, even upon the public service; excepting sailors and soldiers, the nature of whose employment necessarily implies an exception; he cannot even constitute a man lord deputy or lieutenant of Ireland against his will, nor make him a foreign ambassador. For this might in reality be no more than an honourable exile.'

It will be observed that the text books mention two exceptions to the general rule that no British subject can be exiled

> 1. Abjuration and outlawry.
> 2. Act of Parliament.

1. Abjuration and outlawry.
Abjuration as a mediaeval punishment for crime. It is mentioned in Pollock and Maitland's *History of English Law* Vol. II at p. 518:

'True exile is unknown; but the criminal who has taken sanctuary abjures the realm and occasionally, by way of grace, other criminals are allowed to do the like.'

Abjuration died with sanctuary.

Outlawry also was a mediaeval punishment for crime and it was later extended to civil proceedings. Outlawry in civil proceedings was abolished by the Civil Procedure Acts Repeal Act 1879 (42 & 43 Vict. c.59) s.3. It has never been abolished in criminal cases but has passed into disuse, the last judgment of outlawry occurring in 1855.

2. Act of Parliament.
It is still theoretically possible for the King in Parliament to pass an act declaring any person to be an exile. But, as appears above, nothing short of an Act of Parliament will rob a British subject of his right to return to England. The Attorney General's reply to a question by Mr. W. J. Thorne on the 11th December 1936 merely recognizes the existing law on this point.

See Hansard Vol. 318 (1936–37), Col. 2226: –

'Mr. Thorne: I would like to put to the Attorney General a question which I think is a constitutional one and one which was discussed last night. Is a King who has voluntarily abdicated compelled to leave this country?'

The Attorney General: 'No, Sir.'

The Magna Carta of 1215 contained Chapter 42:

'It shall be lawful in future for anyone (excepting always those imprisoned or outlawed in accordance with the laws of the Kingdom, and natives of any country at war with us, and merchants, who shall be treated as is above provided) to leave our kingdom and to return safe and secure by land and water, except for a short period in time of war, on grounds of public policy – reserving always the allegiance due to us.'

This provision was found to be too wide and was omitted from the re-issued Charter of 1216. Afterwards persons could be prevented from leaving the realm without the King's permission, or punished for doing so. Instances are given in Coke 3rd Institutes pp. 177–180. But in later times the exercise of this prerogative to restrain subjects from departing from England in normal times became narrowed down to the issue of the writ *Ne exeat regno* in connection with judicial proceedings. 'The use of such writs in this restricted sphere could not be reckoned an oppressive interference with the liberty of the subject. The perfect freedom to leave the shores of England and return at pleasure, accorded by John's Magna Carta, but immediately withdrawn as impracticable for that age, has in the course of centuries been fully realised.' (McKechnie on Magna Carta pp. 473–477.)

(Signed) Colin H. Pearson

Temple.
3/12/37.

Appendix II

The Duke's Consultations of Jowitt on the Question of the Duchess's Title

(1) *Opinion given by Sir William Jowitt and Mr Patrick Devlin, May 1937*

The Duke of Windsor has been advised that the Letters Patent dated 27th May, 1937, have no effect upon the rank and precedence to be accorded to the Duchess of Windsor.

So far as the Duke's rank and precedence are concerned, these are governed by the Stat. 31, Hen. 8 Cap. 10 and by immemorial custom a wife is entitled to assume the same rank and precedence as her husband, unless such rank and precedence be merely official. In His Majesty's Declaration of Abdication Act, 1936, it was expressly provided that the Royal Marriages Act, 1772, should not apply to the Duke of Windsor. There is, accordingly, no reason why in the case of the Duke's marriage this immemorial custom should not be given its full force and effect.

Nor do the Letters Patent purport to deal with questions of rank and precedence.

With regard to the question of the 'title style or attribute' of Royal Highness with which the Letters Patent do deal, it is to be observed that the Letters Patent of the 27th May, 1937, are issued on the assumption that it is only by their operation that the Duke of Windsor is entitled to this form of address.

The Duke of Windsor is advised that since 1898 he has always been entitled to this form of address and has never ceased to be so entitled.

He first became entitled to this form of address by the Letters Patent of May, 1898 as a child of the eldest son of the then Prince of Wales.

On the accession of Edward VII in 1901 the Duke of Windsor came within the terms of the Letters Patent of January, 1864, as a child of a son of the Sovereign.

On the accession of George V the Duke of Windsor – apart from any patents – further became entitled to this form of address as a son of the Sovereign by established usage – a usage which is recognised in the Letters Patent of 1864.

The Letters Patent of 1917 did not affect the Duke's position.

There are no words in the operative part of any of the Letters Patent to restrict the title of Royal Highness to those only who are 'in succession to the throne'.

The Duke, during his reign as King Edward VIII naturally allowed the attribute 'Royal Highness' to be supplanted by the higher attribute of 'His Majesty' – but upon his abdication he automatically resumed his earlier attribute of 'Royal Highness' as a son of a former sovereign.

Accordingly, the Duke is advised that his right to the attribute of 'Royal Highness' is derived from sources which remain unaffected by and by the Letters Patent of 27th May, 937; and this advice is fortified by the fact that in his speech of 12th December, 1936, upon his accession, His Majesty referred to the Duke as 'His Royal Highness'. In common with the wives of all other members of the Royal Family the Duchess of Windsor cannot lay claim to the attribute of 'Royal Highness' by reason of the provision of any Letters Patent, but only by reason of that immemorial usage which accords to every wife the style and title and attribute of her husband. Inasmuch as the Duke derives this attribute from sources wherein no limitation is imposed upon the use of it by his wife and inasmuch as the Letters Patent of 27th May, 1937, do not purport to deprive the Duke of rights acquired prior to their issue, the Duke is advised that the Duchess of Windsor is by virtue of her membership of the Royal Family entitled in the same way as other royal duchesses to be known by the style and title of 'Her Royal Highness'.

If an announcement is made the Duke of Windsor may desire

(a) to endeavour to get the matter referred to the Lords of the Council or
(b) to abandon the attribute for himself.

In the latter case he might desire to conclude the statement with some such words as follows:

It would follow from this advice that the Letters Patent of the 27th May, 1937, were unnecessary and have achieved no purpose. The Duchess of Windsor would however never wish to adopt any attribute even though entitled to the same by immemorial usage, unless the right were freely accorded to her.

Moreover, it would create difficulty and embarrassment on public occasions if the Duke were to continue to use this attribute and the Duchess were not to use it.

Under the circumstances, though the rank and precedence of the Duke is fixed by Act of Parliament and cannot be altered except by Act of Parliament, and though the Duchess must by usage enjoy her husband's rank and precedence, yet neither the Duke nor the Duchess of Windsor desire to be addressed by the attribute 'Royal Highness' and trust that in future this attribute will not be employed.

The Duke of Windsor recently intimated that he wished to see me and accordingly I went round by arrangement to see him on the afternoon of Wednesday, 13th April 1949.

I did not know on what subject he wished to see me, but I thought it probable it would be on the question as to whether the Duchess should be accorded the title of 'Her Royal Highness.'

I thought this because in 1937 when I was in private practice at the Bar I had written an Opinion on this topic and discussed it with the Duke at the time.

Any embarrassment I might have felt in view of my present position in discussing this matter with the Duke was allayed when he told me that he had mentioned to the King that he was going to ask me to come and see him to discuss this topic and when he added that the King had raised no objection.

My previous Opinion given in 1937 – of which the Duke had a copy – had been that the Letters Patent of 1937 really proceeded upon a misapprehension of the law.

In the view expressed in my Opinion it was erroneous to suppose that the fact of his Abdication and the fact that he had ceased to be in succession to the Throne involved the proposition that he had thereby ceased to be 'His Royal Highness'.

The Opinion was based upon the view that he became 'His Royal Highness' not by virtue of any Letters Patent, but for the simple reason that he was the son of his father who was the Sovereign of this country.

The Opinion pointed out that the Letters Patent issued in 1864 had made it clear that although there was some doubt as to who was entitled to the style 'Royal Highness', it was beyond doubt that the children of the Sovereign were so entitled, and accordingly these children were not dealt with in those Letters Patent.

It was of course clear that the Duchess could not found any claim on the Letters Patent 1937; but supposing that she had a perfectly good claim apart from any Letters Patent, did the Letters Patent of 1937 take that claim away?

In other words, I expressed the view that Letters Patent could modify, control, or even take away that which had been granted by Letters Patent, but that it was questionable whether Letters Patent were an appropriate instrument to take away that which owed its origin to a separate and independent source.

I expressed the view in that Opinion that the Duke was entitled to the style 'His Royal Highness' because he was the son of the Sovereign; that he had never for one moment of time ceased to be 'His Royal Highness' by his Abdication or in any other way; that it was a misapprehension to suppose that there was any need for new Letters Patent if it were desired to create him a Royal Highness; and that the Duchess was entitled to an equivalent rank because she was his wife.

Such, so far as I can recall it, was the substance of the Opinion which I had given in 1937 – an Opinion in which Mr. Patrick Devlin (now Mr. Justice Devlin) had concurred.

At our interview yesterday, I pointed out to the Duke of Windsor that whatever suble arguments lawyers might adduce, the fact was that the Letters Patent of 1937 issued by The King on the advice of his responsible Ministers, plainly contemplated that the Duchess should not enjoy this honour.

The marks of respect which the subject pays to Royal personages are, I said, in no source a legal obligation. They are rather a matter of good manners.

The question for instance whether ladies should curtsey to the Duchess would depend in practice, not upon the view they formed upon a legal question, but upon their desire to uphold and carry out the intention of His Majesty The King as the fountain of honour.

I said, therefore, that if this situation were to be reversed, it could only be effectively reversed by the issue of fresh Letters Patent; that such Letters Patent would not be issued by The King save on the advice of his Ministers, either in this country alone, or possibly throughout the Commonwealth.

The Duke of Windsor expressed his anxiety to end the present situation, which he thought had gone on all too long. It certainly needed tidying up. Its continuance amounted to nothing less than an insult to his wife, to whom he had been most happily married for many years past.

He said that the position which had arisen was exactly what would have happened had there been a morganatic marriage; and this was exactly the position which Mr. Baldwin had said was impossible in this country; and was a position to which the Duke of Windsor, when King, would never have assented.

He thought it might be well for him to get an opportunity of discussing the whole matter with Mr. Attlee.

The Duke of Windsor expressed the view that in so far as legal questions were involved, it was desirable that I should have an opportunity of speaking to His Majesty about his aspect of the case. I said that of course I was available if His Majesty cared to send for me.

I hope I have recorded accurately, though shortly, the substance of what took place.

Appendix III

The Duke's Peace Broadcast from Verdun, 8 May 1939

I am speaking tonight from Verdun, where I have been spending a few days visiting one of the greatest battlefields of the last war. Upon this and other battlefields throughout the world, millions of men suffered and died, and as I talk to you from this historic place, I am deeply conscious of the presence of the great company of the dead; and I am convinced that could they make their voices heard they would be with me in what I am about to say.

For two and a half years I have deliberately kept outside of public affairs and I still propose to do so. I speak for no one but myself, without the previous knowledge of any government.

I speak simply as a soldier of the last war, whose most earnest prayer is that such cruel and destructive madness shall never again overtake mankind. I break my self-imposed silence now only because of the manifest danger that we may all be drawing nearer to a repetition of the grim events that happened a quarter of a century ago.

The grave anxieties of the time in which we live compel me to raise my voice in expression of the universal longing to be delivered from the fears that beset us and to return to normal conditions.

You and I know that peace is a matter far too vital for our happiness to be treated as a political question. We also know that in modern warfare victory will lie only with the powers of evil. Anarchy and chaos are the inevitable results, with consequent misery for us all.

I cannot claim for myself the expert knowledge of a statesman, but I have at least had the good fortune to travel the world and therefore to study human nature. This valuable experience has left me with the profound conviction that there is no land whose people want war. This I believe to be as true of the German nation as of the British nation to which I belong, as it is to you in America and of the French nation, on whose friendly soil I now reside.

International understanding does not always spring up simultaneously

313

of itself. There are times when it has to be deliberately sought and negotiated, and political tension is apt to weaken that spirit of mutual concession in which conflicting claims can best be adjusted. The problems that concern us at this moment are only the reproductions on a larger scale of the jealousies and suspicions of everyday life. In our personal contacts we all strive to live in harmony with our fellowmen. Otherwise modern civilization could never have come into existence.

Are we now going to destroy that civilization by failing to do internationally what we have learned to do individually? In their public utterances the heads of governments are as one in declaring that war would be disastrous to the well-being of their people. Whatever political disagreements may have arisen in the past, the supreme importance of averting war will, I feel confident, impel all those in power to renew their endeavours to bring about a peaceful settlement.

Among measures that I feel might well be adopted to this end is the discouragement of all that harmful propaganda which, from whatever source, tends to poison the minds of the peoples of the world. I personally deplore, for example, the use of such terms as 'encirclement' and 'aggression.' They can only arouse just those dangerous political passions that it should be the aim of us all to subdue.

No, it is in a larger spirit than that of personal or purely national interest that peace should be pursued. The statesmen who set themselves to restore international security and confidence must act as good citizens of the world and not only as good Frenchmen, Italians, Germans, Americans or Britons. The benefit of their own nation must be sought through the benefit of the wider community of which we are all members.

In the name of those who fell in the last war I urge all political leaders to be resolute in the discharge of this mission. I appeal to them in the name of the living, whose existence and happiness are in their hands; and I appeal to them especially in the name of the youth of the present day, with all its incalculable potentialities of future service to the human race.

The world has not yet recovered from the effects of the last carnage, which in each and every country decimated my generation. The greatest success that any government could achieve for its own national policy would be nothing in comparison with the triumph of having contributed to save humanity from the terrible fate that threatens it today.

Somehow, I feel that my words tonight will find a sincere echo in the hearts of all who hear them. It is not for me to put forward concrete proposals. That must be left to those who have the power to guide their nations towards closer understanding.

God grant that they may accomplish that great task before it is too late!

Memoranda of the Duke Concerning His Desire for Official Work in America after 1945

(1) *For Winston Churchill, 15 November 1945*

As American and Anglo-American relations have been a special interest and study of mine ever since my first visit to that country twenty-six years ago, it is a subject with which I am already quite familiar.

I have, of course, had special opportunities of pursuing my studies of these vital but extremely subtle relations and have, in fact, gone out of my way to further them in connection with my five years' Governorship of the Colony of the Bahamas and during the different visits I paid to America during that period.

It is difficult at this distance to define the precise approach to this subject or the lines along which my activities could best be directed in the event of the project we discussed in Paris maturing satisfactorily, which indeed I hope it will. However, this is roughly what I have in mind:

1. To pursue personal and useful contacts I have already made with Americans of different callings and political opinions who realize the vital importance to the future of mankind of a common Anglo-American approach to international problems. My private activities in this direction have been, generally speaking, confined to the Eastern Seaboard of America, but this range of acquaintances could, I am sure, be considerably widened by private visits to the different States; and I have made a practice of concentrating on individuals who have the reputation or are at any rate inclined to be Anti-British. I flatter myself that I have already been able to make a few converts.

2. The assistance and support of Britishers wedded to the same cause should be sought for there must be no one-way traffic in this project and it must not be forgotten that there are Englishmen who are anti-American in their outlook to be converted in the same way as their prototypes on the other side of the Atlantic.

3. The possibilities of the inauguration of schemes for the exchange of students between the two countries – either of school age or, better still, for graduate or postgraduate courses as in the case of the Rhodes Scholarships at Oxford for Americans or the Harkness Fellowships at American universities for British men and women – should be explored. I am convinced, as are many others interested in this subject, that the best and surest foundations for better understanding between Great Britain and America can be brought about if a reasonable proportion of the younger generation could spend their most impressionable years in each other's countries.

4. Public appearances involving speeches or radio broadcasts should be scrupulously avoided at the outset of my mission and then kept to the barest minimum thereafter, and only after consultation with the British Ambassador. So much more can be achieved in the field of furthering Anglo-American cooperation by personal contacts than by publicity, besides which, public utterances on behalf of the British Government are, after all, the role of the British Ambassador.

5. The wornout expression, 'Anglo-American relations', should be eradicated from our vocabulary for there is nothing more calculated to arouse suspicion and a sense of force in the issue on both sides of the Atlantic. A lasting understanding must be built on more solid foundations that that of merely good relations and the fact that the English language is common to our two peoples, so that the nature of my activities in America, therefore, should not be more clearly defined than as being 'within the ambit of the British Embassy in Washington'.

6. To furnish a quarterly report of my work and whatever interesting and useful information I have been able to collect to the King, copies of which would be sent to the British Ambassador in Washington and the Secretary of State for Foreign Affairs in London.

(2) *For Walter Monckton, 8 December 1945*

The problem must be solved mutually with give and take. No one way is advantageous. In return for respecting my brother's feelings, he must understand my difficulties and play his part in helping me to overcome them.

My brother has only a superficial knowledge of the press in America and cannot appreciate the ruthlessness with which it proclaims its freedom or the length it will go for sensationalism.

There are only two questions concerning the Windsors which really interest the press:

1. IS BRITAIN GOING TO GIVE THE DUKE A JOB AND, IF NOT, WHAT ELSE IS HE GOING TO DO?

The press reaction to a negative answer would be deplorable and most unfortunate for both parties concerned. If the present project is agreed upon, then I believe we can get away with it. On the other hand, I believe that although the expression 'within the ambit of the British Embassy in Washington' may well be as far as my brother and the Foreign Office are prepared to go, I am skeptical as to it satisfying the American press, and for this reason a more precise term such as 'ACCREDITED TO THE BRITISH EMBASSY AS SPECIAL LIAISON REPRESENTATIVE IN AMERICA' may have to be devised.

2. WILL THE DUCHESS BE RECEIVED BY QUEEN MARY?

As it seems unlikely that it will be possible to furnish a satisfactory answer to this question in the immediate future, the question of a statement that no quarrel or open breach exists between the Royal Family and myself on this issue but merely a naturally strong disagreement and the fact that there is no quarrel is confirmed by my recent visit to Queen Mary, my conversations with my brother and my willingness to do some work for the British Government.

With regard to the objections that are being raised by Mr. Bevin, most probably on the advice of senior Foreign Office officials, to the effect that the appointment in mind would overshadow the British Ambassador in Washington or give the impression of the existence of two Ambassadors, I contend that there should be far less risk of any misunderstanding were I to work behind the scenes 'within the ambit of' 'accredited to' the British Embassy than if I were to roam around America in free-lance fashion. Besides, my record over a period of nine years and my retiring nature should be sufficient guarantee that I possess the good will and the tact to prevent any infringement on the important and exalted spot of British Ambassador in Washington or treading upon its incumbent's toes.

It should further be emphasized that my work would generally speaking and, anyway, at the outset be confined to making contacts and investigating the trend of American thought behind the scenes and that official speechmaking would remain entirely in the hands of the Ambassador or, in his absence, the Chargé d'Affaires.

The question of taxation should not arise as, if I am 'Accredited to the British Embassy', I would automatically be having diplomatic status.

Source References

This work is mainly based on papers of the Duke and Duchess of Windsor under the control of Maître Suzanne Blum in Paris. Any document in the text the origin of which is not obviously identified there, and for which no reference is given below, may be presumed to come from this general source.

The letters CO, FO, WO and PREM refer to the classes with those designations at the Public Record Office at Kew.

From Abdication to Marriage

5.6	Lord Birkenhead, *Walter Monckton*, (London 1969), p. 169
7.14	J. G. Lockhart, *Cosmo Gordon Lang*, (London 1949), p. 395
7.19	Duke of Windsor, *A King's Story*, (London 1951), p. 280–1
8.8	Birkenhead, p. 125–6
9.31	*A King's Story*, p. 332
10.19	*Ibid.*, p. 314
11.16	Michael Bloch (ed.), *Wallis & Edward, Letters 1931–1937: the Intimate Correspondence of the Duke and Duchess of Windsor*, (London 1986) (hereinafter referred to as *Letters*), pp. 192–4
11.20	*Ibid.*, p. 201–2
12.14	Baldwin's speech on the Abdication Bill reproduced in D. C. Somervell, *Stanley Baldwin*, (London 1951), pp. 120–33
12.24	Quoted in H. Montgomery Hyde, *Baldwin*, (London 1973), p. 520
14.16	*Ibid.*, p. 492
15.1	*A King's Story*, p. 410; J. Wheeler-Bennett, *King George VI: His Life and Reign* (London 1958), pp. 294–5
16.32	*A King's Story*, p. 414; Wheeler-Bennett, p. 287
18.12	*Letters*, p. 233
18.30	*Ibid.*, pp. 241–4
21.9	*Ibid.*, pp. 245–6
22.1	*Ibid.*, p. 244
25.1	Memoir of Lord Somervell quoted in Montgomery Hyde, pp. 566–70
25.20	*Letters*, p. 257
25.26	*Ibid.*, p. 263
27.19	Birkenhead, p. 165
27.28	*Letters*, p. 256
29.27	James Pope-Hennessy, *Queen Mary*, pp. 252–5
30.1	*A King's Story*, p. 334
30.36	*Letters*, p. 233

319

31.16	*ibid.*, p. 238	44.2	Wheeler-Bennett, p. 287
31.20	*Ibid.*, p. 258	53.3	Martin Gilbert, Companion
31.22	John Vincent (ed.), *The*		Part 3 to Volume V of
	Crawford Papers		*Winston S. Churchill,*
	(Manchester 1984), p. 618		London 1982, p. 634
31.27	Mabel, Countess of Airlie,	53.23	*Ibid.*, p. 638
	Thatched with Gold,	53.30	*Ibid.*, p. 643
	(London 1962), p. 200	54.6	*Ibid.*, p. 644
31.31	Birkenhead, p.169	54.12	*Ibid.*, pp. 660–1
32.27	Robert Rhodes James (ed.),	56.1	*Ibid.*, p. 651–3
	Chips: The Diaries of Sir	60.22	Peacock diary quoted in
	Henry Channon, pp. 45–6		Donaldson, p. 290
33.1	*A King's Story*, pp. 326–7		
33.9	Unpublished diaries of		*The Duchess's Status and Title*
	Harold Nicolson at Balliol	68.14	Birkenhead, p. 166
	College, Oxford, 5	68.18	*The Heart Has Its Reasons,*
	November 1958		p. 298
33.36	*Ibid.*, 14 December 1936	71.31	Birkenhead, p. 166
34.15	Vincent, p. 619	73.1	Editorial in *Debrett's Peerage,*
35.17	Rhodes James, p. 104		1973
36.31	Frances Stevenson, *Lloyd*	73.27	*The Heart Has Its Reasons,*
	George, A Diary, London		pp. 340–1
	1971, p. 326	83.6	*Ibid.*
37.1	Vincent, p. 618	83.31	Hoare to Churchill, 5 July
37.10	*Letters*, p. 238		1940, Templewood Papers,
37.14	*Ibid.*, p. 245		Cambridge University
33.34	*Ibid.*, p. 250		Library, XIII/16/37
38.15	Duchess of Windsor, *The*	83.33	Hoare to Churchill, 29 June
	Heart Has Its Reasons		1940, quoted in Martin
	(London 1956), p. 290		Gilbert, *Finest Hour,*
38.33	*Letters*, pp. 268–9		London 1983, p. 613
39.19	*Ibid.*, p. 277	85.14	Quoted in Patrick Howarth,
39.29	*The Heart Has Its Reasons,*		*George VI*, London 1987,
	p. 296		p. 143
40.1	Quoted in Philip Ziegler,		
	Mountbatten, London 1985,		*Fort Belvedere*
	at p. 96		
40.29	Diaries of Sir Ronald Storrs	95.14	*A King's Story*, p. 237
	at Pembroke College,	96.18	Christopher Hussey: *Fort*
	Cambridge		*Belvedere, Surrey: The*
42.26	*The Heart Has Its Reasons,*		*Residence of the Hon. Gerald*
	p. 289		*Lascelles* in *Country Life*, 19
			and 26 November 1959
		96.28	Diana Cooper, *The Light of*
	The Financial Settlement and		*Common Day*, London 1951,
	Quarrel		p. 151
43.3	Frances Donaldson, *Edward*	97.3	*A King's Story*, p. 237
	VIII, London 1974, p. 292	97.14	Book review by Rebecca West
43.6	Book review by A. L. Rowse		in the *Sunday Telegraph,*
	in *Wall Street Journal* etc.,		September 1979, entitled
	entitled *A Candid View of*		*Uneasy Lay the Head*
	an Unsuitable King	97.25	*Letters*, p. 158

97.35   *A King's Story*, p. 316
98.3   Hussey
99.15   *The Heart Has Its Reasons*, p. 325
101.1   Syndicated article of November 1940
101.32   Harold Nicolson, *Letters and Diaries*, Vol. III, London 1968, pp. 98–9
102.24   Hussey, cited article

From Marriage to War

113.4   FO 954/33 f. 69
113.29   Paul Schmidt, *Hitler's Interpreter*, London 1951, p. 75
114.1   Information from Sir Dudley Forwood.
114.24   FO 954/33 ff. 36–8
115.6   *Ibid.*, f. 58
115.10   *Ibid.*, f. 61
115.19   *Ibid.*, f. 62
115.22   *Ibid.*, f. 64
115.30   Vincent, pp. 617–18
116.4   *Ibid.*
116.27   *Ibid.*
117.27   Martin Gilbert (ed.), *Winston S. Churchill*, Part III of Companion to Volume V, pp. 819–21
117.35   *The New York Times*, 23 October 1937
120.36   Ronald Storrs Diary, 23 April 1938
121.1   FO 945/33 ff. 144–53
129.14   Dina Wells Hood, *Working for the Windsors*, London 1957, pp. 35–6
132.18   Nicolson Diary, 5 August 1938
133.1   Quoted in James Lees-Milne, *Harold Nicolson*, Volume 2, London 1981, p. 108
133.11   Birkenhead, p. 169
133.32   *The Memoirs of Princess Alice, Duchess of Gloucester*, London 1983, p. 117

A Year of Conflict

142.14   *The Heart Has Its Reasons*, pp 320–1

143.21   *The Times*, 9 September 1939
145.5   R. J. Minney (ed.), *The Private Papers of Hore-Belisha*, London 1958, pp. 236–40
146.18   Quoted in Donaldson, p. 349
146.24   Nicolson, *Diaries*, 1980 edition, p. 168
147.28   Brigadier Davy's notes in Imperial War Museum
147.34   Despatch 492/S of 19 September 1939 in French Military Archives at Vincennes, 7/N/2817
148.6   WO 106/1653 f. 19
148.12   Quoted in Donaldson, p. 353
148.22   WO 106/1678 f. 2b
148.30   *Ibid.*, f. 3b
149.6   J. R. Colville, *Man of Valour*, London 1972, p. 169
149.15   Roland Vintras, *The Portuguese Connection*, London 1974, pp. 25–6
149.24   WO 106/1678 f. 3b
149.30   Alanbrooke Diary in Liddell-Hart Centre for Military Archives
149.36   Quoted in Donaldson, pp. 353–4
150.1   Pownall Diary in Liddell-Hart Centre
150.18   *The Heart Has Its Reasons*, p. 329
151.28   Quoted in Donaldson, p. 356
152.31   Nicolson Diary in Balliol College, Oxford, 11 March 1940
154.15   Quoted in Martin Gilbert, *Finest Hour*, London 1983, p. 327
156.20   FO 800/326 f. 193
156.30   *The Heart Has Its Reasons*, p. 334
157.14   FO 800/326 f. 187
157.30   *Ibid.*, f. 190
158.6   *Ibid.*, f. 196
158.17   Templewood Papers, Cambridge University Library, XIII/20
158.26   *Ibid.*, XIII/16/29
159.6   Quoted in Gilbert, p. 614
159.25   *Ibid.*, p. 613

159.39   *Ibid.*, p. 614
160.5   Templewood Papers, XIII/20
160.10   *Ibid.*, XIII/16/37
160.32   Gilbert, pp. 613 and 698
161.8   FO 371/24249 f. 148
161.20   Storrs Diary, 14 July 1940
161.22   Gilbert, p. 699
161.26   FO 371/24249 f. 155
162.2   *The Heart Has Its Reasons*,
            p. 342
162.8   FO 371/24249 f. 149
162.11   *Ibid.*, f. 150
162.14   See Duke's letter to Winston
            Churchill of 30 June 1941
            in FO 954/33
162.24   John Charmley, *Lord Lloyd and
            the Decline of the British
            Empire*, London 1987,
            p. 248
163.17   FO 371/24249 f. 208
164.9   *Ibid.*, f. 161
164.15   *Ibid.*, f. 163A
164.19   *Ibid.*, f. 184
164.24   *Ibid.*, f. 187
166.1   *Documents on German Foreign
            Policy*, Series D, Volume X,
            London 1957, No. 152.
167.22   *Ibid.*, No. 211
168.1   *Ibid.*, No. 290
168.23   *Ibid.*, No. 264

The Bahamas

For a detailed account of the
Windsors' sojourn in Nassau,
and also a full description of
sources, see Michael Bloch,
The Duke of Windsor's War,
London 1982, New York 1983,
pp. 105–360

172.28   Sir Alan Burns, *Colonial Civil
            Servant*, London 1949,
            pp. 89–90, 269, 272
173.24   Geoffrey Bocca, *The Life and
            Death of Harry Oakes*,
            London 1959, p. 89
174.5   FO 371/24249 f. 200
179.30   Telegram 436 of 1940,
            Bahamas Record Office
180.22   National Archives
            Washington, 844E/001/60
182.18   FO 371/24263 ff. 243–5

184.18   *Nassau Guardian*, 16 August
            1941
185.23   Account of interview with
            Duke on security of
            Bahamas, 1941, in archives
            of H. Montgomery Hyde
186–90   Most of the correspondence
            quoted on these pages
            may be seen in Anthony
            Eden's papers in Public
            Record Office, file FO
            954/33
190.13   PREM 4/10/4
191.25   FO 954/33
192.26   British Press Service Report
            789/1941 of 24 November
198   For official correspondence
            on the Riots and their
            aftermath, see CO 23/731
            and FO 371/30644
200.19   *The Heart Has Its Reasons*,
            p. 355
200.29   Charmley, p. 248
201.30   *The Heart Has Its Reasons*,
            pp. 347–8
203.24   CO 23/734; CO 23/744
204.26   CO 23/714

The Quest for a Post

215.32   *The Heart Has Its Reasons*,
            p. 358
226.9   Quoted in Howarth,
            pp. 188–9

The Death of Queen Mary

275.fn8   Lees-Milne, pp. 268–9

Postscript

294.5   Letter from Lord Beaverbrook
            to his son, 13 January 1954
            (wrongly dated 1953), in
            Beaverbrook Papers,
            House of Lords. 'The Duke
            of Windsor is not going to
            get any appointment now
            or in the future. The reason
            is her ladyship's
            memoirs. . . .'
296   The Duke of Windsor, *A
            Family Album*, London
            1960, pp. 4–9

Index

Index